THE TWO ELEANORS OF HENRY III

THE LIVES OF ELEANOR OF PROVENCE AND ELEANOR DE MONTFORT

For my wife

THE TWO ELEANORS OF HENRY III

THE LIVES OF ELEANOR OF PROVENCE AND ELEANOR DE MONTFORT

DARREN BAKER

PEN & SWORD HISTORY

AN IMPRINT OF PEN & SWORD BOOKS LTD.
YORKSHIRE - PHILADELPHIA

First published in Great Britain in 2019 by
PEN AND SWORD HISTORY
An imprint of
Pen & Sword Books Ltd
Yorkshire – Philadelphia

ISBN 978 1 52674 751 8

A CIP catalogue record for this book is available from the British Library.

Printed and bound in Great Britain by
TJ International Ltd, Padstow, Cornwall
Typeset in Times New Roman 11.5/14 by
Aura Technology and Software Services, India

Pen & Sword Books Limited incorporates the imprints of Atlas, Archaeology,
Aviation, Discovery, Family History, Fiction, History, Maritime, Military, Military
Classics, Politics, Select, Transport, True Crime, Air World, Frontline Publishing,
Leo Cooper, Remember When, Seaforth Publishing, The Praetorian Press,
Wharncliffe Local History, Wharncliffe Transport, Wharncliffe True Crime and
White Owl.

For a complete list of Pen & Sword titles please contact
PEN & SWORD BOOKS LIMITED
47 Church Street, Barnsley, South Yorkshire, S70 2AS, England
E-mail: enquiries@pen-and-sword.co.uk
Website: www.pen-and-sword.co.uk

Or
PEN AND SWORD BOOKS
1950 Lawrence Rd, Havertown, PA 19083, USA
E-mail: Uspen-and-sword@casematepublishers.com
Website: www.penandswordbooks.com

Contents

Contents

Preface

There have been three queens of England named Eleanor. The first and most famous of them was Eleanor of Aquitaine. She had two husbands, both of them kings, ten children, and went on crusade. The third was Eleanor of Castile. She had only one husband, but sixteen children and she too went on crusade. After her death, she was immortalised with memorial crosses erected in her memory. In between them was Eleanor of Provence. She had only five children, no crusade to her credit, and her husband could not compare to the husbands of the other two Eleanors. Worse, she was blamed for him being a seemingly weak and incompetent monarch. 'She trod on his back', said one chronicler.

It was this picture of Eleanor of Provence that informed Agnes Strickland six centuries later when she embarked on the first major attempt to introduce this queen of England to the general public. Popular historians of the twentieth century like Thomas Costain also fell back on these unflattering depictions of Eleanor. But there was no denying her tenacity and strength of purpose, which led one chronicler to sneak in a description of her as *virago*, a woman in the heroic tradition of great deeds. Indeed, it was Margaret Howell who first picked up on this quality in her biography of Eleanor in 1998. She was a 'woman of great vitality', who also had an 'unusually exciting life-story'. It is that story we shall consider here, in the foreground of the man whose reign made it possible.

King Henry III also received his share of criticism from his contemporaries. He was the longest-ruling monarch of medieval England and most of those fifty-six years were peaceful and prosperous. But political changes at home brought on by Magna Carta and the rise of Parliament, compounded by events abroad like the twilight of the crusades and war between the papacy and Holy Roman Empire, culminated in reforms and a showdown between Henry and radicals led by Simon de Montfort. Like Eleanor of Provence, Simon came to England from the Continent and owed everything to the king. That included marriage to Henry's sister, the other Eleanor of our story.

As a Plantagenet married to a Marshal and then to a Montfort, this Eleanor would bear the names of three of the most distinguished families in English history. The portrait of her that emerges in Mary Green's Victorian work is, however, much like Strickland's Queen Eleanor. She is a woman found wanting in the grand scheme of things, chided for being assertive and too insistent on her rights. Green did not get her material just from churlish chroniclers, either. One contemporary who knew Eleanor de Montfort and counted her as a friend noted her need not only to stand out, but stand up for herself. As with Howell's work on Queen Eleanor, it would take a century and a half before a new biography offered new perspectives on this sister and wife of two historic antagonists. The subtitle attached to that work, by author Louise Wilkinson, says it all about her strengths and weaknesses: *A Rebel Countess in Medieval England.*

It is impossible to separate these women from the men whose relationships and conflicts with each other helped shaped their lives. Both marriages had their problems like any other, but they were long and enduring, and both men were faithful and adoring husbands. The loyalty each spouse inspired in the other, and later in their children, is one reason why these two families were so evenly matched. In that sense, this work might be thought of as the story of two power couples. Whatever Henry or Simon were planning or doing, we can be sure there had been consultation at some point with their respective Eleanors.

These women had, of course, lives apart from their husbands. The countess was a major lord in her own right when she married Simon and she managed their estates in his long absences. The queen had her own household, circle of advisers, and network of patronage. They also had each other. The scanty records show that both Eleanors were in close contact when Henry and Simon's relationship was at one of its lowest ebbs. Although the friendship between these sisters-in-law was unable to overcome the divisions that engulfed them and the realm, there is a certain poignancy in the settlement that followed. With Simon dead and bitterness prevailing on both sides, Eleanor de Montfort needed someone to intercede for her in England. Eleanor of Provence was the natural choice.

The idea for this dual biography came as I was finishing up my biography on Henry, which itself followed one on Simon. One thing that struck me about both men was their relative youth when they entered the world stage. Henry was 9 when he succeeded his father King John, and Simon was born and raised amidst the Albigensian Crusade directed by his namesake father. The same can be said for Eleanor de Montfort, who like Henry was 9 years old when she was married to the much older William Marshal II. Eleanor of Provence was 12 when she left her homeland to marry Henry, never to see it again. All four of them entered adulthood with already enough experience for a lifetime. That gave them a clear understanding of what their world was about.

In coming to our own understanding of their lives, it is important to remember that they lived to be relatively old people. Their marriages and relations to each other spanned decades of the thirteenth century, as thrilling and tremendous an age as any in English history. The people they ultimately became owed to ever-changing circumstances and events. To make that development obvious, this dual biography is strictly chronological. In this way I hope to capture their personalities in the marriages and alliances that played out around them, in their hopes and endeavours for their husbands and children, and inevitably in the political struggle that wrenched their families apart. Much of their story may seem familiar to readers of my earlier biographies, but I like to think of this volume as the concluding part of a trilogy in the lives of these four remarkable people.

This work would not have been possible without the scholarship of Margaret Howell, Louise Wilkinson and a host of others to whom I owe a debt of gratitude. Away from the field, I would like to mention a few at the University of Connecticut who brought strong and dynamic female characters to life with ease and enthusiasm during my undergraduate years. I still vividly recall the biblical Judith of German Professor George Reinhardt, Queen Nitocris of Greek Professor Thomas Suits, and then there was Professor Ludmilla Burns herself, who could have been any of the heroines of her Russian studies classes. No longer with us, they forever have my heartfelt thanks for the memories and inspiration. So too does Magdalena Sánchez, today Professor of History at Gettysburg College, whose research has, by happy coincidence, landed her in Savoy, which plays a prominent role in this book.

Timeline

1215 – Birth of Henry III's sister Eleanor Plantagenet

1223 – Birth of Eleanor of Provence

1224 – Princess Eleanor married to William Marshal II

1230 – Eleanor Marshal joins her husband on the king's expeditionary force in Brittany

1231 – William Marshal II dies

1232 – Eleanor Marshal makes an ill-advised settlement with Richard Marshal

1234 – Eleanor Marshal becomes a bride of Christ

1236 – Henry marries Eleanor of Provence, gives Odiham Castle to his sister

1238 – Simon de Montfort marries Eleanor Marshal, the king and queen escape an assassination attempt, Henry de Montfort is born

1239 – Queen Eleanor gives birth to Edward, Henry denounces Simon and Eleanor and drives them from the country

1240 – Simon de Montfort Jr is born, birth of Queen Eleanor's daughter Margaret, the Montforts go to Italy

1242 – Henry and Queen Eleanor go to Poitou, their daughter Beatrice is born, birth of Amaury de Montfort

1243 – Henry and Eleanor, the Montforts return to England

1244 – Henry grants Kenilworth Castle to the Montforts, Guy de Montfort is born

1245 – Queen Eleanor's second son Edmund is born

1248 – The Montforts go to Gascony

1250 – Henry and Eleanor vow to go on crusade

1251 – The king and queen's daughter Margaret marries Alexander III of Scotland

1252 – Henry argues with his wife, with Simon, Richard de Montfort is born

1253 – Queen Eleanor regent, her daughter Katherine is born

1254 – The queen summons her Great Parliaments, Edward marries Eleanor of Castile, Henry and Queen Eleanor meet King Louis and Queen Margaret of France

1255 – Edmund is declared the King of Sicily

1257 – Katherine dies, the king and queen have a nervous breakdown

1258 – Queen Eleanor plots to expel the Lusignans, reforms begin, birth of the Montforts' last child Eleanor de Montfort

1259 – The Montforts obstruct the peace treaty with France, break with the royal pair

1260 – Daughter Beatrice marries John of Brittany, showdown over Parliament, Edward joins Simon against the king and queen

1261 – Birth of Eleanor of Provence's first grandchild, Henry overthrows the Provisions of Oxford, the Montforts go to live in France

1262 – The king and queen go to France, arbitration with Simon before Queen Margaret

1263 – Simon returns and leads an army that targets the Savoyards, Queen Eleanor harangued by a mob at London Bridge, Simon takes over the government, both sides plea before Louis, Queen Eleanor and Edmund remain in France

1264 – Civil war breaks out, Henry and Edward are captured, Simon's regime begins, Queen Eleanor prepares to invade, gives priority to peace negotiations

1265 – Edward defeats Simon at the Battle of Evesham, Simon and Henry de Montfort are slain, Queen Eleanor and Edmund return to England, Eleanor de Montfort and her children go into exile in France, she retires to the convent of Montargis

1266 – Negotiations begin on and off between the king and his sister

1269 – Edmund marries Aveline de Forz

1271 – Eleanor de Montfort's sons Simon and Guy hack their cousin Henry of Almain to death in Italy in revenge for their father, Simon dies that year

1272 – Henry III dies

1273 – Edward reconciles with his aunt Eleanor de Montfort near Paris

1274 – Edward's coronation, last time all of Eleanor of Provence's children are together, her beloved grandson Henry dies

1275 – Margaret and Beatrice die, Eleanor de Montfort dies

1278 – Young Eleanor de Montfort marries Llywelyn ap Gruffudd, becomes Princess of Wales. She dies in childbirth four years later.

1287 – Eleanor of Provence enters Amesbury nunnery, dies there four years later

England, Scotland and Wales.

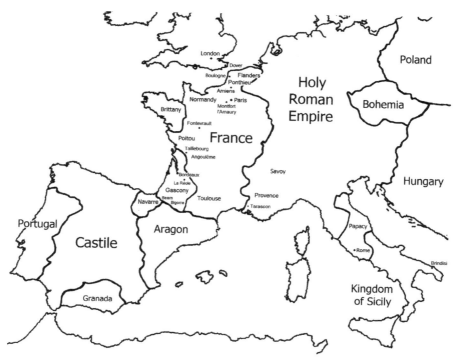

Western Europe around 1260.

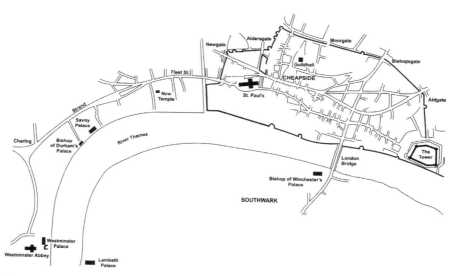

London in the 13th century.

Introduction

Knowing Glances

London, 20 January 1236, and the King of England has arrived with his new bride, whom he married six days earlier in Canterbury. The wealthiest citizens have greeted them as a mounted troop, each wearing costly garments and bearing 360 gold or silver cups to be used at the upcoming coronation banquet. They get into formation behind the king's trumpeters, who lead the procession through the city gates to Westminster a little under two kilometres down the road. After the anointing and crowning of the new queen in the abbey, the party proceeds to the Great Hall, where the king and queen take their place at the table on the dais.

They are Henry and Eleanor, the same names borne by the fabled King and Queen of England two generations back, Henry II and Eleanor of Aquitaine. That marriage had been spectacularly disastrous. When that Eleanor joined her sons in a rebellion against that Henry, he had her locked up in a castle until his death sixteen years later. Like the first Eleanor, the new one is beautiful and comes from a land in the south of modern-day France, but there the similarities end. She is not ten years older than her husband as her predecessor was, nor is this her second marriage. She is, in fact, no older than 12, which is clear from her small stature. As for whether she will turn out to be an equally capable and feisty queen, they will have to all wait and see.

Her husband is also nothing like the informal, power-hording womaniser his namesake grandfather was. Henry III came to the throne as a boy under desperate circumstances. The country had been plunged into a civil war brought on by the repressive policies of his father, King John, and before him, his uncle Richard the Lionheart. Faith and his regent William Marshal got Henry through those dark days, then through another rebellion instigated by Marshal's son. After nearly twenty years on the throne, he is only now finding his way.

Unlike his father and grandfather, Henry eschews hunting, wenching with maids and bullying his barons. He is 27 and lonely when he marries a girl, by proxy, across the Channel. Political intrigue scuttles it, which was just as well, for he had discovered Eleanor. So smitten is he with this daughter of the Count of Provence that he takes her without a dowry. The way to this moment has been pretty haphazard, the whole two decades of his reign really, but now that the king is married, perhaps things will finally settle down.

Fortunately for Eleanor, England had been conquered by the Normans 170 years earlier. The court still speaks the French brought over by their ancestors, so she can at least communicate with her husband and anybody moving in their orbit. It will not be entirely easy, because their French is Anglo-Norman and hers is Occitan, which bespeaks the sunny, romantic culture of the south she grew up in. Indeed, if she has to guess at any particular conversation, it is probably about the weather up there in the north. She heard that it was bad, but even the locals cannot believe the deluge of rains that have fallen that winter. But where romance is concerned, she adores the tales of King Arthur and this is the land where he supposedly performed all those amazing feats. Maybe her new husband will take her to see the sites.

As the banquet commences, Eleanor notices a man standing in close proximity to them, holding a basin of water for the king to clean his hands in before, during and after the meal. But he is clearly no servant. Besides wearing stately robes, he talks to Henry with a familiarity that suggests they are friends. More intriguing, his accent is very close to hers. Someone in her party whispers that it is Simon de Montfort, the son of the crusader who set most of their region ablaze three decades earlier. Simon too grew up in the south of France until his father was felled in the conflict. When the crusade was over, he ventured to England to claim the earldom of Leicester through his grandmother's noble lineage. The earldom came with the office of steward, which is what this tall and handsome knight, then in his late twenties, is doing in attending the king at the feast.

Simon looks at the party from Provence with equal suspicion. He survived a purge of foreign courtiers only a few years before and is worried this new crowd from abroad might re-ignite that peculiar English obsession with aliens. His position seems safe because he is one of Henry's most trusted confidants. He has recently shown his

loyalty to him by proposing marriage to two widowed countesses on the Continent, presumably at the king's urging. Henry has grand ideas about creating alliances across the Channel as a means of recovering the lands seized by the French from his father. 'Do that', he intimated, 'and I'll find you a suitable bride here if it doesn't work out'. Simon returned empty-handed.

Widows abound in this feudal society and the king gets to decide who marries the rich and powerful ones. None is more desirable than his own sister, who is also named Eleanor. She was younger than her new sister-in-law when she was betrothed to William Marshal II, son of her brother's first regent. Because of her extreme youth at the time, it was years before she and William began cohabitating. Their marriage was successful but childless. When he died suddenly in 1231, he was succeeded as the Earl of Pembroke by his brother Richard, who incited that latter-day rebellion against Henry. In the political settlement that followed, Eleanor was obliged to never remarry, thereby ensuring that her share of William's estate eventually returned to the Marshal family. For that, she had to swear a vow of chastity in front of the Archbishop of Canterbury, the same humourless man who had just crowned the new queen.

It is a decision she regrets. Eleanor likes fancy clothes and socialising and is not at all inclined to keeping a low profile and acting like the nun people expect her to be. What they do not know is that this beautiful and vibrant princess, just then passing her twentieth birthday, yearns to become a mother. Her situation is hopeless without a man brave and audacious enough to take on Church and State. From all the chatter at court, this French fellow standing behind her brother fits that bill. And so, as the king looks lovingly at his new bride, his sister and the steward exchange knowing glances across the way.

Within two years, Eleanor Marshal and Simon de Montfort would be married in a ceremony marked by no elaborate celebrations. Everything was done in secret, arranged by Henry in the expectation that no one would approve of it. He could not have been more right, but he weathered the storm that arose on account of it as he did all the other ones. And yet within two more years his friendship with Simon was in shambles and the relations between these two ambitious, very gifted men would lead, over the course of three decades, to a constitutional crisis that changed England forever.

Key to the outcome of these events were the two women in their lives, Eleanor of Provence and Eleanor de Montfort. In the course of time, these two Eleanors became friends as well as sisters-in-law, drawn together by motherhood and family and their mutual interests in learning and religion. But they were every bit the political animals their husbands were and threw themselves into the fray with the same determination. It was not just about standing by their men. Their own rights and security, and those of their children, were at stake, and they were fearless and formidable in advancing and protecting them. They did so, however, at the cost of their own relationship. In the end, as one left for exile, the other came home, and they missed each other by a single day.

1

No Greater Treasure 1215–1235

The legacy of King John, his youngest child, lots of marriages

On 19 May 1232, the body of King John was reinterred in a new tomb at Worcester Cathedral. Those of his five legitimate children in attendance were Henry, now the king, and Eleanor, John's youngest daughter. Henry was 9 when their father died in the early hours of 19 October 1216, but his sister was barely a year old at the time and so had no memory of him. She may have asked to be there specifically to see what he looked like in that state of preservation. The figure revealed in the coffin was about five feet seven inches tall, wearing his crimson coronation robe and cap. After he was translated, an effigy showing a crowned, bearded king flanked by the images of two canonised bishops was placed on top of his tomb chest. John had asked to be buried in Worcester because of his attachment to these local saints. It was hoped they would shield his soul in the afterlife.[1]

He certainly needed it. In his seventeen years on the throne he lost most of his dynastic lands on the Continent, was implicated in the murder of his nephew Arthur and other opponents, introduced a national tax, and subjected England to an interdict before making it a papal fief. The barons and clergy, harassed and bullied by him to no end, rose up and imposed a charter of liberties on him. A struggle ensued over Magna Carta, as the charter was later called, culminating in civil war and an invasion from France. The situation had mostly stalemated when John died of dysentery, aged 49. Since the king himself was the most objectionable feature of his reign, his death made it possible for the regency council instituted for his underage son to expel the French and reconcile the warring barons.

John's rule had begun to flounder when, having just succeeded his brother Richard I in 1199, he married Henry and Eleanor's mother

Isabella a year later. She was just a child then, no more than 12-years old, but as the heiress to the county of Angoulême in Poitou, John hoped to fortify his hold over this Continental lordship he had inherited from his mother Eleanor of Aquitaine. Isabella was betrothed to a leading Poitevin noble at the time, Hugh Lusignan, who felt aggrieved and complained about it to John's overlord King Philip Augustus of France.

Philip had been looking for any excuse to seize Normandy and other lands from the English and this was as good as any. By 1204, John had lost all but the southern lordships of Poitou and Gascony. As he plotted to get his lands back, and quarrelled with the pope and everybody else in the meantime, he and Isabella started a family with the birth of Henry in 1207, another son Richard in 1209, and a daughter Joan a year after that.

In 1214, John had a plan in place to defeat the French and went to Poitou with his wife and children, Richard and Joan. Another daughter was born to them there, named after Isabella in honour of the birth taking place in her homeland. To shore up his elaborate framework of alliances, and to make amends somewhat, John betrothed 4-year-old Joan to the son of Hugh Lusignan, who was another Hugh, just then in his late 20s. All the scheming and money came to nothing, however. John's allies in the north were crushed and he returned to England to face the consequences.

In the ensuing war with his rebellious barons, John put his children in various castles for protection. His wife Isabella was also under armed guard when she gave birth to Eleanor, probably in 1215. As the fifth child, and daughter no less, the chroniclers did not see any need to note when or where she was born, but Winchester or Marlborough seem the most likely locations. The landing of French forces in the spring of 1216 brought mother and infant to Bristol in case they needed to escape abroad.[2]

After John's death, Isabella left Eleanor with her wet nurse to help arrange the coronation of her son Henry in nearby Gloucester. It soon became clear that the regency council was not going to allow Isabella any role in the young king's affairs, because she was both a woman and foreigner. John had also been dismissive of her abilities, keeping tight control of her household and whereabouts throughout their marriage. In 1218, she left England to check on the welfare of Joan in Poitou and to see to her own position as the Countess of Angoulême.

The care of her other children was left to the direction of Peter des Roches, the Bishop of Winchester, John's most trusted adviser and member of the regency council. Worried about any one guardian having too much influence over the royal brood, Roches gave each sibling a separate household run by his adherents, to be reared and educated according to their status.[3] While the boys were taught letters, manners and knightly pursuits, the girls were prepared for marriage, motherhood and managing a home and household. As with most noble families of that era, they grew up speaking the French of their Norman ancestors and the English of the servants who managed their day-to-day upbringing. The girls were probably taught to read to some degree, both Latin and French, to facilitate their piety, skills in correspondence, and also escaping with a romance novel when the occasion arose.[4]

In the plainest terms, a royal princess was groomed from childhood to become the wife of somebody who could advance the interests of the monarchy, usually a foreign potentate. It was not enough to be physically healthy and beautiful, she also had to learn the finer points of good breeding, to be able to carry herself on foot or horseback with elegance, speak in a gracious and accomplished fashion, and exude a spiritual and calming air in all undertakings.

The governess assigned to make sure Eleanor had these qualities was Cecily de Sandford, a married woman of noble extraction. She was praised in her day for exquisite manners and strong sense of religious devotion.[5] It would be under her tutelage that Eleanor, like her sister Isabella, was expected to become imminently desirable for the day an embassy arrived from abroad to 'view' her on behalf of a potential ally.

The political situation of her brother's minority upset those plans practically from the start. The successful conclusion of the civil war and settlement owed much to the efforts and prestige of Henry's regents, the aged knight William Marshal and papal legate Guala Bicchieri. By 1220, Marshal was dead and Guala had gone back to Italy. Apart from a new legate, who served only a short time, Henry's regents were now Roches and Hubert de Burgh, the justiciar who was another holdover from John's government. The most pressing issue was to reassert royal control throughout the realm. The sheriffs and castellans who had remained loyal were loath to give up the power they had accumulated during the troubles. They argued that a king put them where they were and only a king could remove them, something not possible until Henry came of legal age.

Many of these men were aliens brought to England by John, who had given them heiresses and positions of power in return for their absolute loyalty. Roches was one of them. He rose from obscure origins in the Loire Valley in France to become one of John's steadfast cronies and was rewarded with the richest bishopric in England. When he resisted the drive to reclaim castles and sheriffdoms for the government, the justiciar denounced the influence and control of foreigners like him.

Hubert was being politically disingenuous, because there were plenty of English barons equally ensconced in their own private principalities. They included magnates like Ranulf de Blondeville, the Earl of Chester. Another was the man who succeeded William Marshal as the Earl of Pembroke, his son William II. Although the younger William had backed the French against John, he switched sides after Henry became king and came into possession of Marlborough and Fotheringhay Castles before hostilities ceased. He too was unwilling to hand them over to the council.[6]

A widower in his thirties with no children, William hoped to remarry. As one of the greatest landowners in the realm, with estates throughout England, Wales and Ireland, he had to run his prospects by the king and council. The most eligible bride then in England was Margaret, the oldest sister of King Alexander II of Scotland. Back in 1209, the then kings of England and Scotland, John and William the Lion, decided to deal with Scottish claims to the three northernmost English counties by betrothing William's 15-year-old daughter Margaret to 2-year-old Henry. With new kings now on both thrones, the treaty was reworked to marry Alexander to one of Henry's sisters. The council under Hubert would then find respectable husbands for Margaret and her sister Isabelle, who had accompanied her to England.[7]

In terms of wealth and standing, Marshal led the field of prospective bridegrooms for Margaret. He was just then considering two aristocratic brides on the Continent, but a princess was a far better catch. The council, however, had doubts about his loyalty to the Crown. If it was going to take a princess to keep him from marrying someone from abroad, they preferred it be an English one, the king's 5-year-old sister Eleanor.[8] Unlike with Margaret, Marshal would have to wait years before he and Eleanor could live together and start a family, but becoming brother-in-law of his own lord king would give him enormous prestige and clout.

Why Eleanor was chosen and not her sister Isabella, who was a year older, had to do with developments in Poitou. In 1219, Isabella of Angoulême sent a letter to her son Henry explaining that Hugh Lusignan was no longer willing to wait for Joan, now 10-years old, to grow up.

He wanted a wife and children, and so to keep him from marrying into a family hostile to England, Isabella married him herself.[9] Certainly her marriage to Hugh put Isabella in good position to defend Henry's interests in the region, and the return of Joan would help settle the problem of the treaty with Scotland. In her letter, Isabella promised to send her daughter back to England, but conditioned it on receiving the dower lands given to her by John and the £2,333 he 'ought' to have willed her.[10] As for the various lordships in Poitou meant to go to Hugh as Joan's marriage portion, they were keeping them too.*

It sounded like extortion that did not bode well for the future, but all Henry and the council could do was protest and complain about it to the pope. In the summer of 1220, just after his second coronation in Westminster Abbey, the king travelled to York to make final arrangements for Alexander's marriage to Joan. The wedding was to take place by 13 October, but assuming the bride had not been repatriated by then, the next oldest sister would become his wife. Six-year-old Isabella was escorted to the negotiations so Alexander could view her. Henry and Hubert also promised to find husbands for Margaret and her sister Isabelle within a year of that date or return them to Scotland.[11]

A harder problem was finding a marriage portion for whichever of the English princesses, Joan or Isabella, reached the altar. The government was broke, with not even £200 left in the treasury. The best they could offer Alexander was to write off the £3,333 Scotland still owed for Margaret's dowry of £10,000 under the original treaty and to give him Fotheringhay Castle, which Marshal claimed he was willing to give up 'to obtain the preferment' of Eleanor.[12]

As the date for the wedding neared, Henry and the court again went north to tell Alexander that Joan was still abroad, but an agreement, all to Hugh's advantage, had been reached for her return. She arrived early the next year and the wedding took place in York on 19 June 1221. Noting her

---

* A marriage portion (or dowry) was the money or property given by the bride's family for her security. Although it came under the legal control of her husband, the marriage portion reverted back to her upon his death or to her family after her own death. A dower was the property of the groom to be settled on the bride in the event of his death. She was to keep it for her lifetime, then it reverted to their children or to the husband's family in the event there were not any.

young age at the time, the Lanercost chronicler later remarked that Joan grew up to be something of a beauty.[13] Then, on 3 October of that year, Margaret finally got married. The ceremony was held in London and the bridegroom was none other than Hubert de Burgh. To court observers, it looked as if the 50-year-old, twice-widowed commoner Hubert had been angling to marry the Scottish princess all along in order to ennoble his status. Indeed, he had insinuated himself into friendship with the King of Scotland, now his brother-in-law, with gifts beforehand.[14]

Despite his agreement to hand over Fotheringhay, Marshal had to be shamed into doing it. He was told to surrender Marlborough and another castle as well or risk forfeiting his chance to marry Eleanor. The hard line reflects Hubert's intention to make an example out of Marshal for the other obstinate potentates to see. Slowly and reluctantly, they too began to comply and yet Marshal was still denied his bride. In 1222, he complained about it to the pope, who responded by telling Stephen Langton, the Archbishop of Canterbury, to make it happen, but on condition that it did not create a scandal.[15]

He was referring to the fact that Eleanor was only 7, five years below the age of consent decreed by the Church. There was also the obstacle to the nuptials raised by the barons and bishops of England. Magna Carta prohibited the disparagement of women, which is to say marrying them to men of lower social rank. That had been the case of Margaret's marriage to Hubert, but the Scottish court, where Magna Carta did not apply, saw the groom as the powerful justiciar and not the son of an unknown gentrified family in Norfolk. Marshal, on the other hand, was descended from the ancestral nobility through his mother, and his father was, of course, the William Marshal of legend. Junior even had a biography of his father commissioned at this time to dispel murmurs that his blood was not good enough for Eleanor.[16]

She was a princess just the same, and royal marriages were expected to form profitable alliances for the kingdom. Henry said as much in a letter he wrote to the pope justifying marrying Eleanor to one of his subjects instead of to a foreign prince. 'We have no greater treasure than our own marriage and those of our sisters.' But Marshal was still a great potentate, who had recently recovered two castles for the king from the Welsh, and there was always the worry that he might marry someone from abroad. The English nobility and clergy nevertheless needed more convincing, and Marshal suspected it was the jealousy of certain rivals, particularly the Earl of Chester, that was keeping the marriage from going forward.[17]

Hubert himself was anxious for it because, in reclaiming the castles and sheriffdoms for the king, he had undercut his own rivals for supremacy on the council. With Roches and the other aliens now out of the way, he wanted to bind Marshal to the Crown as a firm supporter. It was of particular importance then because the Lacy clan in Ireland was going on a rampage and the Earl of Pembroke's recent military success against the Welsh made him the right man to go there and suppress them. Sending him there as the king's brother-in-law would not only enhance his authority, but interpose a separation of several years after the wedding to allow his much younger bride to develop physically.[18]

On 23 April 1224, after a wait of three years, William Marshal and Eleanor Plantagenet were married. The date is given in a chronicle connected to Canterbury, so presumably Archbishop Stephen officiated. The wedding day was not the first time the by now 9-year-old girl and 35-year-old man saw each other. Since Marshal was no foreign ruler, there would have been no prior 'viewing' for his benefit, but Henry had arranged for him to escort Eleanor to a certain function two months earlier. A little over a week after the wedding, on 2 May, Marshal received his appointment as justiciar for Ireland and off he went.[19] Eleanor, now the Countess of Pembroke, went back to the care of her governess Cecily in anticipation of his return some day.

Marriage to William Marshal II, accompanying him and the king abroad

Marshal's departure coincided with the greatest crisis of Henry's minority. The last castle to hold out against the king was at Bedford, where the garrison was under the command of John's famous alien captain Fawkes de Bréauté. Their decision to put up a fight could not have come at a worse time. King Louis VIII, who had attempted to take the English throne from John when he was the crown prince of France, refused to renew the truce with England. While Henry hammered away at Bedford, Louis bought off Hugh Lusignan and marched into Poitou. By the time Bedford surrendered in August 1224, Poitou as an English lordship was lost and Gascony was now in danger. To fund a relief force,

Henry agreed to reissue Magna Carta in return for a tax. In the spring of the following year, the force left under the nominal command of the king's 16-year-old brother Richard.[20]

The papacy was mortified by these events. Henry was technically a ward of the pope and the army used by the overly pious Louis to conquer Poitou had been assembled for a crusade. When the pope complained, Louis threatened to invade England and take the Crown there after all. To show he meant business, he began courting the Holy Roman Empire for a marital alliance.

Henry sent the Bishop of Carlisle to Germany to thwart those plans, namely by negotiating a marriage between his sister Isabella and the imperial crown prince. Henry himself would marry another Margaret, the daughter of the Duke of Austria. Emperor Frederick II found himself unable to choose between England or France and decided to make it an all-German wedding by marrying his son the crown prince to the duke's daughter.[21]

In 1226, Louis finally got around to crusading against the Albigensians of southern France. Henry's court astrologer, a fellow by the name of William Pierrepont, declared that a terrible fate awaited the King of France. Sure enough, he died of dysentery, aged only 39.[22] Since he left behind an underage heir, also named Louis, Henry saw his opening to recover the lands lost by his father on the Continent. He proposed to marry himself to Yolanda, the daughter of the Duke of Brittany, as a way of gaining a foothold next to Normandy, but Louis's widow Blanche of Castile, now the queen regent, outbid him and took Yolanda for one of her many sons.[23]

By this point Marshal was no longer the justiciar of Ireland. His mission had been mostly successful, but in June 1226 he resigned his appointment under a cloud of suspicion. When he declined to meet Henry in Wales to talk about it, the king sent him a letter assuring him of his trust and reminding him that he had given him his sister in marriage. If, however, Marshal insisted on evading him, he would have to surrender two more castles.[24]

Marshal might have believed it was Hubert behind the coolness between the brothers-in-law. The justiciar of England was then at the height of his power, marked by his enfeoffment with the earldom of Kent. The king had done it for Margaret's sake, to give her husband a title more befitting to her royal background, but little excuse could be found for all the castles and lands he was bestowing on Hubert and his family at the same time. One of Hubert's nephews even took over Marshal's old job of justiciar for Ireland.[25]

Another nephew of his was given Berkhamsted Castle over the claims of Henry's brother Richard, who had just returned as the saviour of Gascony. The king had belted Richard the Earl of Cornwall for his efforts, but did not give him much property to back up the title. An argument between the brothers over this issue led Richard to meet Marshal in Marlborough and together they joined forces with several other earls to air their grievances to Henry in August 1227.

Mostly it was their distrust of the Earl of Kent and the way the king had been redrawing the forest boundaries since declaring himself of age the previous January. Some promises were made and that was the end of the standoff.[26] All the earls went home except Richard of Cornwall. He had received some minor grants, but felt he deserved more rewards and respect as the heir to the throne. He decided to go north to see if he might not obtain them by taking a Scottish princess for a bride.

It was not Margaret's sister Isabelle. In 1225, she was married to 16-year-old Roger Bigod, the future Earl of Norfolk, as part of sending him north to become a ward of her brother the king.[27] Alexander II had one more sister, Margery. She was a decade older than the 18-year-old Richard, but it seems he was more interested in what marriage portion she might provide than either her age or why she was still unmarried. Henry was not amused by his brother presuming to act on his own in the matter and labelled him 'rebellious'. The Scottish nobility also saw something untoward in Richard's suit and advised Alexander to reject it.[28]

In all these developments at court, William Marshal had to busy himself without his wife by his side. Henry had made him wait three years to marry his sister, he was now making him wait longer before engaging in spousal relations with her. It was known in the Middle Ages that the chances of a young woman having a safe pregnancy and childbirth were better the older she was. The Marshals likely did not consummate their marriage until October 1229, when Eleanor was 14 and her husband 40. In that month on the eighteenth, Henry granted Marshal ten manors, meant to comprise Eleanor's marriage portion.[29]

In fact, it was the second time these manors had been granted to Marshal as a marriage portion. The first time came in 1214 with his marriage to Alice de Bethune, who died less than a year later. King John seized the manors when Marshal sided with other rebels to depose him.[30] He eventually got them back, but held them only at the king's pleasure. Now, in making the grant permanent, Henry was giving Marshal what was his to begin with. The marriage did not cost the king a thing.

There was a reason for the grant and consummation at this particular time. Relations between France and Brittany had broken down and the duke switched his allegiance to England. Hoping this development had put the queen regent Blanche of Castile in the mood to compromise, Henry offered to marry his sister Isabella to the young King Louis IX, both of whom were about 15. The French could keep the counties of Maine and Anjou as her marriage portion, but they would have to give back Normandy to Henry. Blanche, however, had already shown she was more than willing to pound the duke and other dissenters and so ignored the King of England. Henry realised the only way he was going to get anything back from the French was by taking it by force.[31]

In the summer of 1229, he summoned the feudal host to gather at Portsmouth on the south coast. Marshal was going as one of the senior commanders and Eleanor was to accompany him, perhaps in the hope they might conceive a child during the campaign, just in case he did not make it back. Henry was so hopeful of a pregnancy that he promised William he would allow his brother Richard Marshal, a French peer who had lived in Normandy for the past decade, to succeed him as the Earl of Pembroke in the event he died without an heir.[32]

For logistical reasons, the fleet did not sail until the end of April 1230. On the morning of 2 May, Henry ordered his ship and several others to make landfall at the island of Jersey. He was concerned about Eleanor, who had become unwell during the voyage. What was described as 'fatigue' in an official letter may have been seasickness or morning sickness, perhaps even a miscarriage. The remarkable thing about this episode is that Henry, with so much riding on the outcome of this venture, had not only diverted part of the fleet on his sister's behalf, but refused to abandon her there. Whatever afflicted her, she was soon fit to travel and at three the next morning, they left to join the remainder of the fleet in Brittany.[33]

The success of the expedition depended on Hugh Lusignan and other Poitevin nobles returning their homage to Henry. The negotiations that took place gave Eleanor the opportunity to see her mother. She had been no more than three when Isabella of Angoulême left England and so she probably had no real memory of her. Although Isabella had started a new family with Hugh, with six children already and another three to come, she may have kept informed of her daughter's wellbeing and upbringing through Robert de Courtenay, a distant relative of hers residing in England. He was Eleanor's guardian at the time of her marriage to Marshal and Henry may have chosen him specifically because of his connection to their mother.[34]

It was a hefty pension and free hand to bully their neighbours that had made Hugh and Isabella defect to the French in the first place. In June 1230, a royal steward wrote home that the couple had renewed their treaty with Blanche and that doomed the enterprise. Henry found some allies, but could not bring himself to launch a war of re-conquest, and Hubert, who saw nothing in it for himself, made sure he did not.

Eleanor went back to England that summer, but returned in September as Henry and her other brother Richard of Cornwall prepared to go home to recuperate from a bout of dysentery. Apart from keeping Marshal loyal and happy, the king wanted his sister there as a figurehead for the Plantagenets in their struggle with the Capetians. To Henry, appearances meant everything.[35]

Teenage widow, an ill-advised settlement, lord of her estates

One of those who succumbed to dysentery while on the Continent was Gilbert de Clare, the Earl of Gloucester. He left behind a widow Isabel, who was the second of Marshal's five sisters. Richard of Cornwall, once sufficiently recovered, saw his chance and moved in to marry her. She was nine years older than him and had six children, but was said to be a beauty and stood to inherit one-third of her late husband's estate as her dower.

Marriage to Isabel de Clare would also make Richard a brother-in-law of the Earl of Derby, uncle of the Earl of Norfolk, and stepfather of the future Earl of Gloucester, useful associations come the next showdown with his brother the king. Henry could sense what Richard was after and expressed his disapproval. He was also against the marriage because it robbed him of two valuable matches, Richard's and Isabel's, to engineer for the Crown's political and financial advantage.[36]

Eleanor and her husband, who had returned from France in February 1231, were at the nuptials that took place on 30 March. One week later, Marshal was dead. There was no word on what killed him, just that he became ill, died, and was buried at the New Temple Church in London next to his father. Eleanor's grief is unrecorded, but can be measured in the response of her brother. According to Matthew Paris, Henry loved William Marshal II 'immoderately' and cried out to heaven when he saw his body. He tried to comfort his sister with gifts of venison and his own best wines.

The personal loss aside, there was work to be done. Marshal had been a major landowner and here it was hoped that at least Eleanor was pregnant. Otherwise William's heir was his brother Richard Marshal, a liegeman of the King of France. Despite his earlier promise to William, Henry had no desire to have somebody of such dubious loyalty succeed as the Earl of Pembroke. At the end of May, when Eleanor would have known that she was not with child, Henry ordered the confiscation of the Marshal estates.[37]

That put the tenants of these lands in Wales and Ireland in an uproar. Rumours began circulating that Richard Marshal was planning an invasion and was getting help for it from his new brother-in-law Richard of Cornwall, who was still sore at Henry for not granting him the county of Cornwall in fee. The Welsh prince Llywelyn ap Iorwerth took advantage of the situation to strike. Henry could only muster a lacklustre response from among his barons to turn him back and so he agreed to make peace with both Richards. He was building a castle in Wales when Marshal appeared on 8 August 1231 and did homage for Pembroke. Two days later Richard of Cornwall came and received the grants he was looking for.[38]

Interestingly, in that same month Henry received another visitor from France looking for an English earldom. He was Simon de Montfort, the son of the Albigensian crusader of the same name. The grandmother of this younger Simon had been the sister and co-heir of the fourth Earl of Leicester when he died in 1204. When her Montfort brood threw their lot in with France, King John seized the earldom and gave it to Ranulf in compensation for the lands lost by the Earl of Chester on the Continent. Since Simon was a first cousin once removed of the old earl, who had no children, Ranulf agreed he could take possession of Leicester. Henry saw something in Simon to suggest he was a man worth having at court and accepted his homage for the earldom, but not with the title of earl yet.[39]

If on his deathbed Henry was asked which of the 672 months of his reign he would do all over again, then August 1231 would be it, for no two people caused him as much sorrow and anguish as Richard Marshal and Simon de Montfort (and Richard of Cornwall had his moments). There was Marshal to begin with, although his first opposition to the king was entirely reasonable. In October 1231, Henry had decided, presumably out of nowhere, to marry Margery, the youngest sister of Alexander of Scotland and the woman Richard of Cornwall had tried to scoop up four years earlier.[40] The match made no sense politically, because the two kings were already brothers-in-law. But Henry was now 24-years old and, having never been with a woman before, he was probably feeling lonely. He asked Hubert to come up with a bride and Margery was it.

It was Margery all right, said court cynics, because if the king married her, he would become Hubert's brother-in-law. The justiciar had only reversals to show lately and was hoping this would help him retain his hold on power. Henry had been recently ill and that certainly informed Hubert that if the king were to die unmarried and childless, he would be succeeded by Richard of Cornwall, his sworn enemy.

Marshal and the other magnates did not object to the marriage on these grounds, rather it was their opinion that it was degrading for the king to marry the younger sister (Margery) of the wife (Margaret) of one of his subjects (Hubert). Henry did not care and made plans for a wedding in York anyway. He was eventually dissuaded, chiefly at Marshal's insistence, and went back to spending the better part of his time settling the squabbles, jealousies and inheritances that came with the drearier side of kingship.[41]

The most complex of these issues was the Marshal estate. As William Marshal's widow, Eleanor was entitled to receive the manors that comprised her marriage portion, plus a third of her late husband's property as her dower. Contemporary assessments put the value of her marriage portion and dower in England at around £530. The estate in Wales and Ireland was probably worth four times that amount.[42] Altogether her one-third dower would earn her some serious money in an age where £100 a year was considered affluence.

Rightly suspecting that the four surviving Marshal brothers would take a dim view of the settlement, Henry's delaying action in allowing Richard to succeed at Pembroke had at least as much to do with securing Eleanor's inheritance as it did with questions about Marshal's loyalty. Indeed, when Marshal first arrived that summer and found the estate in Crown hands, Henry told him, rather absurdly if the story from chronicler Roger of Wendover can be believed, that his sister might yet be pregnant. They would all have to wait until they could be sure she was not. In the meantime, Henry assigned Eleanor several properties in anticipation of the final settlement.[43]

Magna Carta stipulated that a widow should have her dower and marriage portion within forty days of her husband's death. Since they were already well beyond that deadline, Marshal felt no obligation to pursue the settlement. Admittedly, there were a lot of properties to assess and family and tenants to consult before Marshal reached a final decision. Not until June 1232 did he name nine properties for Eleanor's Irish dower.

Only a month later, however, he thought better of it. On 29 July, he met the king at Woodstock and offered Eleanor a lump sum annuity of £400 for her dower in Wales and Ireland.[44] While far short of what she might get in the best-case scenario, it would spare them all a protracted struggle, as well as her the trouble of having to manage a vast, scattered estate. Together with her English properties, she could enjoy an income of nearly £1,000, a stupendous sum for a 16-year-old girl. At Henry's urging, Eleanor accepted the deal.

The offer likely came about as a result of the fall of Hubert de Burgh. Henry sacked his chief minister after he was implicated in recent attacks against papal clerks.[45] Taking his place in the king's counsels was his avowed enemy, the formerly disgraced Roches, but Henry was also keen to cultivate Marshal as an active member of the court. Clearly the issue of his sister's dower had to be settled before they could become regular intimates. Lest Eleanor got the idea, however, that her interests were being sacrificed for political expediency, Henry granted her numerous favours and made lots of gifts of venison for her table, a sure sign of royal favour.[46]

By Christmas 1232, it all began to unravel. Roches had promised Henry that, given another chance, he would restructure his finances so that, instead of scrounging for money all the time, the king would have the same treasures enjoyed by his father and grandfather. Roches was just then in a good position to make it happen. The confiscation of Hubert's assets followed the death of the childless Ranulf of Chester, the largest landowner in the realm, providing the regime with two huge windfalls of patronage to disburse. The capital, both political and financial, was enormous if handled adeptly.

But Roches was out to settle a few scores for his earlier ouster. He insisted that Henry start acting like a real king as his father had been and right all the wrongs Roches and his men had suffered. With his eye on the promised treasure, Henry adopted this autocratic line and began dismissing officials and abrogating charters contrary to the protections of Magna Carta.[47]

This was the reason Marshal gave for the rebellion he raised in the autumn of 1233. The king had surrounded himself with foreign favourites who were out to undermine Magna Carta. In truth, he was much more a foreigner than Roches and his circle, and his own conduct in settling Eleanor's dower showed the charter of liberties was hardly anything sacred to him. He and his allies, moreover, had also benefited in the realignment of wealth and power, only nowhere near as much.

At first, Marshal merely sulked, but when some of his men and kinfolk cut deals with Henry, he felt betrayed and set out to punish them. Spurred on by the diehards in his camp, Marshal forgot all about his father's legendary loyalty to the Crown and joined an insurrection that bested Henry at every turn. He and his riders even teamed up with the Welsh in sacking Shrewsbury and putting the town to the torch. With no one able to match him in the field, and Marshal contemptuous of his latest peace offer, the king lured him to Ireland to defend his estates there. The Earl of Pembroke was cut down in a skirmish and died on 16 April 1234.[48] He was not brought back to London to lie next to his father and brother at the New Temple.

In the shakeup that followed, Roches and other ministers were disgraced and dismissed. To obtain peace with the rebels and the Marshals in particular, Henry would have to pardon the third son, Gilbert, and allow him to succeed his brother, who had left behind a wife in Normandy but no children. One of Gilbert's grievances was sure to be Eleanor's dower and the arrears owed her by the late Richard, who had failed to pay her the first year's annuity of £400. Although Henry had every right to order the seizure of Richard's goods to make up the default, and did order them, it likely only aggravated the now dead man's defiance.[49]

The mediator between Gilbert and the king was Edmund of Abingdon, the newly consecrated Archbishop of Canterbury. Like the majority of bishops, he never hid his disgust for the foreigners at court, even accusing them of murdering Richard Marshal, but he worked tirelessly to end the conflict. Aware that Eleanor's dower was a sticking point, he may have prevailed upon her and Henry to make it as palatable as possible to the Marshals. The only thing for sure is that, sometime during the negotiations, Eleanor knelt before Edmund and took a vow of perpetual widowhood. He then placed a gold ring on her finger signifying that she was henceforth a bride of Christ sworn evermore to earthly chastity. At 19-years old, Eleanor had declared she would never marry again.

It seemed like a concession to the Marshals on the face of it. Were Eleanor to take another husband, as seemed likely given her youth, her dower properties would come under his control and he might cause the family endless trouble trying to recover them should she pre-decease him. The Marshals would, moreover, regain her marriage portion were she to die childless. At a meeting in Marlborough on 12 August 1234, Henry worked out an agreement between Eleanor and Gilbert to finalise her English dower. Ten days later, the king confirmed Gilbert Marshal as the new Earl of Pembroke.[50]

But it was not just for one disgruntled baron that Eleanor chose to become a widow for life. Like her brother and most people of that era, she was very pious and had visited religious houses following her husband's death. She was not alone in making her vow, either. Kneeling at her side before Edmund, also swearing perpetual widowhood, was her former governess Cecily de Sandford, a woman of strong faith who doubtless still exerted influence over her.

A worldly element could have also informed Eleanor's decision. As one of the richest landowners in the realm, she wielded power independent of being the sister of the king. Marriage meant she would have to give it up and revert to the role of the submissive wife, perhaps constantly pregnant as her mother had been and always running the risks to health and life that came with childbearing. Meanwhile, her husband would be making all the rounds concerning her property, doing all the business with them, and getting all the attention and entertainment she enjoyed now.

Last but not least, there was her status as treasure of the realm to consider. Magna Carta protected widows from being forced into remarriage, but there would always be pressure on Eleanor, as the king's sister, to enter into an international marriage alliance for the sake of the kingdom. That would not only take her away from her properties, but from her family and home altogether, probably never to see them again. Her husband could be an old ogre with a wandering eye or need to be on horseback all day long, and even if he was not, she might have to endure a weird and lonely life in a strange court.

Case in point was her 20-year-old sister Isabella. In February 1235, she was betrothed to the twice-older, twice-widowed Frederick II of the Holy Roman Empire. He was the father of the crown prince she might have married eight years earlier, who was now languishing in prison, and would die there, after raising his own rebellion. Frederick's prestige allowed him to ask for an incredible £20,000 dowry for her, and the king and council, after discussing the matter for three days, agreed that an alliance with the emperor was worth having.[51]

Isabella was given a spectacular send-off in May, which ended with Henry and his sister in tears as they said goodbye to each other. Her departure would have left Eleanor next in line should a similar match with a foreign potentate present itself. Now that she was off the marriage market, Eleanor threw herself into estate management with gusto and she was not shy about using her connection to the king to get things done or to intercede for her tenants with him. Henry was generally obliging towards her, but would also call her out when she overstepped her authority.[52]

Where she needed him most was again the issue of her dower. She had no sooner reached an agreement with Gilbert Marshal for the rest of her properties when the king had to order more seizures on account of his failure to keep up payments to her. Like his brother Richard, Gilbert also defaulted on the first annuity of £400 he owed her. He was probably not being difficult, just lacked the cash, and more agreements and sureties were arranged to ensure Eleanor received what was due her.[53] To show he appreciated his efforts, the king gave Gilbert his consent in July 1235 to marry Margery, the Scottish princess whose hand he himself had sought four years earlier. Henry was hoping the match would heal the rift not just between him and the Marshals but a more serious one that had developed between him and his brother-in-law up north.

Alexander of Scotland had allied himself with the Marshals during their insurrection. He did not like the treatment meted out to his brother-in-law Hubert de Burgh (Margaret's husband), and his other brother-in-law Roger Bigod (Isabelle's husband) was a Marshal nephew. Henry was hoping the wedding between Gilbert and Margery on 1 August in Berwick would mollify Alexander because the Scottish king and Gilbert's interests in Ireland were similar.[54]

But Alexander's biggest gripe was his marriage to Joan. She had never been given an adequate marriage portion, nor had she given him an heir to the throne after thirteen years of marriage. It did not occur to Alexander that his failure to give his wife independent means or a vibrant social life at court did not help the situation any. Henry was close to all his sisters and Joan's plight moved him in October 1234 to grant her a manor in Huntingdonshire, both to provide her with an income and perhaps a place to stay when her husband was at his surliest.[55]

Eleanor continued enjoying her brother's favour as she went about establishing herself as a lord, the dowager Countess of Pembroke. She received various gifts of oak to carry out construction works at her manors, more venison for her table, and licenses to hold markets. In all likelihood, she was with the court for Christmas in Winchester at the end of 1235.[56] She would have found Henry busy making sure everything was splendid, not just because he was keen on pageantry, but more so on this occasion because he was expecting a special party to arrive just after the festivities. In all the recent marriage activity, the king had finally managed to find himself a wife. Two, in fact.

2

An Elegant Sort of Beauty 1236–1237

Checking the French, Henry's first marriage

The Marshal insurrection had been a turning point in Henry's reign. Although convinced the Earl of Pembroke had been a traitor, the king admitted he himself had acted outside the law. Under pressure from the Archbishop of Canterbury and other clergy, he reissued Magna Carta as surety against it happening again, but privately he blamed Roches, his boyhood mentor, for leading him astray. It was because of him and the other holdovers from his father's administration that things grew so out of hand, making him look bad and, worse, a laughingstock. Far from having any of the promised treasure to show for it, he was more broke than ever, unable to stop the French from wiping out his earlier gains on the Continent. He decided to make a clean break and started by vacating the great offices of state like justiciar and chancellor. Henry would rule with the help of his council and household, but no more would he leave himself open to the advice or designs of a single minister or personality.[1]

His first order of business was to create a home life for himself. A natural family man, Henry was frustrated that nothing had come of any of the earlier marriage proposals for himself. He charged Hubert with sabotaging the first of them, in 1226, by allegedly telling the family of Margaret of Austria that the king was weak, womanish, quarrelsome and deceitful. If that were not enough, he suffered from leprosy and was impotent.[2]

Looking around the map of Europe, Henry set his sights on Joan, the heiress of the county of Ponthieu just across the water. It was neither big nor rich, but its close proximity to Normandy made it ideally suited for another recovery operation in the future. He sent an embassy to Joan's parents that resulted in an exchange of marriage vows by proxy with the 15-year-old girl. On 8 April 1235, Henry wrote to Joan's father, asking him to send her to England by 27 May so they could have a real wedding on that day, the feast of Pentecost.[3]

Although Joan and Henry were married in the eyes of the Church, they were both great-great-grandchildren of King Louis VI of France, putting them within the four degrees of consanguinity prohibited by that same Church. They would need a dispensation from the pope in order to make their union binding. Henry sent proctors to Rome to obtain the dispensation, but Blanche of Castile had her own group of men there to lobby against it. Ever eyeing Henry's intentions, she knew what he was after by marrying Joan. So worried was she at the prospect that she threatened to strip Joan's parents of their county if the marriage went forward.[4]

Determined not to be frustrated again in his search for a wife, Henry had been negotiating for another bride even as he was in the process of marrying Joan. She was the niece of Amadeus of Savoy, whose county south of Lake Geneva controlled the strategic Alpine passes between France and Italy. The niece was actually further south in the county of Provence, but the whole region piqued Henry's interest because Savoy and Provence were part of the Holy Roman Empire. His marriage to a daughter of both dynastic houses, coinciding with the wedding of his sister Isabella and Emperor Frederick, was bound to give him plenty of diplomatic leverage against France.[5] Blanche, however, was not overly concerned because both counties were nowhere near the lands Henry wanted back. There was also the fact that she had arrived there first.

Since taking control of the French monarchy, Blanche of Castile had vigorously pursued the expansionist policy begun by her father-in-law Philip Augustus. In 1229, she set her sights on Toulouse in the south. That county had been ravaged for two decades by the Albigensian Crusade, led first by Simon de Montfort's father until he was killed in 1218, then by Blanche's husband Louis until he too met an untimely end. The Count of Toulouse, Raymond VII, was desperate for reconciliation and willing to give up the heretics he had long protected in order to gain it. The stiff terms imposed by Blanche included marriage between Raymond's only child Jeanne and her son Alphonse. Should the couple produce no heirs, Toulouse would pass to the monarchy after Raymond's death.[6]

If Blanche was hoping Raymond would try to recoup his losses elsewhere, he did not disappoint. Looking eastward, he pressed his family's ancestral claims to Marseille and nearby territories. They were under the control of Provence, which normally could have sought aid from the empire in turning Raymond back, but Frederick was too preoccupied with his Italian subjects. Blanche presumed to help settle the quarrel by sending an emissary to Raymond and to the Count of Provence, Raymond Berenger V. His wife was Beatrice of Savoy, sister of Amadeus. The emissary was to determine the extent of their grievances, but while in Provence he asked for a look at the count's eldest daughter Margaret. He reported to Blanche that the 12-year-old girl was 'pretty of face, but prettier of faith'.[7]

That was all Blanche needed to know. Raymond Berenger and his wife Beatrice of Savoy had no sons, only four daughters. A marriage between her son King Louis IX and the eldest of the daughters would make it easy for the monarchy to absorb that county as well. The count and countess suspected as much, but a marital alliance with France was their best chance to keep both their neighbour Raymond VII and their overlord Frederick in check. Blanche, moreover, allowed the impoverished couple to secure Margaret's dowry of £6,667 with a meagre down payment and lien on Tarascon Castle near the Mediterranean coast.[8]

Of course, it was not just to annex Provence that Blanche was eager for the match to go forward. Her son needed a wife to produce heirs, and a pretty and pious one would do. There was never any thought given to the abilities Margaret might possess for governmental affairs or even running a household. Although Louis was now 19, the age at which Henry declared his majority, Blanche intended to go on ruling as before. When anyone spoke of the Queen of France, it was still going to be her.

The first sign of her controlling nature came after Margaret was escorted to her wedding at Sens on 27 May 1234. Her uncles William and Thomas of Savoy, experienced men of the world, had been expecting to stay on at the court in Paris, but Blanche sent them and the entire party, including Margaret's damsels and nurse, home with money for their travel expenses. The young bride was left on her own. Louis, on the advice of his priests, waited three days before they consummated their marriage, spending all that time in prayer and devotion. Blanche may have had some input in that decision. She had a good idea of how much time the young couple ought to spend in each other's company and was always ready to intrude to enforce their separation.[9]

William and Thomas were not the only siblings of Amadeus and Beatrice of Savoy. There were ten in all, including brothers Peter, Boniface and Philip. To provide for all these younger sons, their father had angled positions in the Church for them. By 1226, William was the Bishop-elect of Valence, a small town located between Lyon and Avignon. He was never consecrated in the post because he longed for something better. He and his brothers were a warlike, sophisticated lot, more at home in international diplomacy and conflict than in chanting hymns and prayer, and would gladly lead papal armies if given the chance to do so.[10]

In agreeing to marry Margaret to the King of France, Raymond Berenger and his Savoyard in-laws were hoping to become junior partners in the marital alliance. Blanche's rebuff left them exposed to her machinations. But they found that they still had a role to play in European affairs because the King of England and Holy Roman Emperor were both wary of her. Six months after the Franco-Provencal wedding, Frederick proposed an alliance with England by taking Isabella Plantagenet as his third wife.

Henry had also turned his attention to this region with his own view to containing Blanche. If she thwarted him in Ponthieu, as was likely to be the case, he would do the same to her in Provence. And so, well before he married Joan, Henry had sent ambassadors to Raymond Berenger and Beatrice to inquire about their next oldest daughter, Eleanor.[11]

Presuming she was 12 when the ambassadors arrive, Eleanor was born in 1223. She was actually the fourth child. Twin boys had been born before Margaret's birth in 1221, but died shortly afterward. Another pair of daughters would come along later, Sanchia in 1228 and Beatrice in 1231.

Until she left for married life with Louis, Margaret was Eleanor's closest childhood companion. As the children of aristocrats, the girls were raised to carry themselves well in society. For this, they had the court of their parents, which continued the tradition of culture and literacy that distinguished their region of Languedoc. The girls likely learned how to read their native Occitan, which was linguistically close to French, and enough Latin to be able to navigate the religious ceremonies and letter writing that dominated their lives. They learned how to ride a horse, master a hawk, play chess and show a discerning eye for clothes and jewels. All these skills were acquired and managed with grace and finesse, which served to enhance their natural beauty and make them desirable on the marriage market.[12]

It is doubtful if much of this mattered to the ascetically-inclined Louis. The pomp and high life he could do without. Margaret had to be pious and fruitful, that was what counted. Henry was a completely different story. So spare and gloomy was his first coronation that he went all out for his second one in May 1220.[13] Henry never outgrew his love for spectacle and showmanship and whoever ended up by his side had to accept the importance he placed on pageantry and splendour in his concept of monarchy.

Whatever his ambassadors reported from their mission to Provence, Henry went ahead with his marriage to Joan and sent proctors to Rome for the dispensation. When the party from Ponthieu failed to show up for their official wedding in May, it was clear that Blanche had made her move. On 22 June 1235, Henry wrote a letter to Count Amadeus of Savoy of his desire to marry his niece Eleanor, but that he had already married the daughter of 'a certain nobleman'. Not to worry, he expected the matter to be resolved soon.[14]

Two emissaries were dispatched to Savoy with the letter, Richard le Gras and John of Gatesden. In all likelihood, they also went south to Provence to meet Raymond Berenger and Beatrice and to view Eleanor. Roger of Wendover gives us an idea of the atmosphere of these bridal inspections in the case of Henry's sister Isabella when Frederick's agents came calling.

> She appeared before the messengers of the emperor, a lady in her twentieth year, beautiful to look upon, adorned with virgin modesty, and distinguished by her royal dress and manners. After they had refreshed their sight for some time with gazing on the lady, they decided that she was most worthy in all respects of the imperial couch, and confirmed the marriage on the soul of the emperor by oath, presenting her with a wedding ring in his name.[15]

Three days after writing his letter to Amadeus, Henry received a visitor at court, Master Peter the surgeon, a Gascon by birth. He had a gift for the king, a stone attached to a chain to be worn around the neck. It was a talisman against thunder. Like many people of that day, Henry was afraid of atmospheric disturbances and not at all shy about letting everyone know it. If it seems Master Peter had been sent to Henry by Eleanor's family, then they knew of his fear of thunder and wanted to show with the pendant that they had his best interests at heart.[16]

And yet Henry did not drop Joan just like that. Not for another three weeks, on 16 July 1235, did he order his proctors in Rome to suspend his application for the dispensation. Without it, their marriage was automatically annulled, which is to say it was never valid from the beginning. But because Blanche had denied Joan a king for a husband, she was obliged to find her an alternate of equal rank. She found one later that year when her nephew Ferdinand III, the king of her native Castile, became a widower. He was in his mid-30s and had ten children, seven of them sons, so there was no apparent need for him to marry again, except perhaps to keep him from producing more offspring out of wedlock. Within two years, Joan was married to Ferdinand and eventually gave him another five children.[17]

Sometime before 10 October 1235, Henry's emissaries were back from Provence. On that day he wrote separate letters to Raymond Berenger and Beatrice expressing his wish to marry their daughter. Five days later, having secured the consent of his council, he dispatched a diplomatic team to manage the business side of the marriage.

He would have been told that the count and countess were impoverished and had been unable to afford the costs of their eldest daughter's dowry. But Henry was nothing if not hopeful and prepared six letters, each bearing a different sum for a possible dowry, starting at £13,333 and going as low as £2,000. On 19 October, he suddenly realised he was tempting fate and dashed off another letter to his envoys to tell them to forget the money if need be, they were to bring the girl back to England even with no dowry.[18]

For his part, Henry had to nominate a dower for his future wife. As in the case of his sister's dower, Eleanor of Provence would be entitled to a one-third property settlement after his death, which would be hers for life, then revert back to the Crown. Eleanor Marshal's dower had not been nominated beforehand, hence all the trouble she had with her in-laws. Previous queens of England had had the same dower, consisting of various towns and tenements, but they would have to go to the first queen in line, Isabella of Angoulême, in the event Henry predeceased her as well. In this case, he stipulated that Eleanor was to have a total of fourteen cities, including Gloucester, Cambridge and Bath.[19]

Perhaps as expected, Raymond Berenger was unable to come up with even £2,000 for Eleanor's dowry, but the wedding went forward as instructed. On 23 November 1235, at Tarascon Castle, Eleanor exchanged vows with Henry through his proxy Robert de Mucegros, who had earlier accompanied Isabella to Germany for her marriage. Sometime later the party moved upriver to Vienne, just south of Lyon, where the ceremony was repeated on 15 December with a view to confirming the marriage contract.[20]

It was probably here that Eleanor said goodbye to her parents and younger sisters and left with a retinue led by William of Savoy, numbering as many as 300 horsemen according to Paris. It took them five days to cross the territories controlled by Theobald, the Count of Champagne. As he was distantly related to Henry, he covered their expenses. For their journey to the northern coast, they received an honourable escort from the French royal family, namely Louis, Margaret and Blanche.[21]

The wedding of Henry and Eleanor, her coronation, their honeymoon

Henry's state of nerves over Eleanor's impending arrival can be seen in his itinerary at the time. Unlike his father, who regularly kept his court on the move, Henry was more sedate, preferring to spend long stretches at Westminster, Windsor, or his palatial retreats upcountry. On 17 December, he was at Clarendon, four days later Southampton, the next day Waltham. Christmas Day was spent in Winchester, then nearby at Marwell Manor. At the beginning of the new year he was in Marlborough, then Reading, and at Windsor on 11 January. Finally, he received word that Eleanor's party had arrived at Dover, apparently sooner than expected. He hurried to Canterbury to meet them. Again, it was probably nerves that made him, in the words of Paris, 'rush into the arms of the messengers' before turning his attention to Eleanor.[22]

He was at that time 28, she 12 or little older. Paris made a contemporary illustration of the two that shows a fully grown man next to, for all intents and purposes, a child, very demure in stature and boyish in appearance. Fortunately for Eleanor, Henry was an ingratiating sort who would have done everything possible to make her feel comfortable.

That would have started with making himself understood, for he spoke what was probably a mingling of the Poitevin French of his mother and early minders and the Anglo-Norman of his court. Her Occitan was close enough to any sort of French for the two of them to be able to get through the basics of their wedding day, which fell on 14 January. Edmund of Abingdon, the archbishop, conducted the ceremony and nuptial mass in the cathedral of Canterbury in front of her entourage and an impressive gathering of the nobles and prelates of the kingdom.[23]

After that came the blessing of the wedding bed and consummation of their marriage. Here again, Eleanor benefited from having a husband who was sensitive and equally inexperienced in these matters. His only known personal attachments to women up to that point had been with two nuns and his three sisters. It could have come from an innate shyness or reverence for the Virgin Mary, which was in vogue at that time, perhaps even a fondness for saints that went back to his days of tutorship under Peter des Roches, the Bishop of Winchester.[24] Excessive piety and modesty among first-time royal couples was not an unknown quality, as Louis and Margaret's example shows, but for those like Roches who knew the lustful King John, or else knew of the two dozen or so illegitimate children sired by him and the first two English kings named Henry, this Henry must have seemed like a strange bird.

The newlyweds spent the next few days in Canterbury getting to know each other. Henry was a natural when it came to putting people at ease and would have organised their itinerary to suit Eleanor's needs. Doubtless he showed her the shrine of St Thomas Becket, the archbishop murdered in the cathedral by retainers of Henry's grandfather Henry II. The translation of Becket's remains to a glittering new shrine in 1220, some fifty years after he was cut down, had been an impressive ceremony, drawing dignitaries from around Europe and marking the first appearance of the then 12-year-old Henry on the international stage, the same age as his wife was now.[25] By his side, Eleanor was going to have to get used to grand entrances and state occasions, starting with her own coronation.

It took place on 20 January, a Sunday. According to Paris, London was adorned with 'flags and banners, candles and lamps, with wonderful devices and extraordinary representations, and all the roads were cleansed of mud and dirt and everything offensive'. A blue ray-cloth was laid between the grounds of Westminster Palace and the abbey church. The king's procession appeared first. Wearing his coronation regalia, Henry walked beneath a canopy of purple silk held aloft by four silver lances, each borne by a baron of the Channel ports.

Eleanor followed underneath her own canopy, her hair worn loose with a circlet of gold on top, and two bishops at her side for support. After the appropriate prayer, she was led to the high altar, where she knelt as another prayer was recited. Upon rising, her circlet was removed and Archbishop Edmund anointed her head with holy oil. A ring was produced, blessed and placed on her finger. Then came the high point, the blessing and raising of the gold crown of lilies, which was placed on her head. Thus she became *regina Dei gratia*, queen by the grace of God, the first in the land since Henry's mother Isabella, who had left nearly two decades earlier to find the power and respect always denied her as Queen of England.[26]

In addition to producing an heir, Eleanor of Provence's primary duty as queen was to intercede with her husband on behalf of their subjects. She was guided through the ritual of intercession immediately after her coronation by making an appeal on behalf of William de Panchehall, who had committed a forest offence. She did not know William, was simply told that this was the scoundrel whose pardon she should seek from the king.[27] Henry was more than willing to grant her this favour, but given his penchant for micro-management, he probably knew what William had done wrong and cleared him as the lucky fellow beforehand.

The day ended with the banquet described in the Introduction. It is unlikely Eleanor was present longer than she had to be, both on account of her age and Henry wishing to shield her from the excesses of English behaviour, whether it was drunkenness or grappling over rights and presumed slights. Indeed, Simon de Montfort's role as the hereditary steward of the banquet did not go uncontested by Roger Bigod, the Earl of Norfolk, and there was no traditional chief butler because the Earl of Arundel, who performed that function, had been excommunicated by the Archbishop of Canterbury after an argument over hunting dogs.

The queen herself probably retired to the king's chamber because her chamberlain, as was his right, claimed the whole of her 'bed, basins and other things'.[28] It is hoped she liked green. The posts supporting the canopy of his bed were painted green, with gold stars sprinkled throughout, and he had had his chamber painted in a 'good green colour' to resemble a curtain. There were also murals, including one above his bed depicting the coronation of Edward the Confessor, his idol among his predecessors. Henry intended his chamber to be a centrepiece of his kingship and often received visitors there. Generous, sometimes to a fault, he expected others to be as well. In that year of his marriage, he had a phrase inscribed over the entrance to the chamber that read, 'He who does not give what he has, will not get what he wants'.[29]

Eleanor's chamber, built south of and at a right angle to his chamber on the palace grounds, would also serve as a statement of queenship.

Young as she was at the time, there is no reason to suspect she did not have an opinion of her own on the matter of her quarters. Decorating would have to wait, however, because the rains that fell her first winter in England were among the heaviest in living memory. Edged up against the Thames, Westminster was eventually flooded, making getting around the palace possible only by horse or small boat.[30] Eleanor did not have to endure this feat of travel because the day after her coronation, the whole court packed up and moved ten miles south to Merton Priory, presumably to escape the rising waters.

Since the barons and clergy of the realm were gathered at that moment for her coronation, Henry had called for a *parliament*, a word just then taking off to describe gatherings of state summoned to deal with major issues. In this case, a reform of the laws was needed to codify the rulings that had followed the enactment of Magna Carta.[31] How much Eleanor knew about the proceedings and results of what became the Statute of Merton would have come from her uncle William of Savoy. He and his retainers had not been unceremoniously shipped off as had been the case after her sister Margaret's wedding in France. Henry was still intent on pursuing his claims against the French monarchy and wanted the worldly churchman and his family, with their connections to the papacy and empire, to spearhead those efforts on the Continent.

For now, William was invited to join the king's council, even becoming the nominal head of it. He received, as his reward, custody of the honour of Richmond in the north, which had formerly belonged to the Dukes of Brittany. It was a lavish gesture, but met no apparent opposition from the other councillors. They were in fact happy to have William there, because a major financial crisis was looming on account of Isabella's dowry and the queen's coronation. Meeting these huge costs and putting the Crown's finances on surer footing required inquests into arrears at the exchequer and re-organising the sheriffdoms and royal demesne to generate more income. William may have had some executive ability that helped pull it off, but for the councillors who directed the grinding work of reform, his main purpose there, as a foreigner and newcomer, was to take the flak from all those forced to disgorge land and rents or else pay up their back taxes.[32]

The court was on the move through much of this activity. The first week in February was spent in Winchester, where Henry doubtless delighted in showing his young bride around the city of his birth.

Eleanor would visit other royal palaces and lodges that provided country retreats during her queenship, including Clarendon, Marlborough and significantly Woodstock, just north of Oxford. But it was Windsor, where the court had gone in April, that Henry and Eleanor would come to call their family home.

After spending a month in and around Winchester in May and June, the court headed to Glastonbury, the first stop on a tour of the west country. They were there for only a day (27 June), suggesting the whole point was to see a tourist attraction, the graves of King Arthur and Guinevere. How the two legendary figures ended up there no one had a clue, just that in rebuilding the abbey church in the last century two graves were uncovered that were quickly attributed to them. Eleanor was fond of romances and would have grown up familiar with the wildly popular exploits of Arthur and company. Henry, who almost never journeyed to that part of England, also enjoyed tales of this sort and perhaps thought a visit to the final resting place of the fabled couple would make a nice honeymoon present for Eleanor.[33]

As autumn approached, the court moved north to York, where a meeting was arranged with Alexander and Joan. The King of Scots was demanding Northumbria as the marriage portion he had never received. Henry gave him £54 of land instead, but to Joan he gave the manor of Driffield. It was not only worth more but was for her use only, beyond the control of Alexander as any property in a marriage portion would otherwise be. If Joan had been a party to the talks, it may have been Henry's reward to her for their success, but either way, it gave her financial independence in what was becoming an increasingly strained marriage.[34]

The Scottish royal pair was still childless after fifteen years together (as were Alexander's sister Isabelle and Roger Bigod after eleven years). The lack of an heir was a worrisome thing anywhere in that age, but especially in Scotland, because the nearest and only male claimant to the throne was Alexander's cousin John the Scot. He was currently the Earl of Chester, having inherited the title and his massive estates from his uncle Ranulf, who had died childless in 1232. And John himself was still childless after fifteen years of marriage.

It would not have been the first meeting between new sisters-in-law Eleanor and Joan. In December 1235, in expectation of Eleanor's arrival in England, Henry had summoned Alexander and Joan to London.

No specific reason was given for the summons, but since the nobles and prelates of the kingdom were also being asked to attend, we may assume it was for the coronation of his queen.[35] Joan was thirteen years older than Eleanor, but had been younger than her at the time of her own marriage, which had followed the excruciating manipulations of her mother Isabella of Angoulême and stepfather Hugh. She would have understood and empathised with Eleanor as she adapted to her new life. Her family situation in Scotland, which until a few years previous included a vigorous and capable mother-in-law, had left her feeling lonely, isolated and yearning for companionship.

The two Eleanors, Christmas court, Simon de Montfort

Just after making the manorial gift to Joan, Henry turned his attention to his youngest sister. On 18 October 1236, he gave Eleanor the much refurbished manor and castle of Odiham in Hampshire, probably as a gift for her turning 21.[36] The choice had been made with due consideration. In Henry's mind, in-laws were very much family and he easily referred to Hugh Lusignan as 'father' and William of Savoy as 'uncle'. He doubtless saw his sisters Joan and Eleanor now as his wife's sisters as well. Since Eleanor Marshal was single, apparently for life, she would be available to act as a mentor for the younger Eleanor, to help introduce her to the English nobility and otherwise grow into her role as queen. Giving his sister a residential home between Windsor and Winchester, his favourite city, was Henry's way of ensuring the proximity of his two Eleanors to each another.

Eleanor Marshal's status as a bride of Christ also enhanced the piety of Henry's court. The king was eager for his queen to follow Eleanor's example of religious devotion and partake in festivities that, like her coronation, reinforced the link between divinity and monarchy. Apart from Christmas and Easter, the holiday with the most significance for Henry was 13 October, the feast day of the translation of St Edward the Confessor. It was in building a cult around the Confessor, who was half Saxon, half Norman, that Henry hoped to do away with the divisions that had beset the land since the Conquest of 1066. For the queen's first feast day of St Edward, he had an image of her fashioned in gold to present at the shrine of the Confessor.[37]

In all her travel that first year in England, the queen was accompanied by her own household. Eleanor had the comfort of having familiar people around her. Her damsels included a woman from Savoy, Willelma d'Attelens, whose daughter Isabel lived with them. The man who had exchanged vows with her, Robert de Mucegros, was the steward in charge of her household. Even John of Gatesden, sent by Henry to view her in Provence, was retained as the keeper of her wardrobe and finances. For her moral and physical development, Henry appointed Master Nicholas Farnham, who trained in medicine and theology at Oxford, Paris and Bologna. 'A man of good learning', says Paris, 'adorned by mature and modest demeanour and conduct'.[38]

Inasmuch as Christmas was about celebrating the birth of Christ, Henry liked to spend it in his own birthplace of Winchester. The queen's first Christmas there was brief, however, just two days before the court got underway again. There was a flurry of activity preceding the Parliament scheduled to convene at Westminster in January 1237. The magnates approved a national tax, but tacked on strict controls for spending it. They also asked the king to confirm Magna Carta. This would remove all doubts about the force of the charter, which had been sealed when Henry was still a minor, and it would remind the king and council not to allow reforms to infringe anyone's rights without due process.

Another concession was a shakeup of the council, which saw William of Savoy leave the realm after Parliament concluded, if only for a short spell. To Matthew Paris, he was an evil influence and the chronicler laid into him with some of his most bizarre and xenophobic rants. He sniped that the king and queen did not accompany William to Dover out of affection and good manners, but to make sure he safely got away with packsaddles stuffed with gold and silver.[39]

William's departure coincided with the emergence of Simon de Montfort as one of Henry's closest advisers. He had been absent for much of the recent political controversy, presumably across the water in search of a bride. He was out to marry for money, which he needed to pay off the loans he had taken out to acquire and maintain his Leicester estates. Twice he tried his luck with rich widows, Countess Mahaut of Boulogne and Countess Joanna of Flanders.

It was probably Henry's idea that he set his sights on these older women. Certainly Simon would have needed his permission to pursue them. Should he come into possession of either county through either woman, it would give Henry a strategic foothold next to Normandy. Naturally Blanche saw right through it and had Simon all but chased off the Continent. So worried was she that the young Frenchman had in fact contracted marriage to Joanna that on 12 April 1237, Blanche hauled the countess into court to make her swear they had not been married nor ever would be.[40]

Simon would have wanted a younger bride in any case, one with whom he could establish a family and dynastic clan in his adopted country. Since she needed to be rich, or at least an heiress, he needed the king. If Henry told him to try those widows first, he slicked back his hair and caught a boat over. Having done the king this favour, at a cost to his reputation, he expected his rewards, and Simon de Montfort was forever in a hurry. In October 1236, as Henry was bestowing Odiham on his sister Eleanor, Simon signed himself, which is to say he issued a charter, as the 'Earl of Leicester' for the first time.[41] Considering he had never received the title, and Henry was quite fussy about who his earls were, there must have been some understanding between the two.

By the spring of 1237, Montfort was dominant on the council. He earned a rebuke from Paris when, together with John de Lacy, the Earl of Lincoln, Simon arranged to bring a papal legate into the country.[42] Legates generally aroused fear and loathing among the English clergy because they interfered in everything and outranked everybody, even the Archbishops of Canterbury and York.

That was precisely why Henry asked for one. Like his predecessors, the king considered the archbishops, bishops and abbots of the realm to be his magnates. He expected a say in Church elections as a way of rewarding his followers and ensuring the loyalty and cooperation of the men who occupied these positions, something that had been lacking during Marshal's insurrection. A legate by his side would help put these churchmen in their place.

Henry also wanted the legate, Cardinal Otto, to mediate the ongoing dispute with Scotland. In September, the court went back to York and there Alexander agreed to surrender his claims to Northumbria in return for £200 worth of lands in the northern counties.[43] After the treaty was concluded, the two queens Joan and Eleanor left to undertake a pilgrimage to Canterbury together.

Joan's position in Scotland had become critical following the untimely death of John the Scot on 6 June 1237. She and Alexander needed an heir more than ever and it was hoped that prayer and devotion at the shrine of St Thomas might help.[44] At 13, Eleanor was still too young for pregnancy. She probably joined her sister-in-law to offer company and support, perhaps to pray for her own sister Margaret, who had now been married to Louis for more than three years without any sign of an heir on the way.

The court moved to Winchester for what would be a real family Christmas. Joining the king and queen would be Henry's sisters Joan and Eleanor and two of their kinswomen. One of them was Helena, the Countess of Chester, who was about Henry's age but was technically his niece. She was the daughter of Llywelyn ap Iowerth and Joan of Wales, a natural daughter of King John born in the early 1190s, well before Henry and his younger siblings came along. Helena had been married to John the Scot in 1222 in a match arranged by her father and his ally Ranulf of Chester.[45] The death of her husband John the Scot left her, like her aunt Eleanor Marshal, a widow countess with no children.

The other kinswoman never got a chance for marriage. She was Eleanor of Brittany, Henry's cousin, the daughter of King John's older brother Geoffrey. When Richard I died in 1199, Arthur of Brittany, her younger brother, had pressed his claim to the throne. Both siblings were captured by John in the ensuing struggle, with Arthur disappearing without a trace and Eleanor of Brittany packed off to England to live the rest of her life in honourable confinement. Henry realised she could never be released, but sympathised and ensured her comfort and wellbeing.[46] By this time she was in her 50s, much older than her extended family, but doubtless happy for these rare moments of exposure and togetherness.

After Christmas, the court slowly moved back to Westminster, where on Wednesday, 6 January 1238, it celebrated the Epiphany, the official end of the holiday season. The next day everything would be back to business as usual. Only something unusual was about to happen. Two guests had turned to the king in need and Henry liked to be helpful. So he helped them, but were he later to come up with a name for that particular day and all that followed on account of it, it would probably be Black Thursday.

3

Too Much Goodwill 1238–1241

Eleanor Marshal weds Simon, furore over it

It is possible that Eleanor Marshal accompanied the two queens on their pilgrimage to Canterbury in late 1237. Now 23-years old, she too was overcome by the desire to become a mother.[1] Her vow of chastity should have precluded the thought, but Eleanor was nothing if not headstrong and resourceful, a true child of King John and Isabella of Angoulême. For all her piety, she would not let her vow stand in the way of getting married and having a family if the opportunity arose. It also would not take much to get her brother's permission. Henry was not just a romantic at heart, but all his gifts to her these years suggest a twinge of guilt over the circumstances that imposed perpetual widowhood on her in the first place.

The real problem would be the two men behind those circumstances. There was Edmund of Abingdon, the Archbishop of Canterbury who had administered her vow. He would take it as an affront if she repudiated it and he was not then in the best of moods. His monks were giving him a hard time and he felt overshadowed by the legate, who, as feared, was cleaning house in the English Church. The abuses Otto sought to stamp out included pluralism, greed, absenteeism, concubines, and a priesthood filled with idiots and illegitimate children. Edmund decided to skip the Christmas court and left for Rome on 30 November to complain about the cardinal and the monks.[2] Since the trip in those days took around six weeks, he would be gone until spring at the earliest. If there was an opportune time for Eleanor to get remarried, this was it.

The other man likely to be up in arms was Gilbert Marshal. It will be remembered how her vow of chastity had been taken as part of reconciling the Marshal family to the Crown in 1234. The idea was to keep her single and childless in order to ensure the smooth transition of her English dower lands back to their clan after her death. Gilbert might retaliate against her getting remarried by withholding the annual £400 payment for her Irish dower. Admittedly, he would be risking the king's displeasure. Henry was the surety for the money in the event Gilbert became a deadbeat like his brother Richard had been.[3]

Any question of Eleanor remarrying would have to be taken up by the council. Her vow might make them pause out of respect for Edmund, but they knew the pope would grant her a dispensation if her remarriage created or enhanced a foreign alliance that was also in the papacy's best interest. That, however, was the problem for Eleanor. They would only look favourably upon a match that sent her abroad like her sisters, entailing her to give up her home, family, and the lordship of her estates. Of course, law and custom dictated that she would have to give up official control of her estates to whoever became her husband, but as her mother Isabella had shown with Hugh Lusignan, marriage between equals was more often the norm than not.

Eleanor could achieve that equality by marrying somebody within the realm. A princess first and foremost, she outranked everyone in the pool of baronial bridegrooms. Marrying beneath herself, as it were, would give her automatic leverage, and there would be no need to worry about disparagement because that issue had been dealt with sufficiently at the time of her marriage to William Marshal II.[4] She was, moreover, an adult, able to speak for herself unlike back then. If she was going to break her vow of chastity, doubtless a soul-searching prospect in that age of faith, it may as well be with a man of her own choosing.

How that man came to be Simon de Montfort is up for conjecture, but it is easy to see the attraction between the two of them. As Matthew Paris noted at the time, Eleanor was rich, beautiful, and sister to the King of England, Queen of Scotland and Holy Roman Empress. Her royal extraction meant promising futures for her children. Simon's best qualities were more personal. He was handsome, eloquent and fearless, not afraid to take on people like the Marshals or others who gave her trouble.[5] Equally important for her own nature, he was pious and ambitious. Just coming from nowhere to become Henry's leading councillor spoke volumes about his abilities.

Eleanor and Simon had crossed paths at any number of state occasions over the years. The records show both were in attendance at court when the king and queen came to Worcester in the summer of 1236. This would have been just after Simon's second failed attempt to find a wife abroad.[6] There is no way to know when the two of them fell for each other, how they confided in Henry about it, or what his initial response was. By the time of the Christmas court of 1237, the king had decided to allow them to marry. Amiable and anxious to please, he could hardly do otherwise. She was his adored sister, he his most trusted friend and confidant. But all three were aware that the Church and council would not see it in the same glowing terms. If they were going to pull it off, it would have to be an elopement.

Westminster Palace in the thirteenth century was dominated by the Great Hall, which ran parallel to the River Thames. There were two annexes at the north end of the hall housing the offices of the exchequer, and at the south end stood a complex of buildings that formed a courtyard facing the river. They consisted of St Stephen's Chapel, a Lesser Hall built in line with the Great Hall, and Henry's long, narrow chamber, which ran parallel to St Stephen's. A small chapel for the king's use was built adjacent to the northeast corner of his chamber, opposite to his bed on the other side of the wall. There was an opening in the wall, called a squint, that enabled him to follow mass inside the chapel from his bed if he chose, but more likely the squint was there for moments before sleep.[7] Henry could take a last look at the cross and altar in the candlelight while doing his prayers and devotions.

This little chapel was just the private place of worship needed to solemnise the secret marriage of Eleanor and Simon. Walter, the chaplain of St Stephen's, was summoned there on 7 January 1238 to officiate the wedding ceremony. Says Paris, the only chronicler who describes the event in detail, 'the king in person gave the bride away to Simon, who received her most gratefully'. Paris finishes the passage by noting that not quite a fortnight later, on 20 January, 'a dreadful thunder was heard, which was accompanied by a strong wind and heavy clouds'.[8] That might be used as the date for when word about the marriage got out, for the expected storm was on its way.

Richard of Cornwall was at the centre of it. He was already indignant over another marriage in the works. Previously in late October, it had been decided in council that Richard de Clare, his stepson and heir-presumptive to the earldom of Gloucester, should marry Maud, the daughter of John de Lacy, the Earl of Lincoln. Cornwall resented Lacy and Montfort's grip on the council, but he grudgingly gave his consent to the match because at least Lacy scored his marriage through the proper channels.[9] There was nothing at all to recommend the Montfort

48

marriage. Simon owed everything to Henry and brought no immediate advantage to the kingdom. Not even the prominent roles played by his family in France and in the Holy Land were worth ignoring the council and offending the Church for his benefit.

Henry's brother had already instigated revolt against him twice before, with William Marshal II in 1227 and Richard Marshal in 1233. For this one, he was joined by Gilbert Marshal, who took his expected dim view of the match. By early February, Henry was warning the barons of the Channel ports to be on the lookout for Richard and to disregard any orders he might give them that did not have royal authorisation first.[10] Otto the legate attempted to mediate, but Paris claims that Richard told him to mind his own business.

The demonstrations worked up against the king grew heated enough for old and infirm Peter des Roches, who believed a monarch's will was absolute, to advise Henry to retreat. The king did just that, to the Tower of London. There he received a list of demands that called for the appointment of officers of state and an end to his personal rule that had begun after the last rebellion. This is only guesswork, because the demands were never revealed. Suddenly, out of nowhere, Richard dropped all opposition and went home. Gilbert and the others, looking like complete fools, did the same.

Paris says that Montfort and Lacy had sought out Richard individually and humbled themselves before him with gifts.[11] Their supplication was welcome, but what really did it for him was the £4,000 that Henry had transferred to him from the tax recently collected. Richard's main concern then was to go on crusade, a hugely expensive prospect, and figured he could use the controversy of his sister's marriage to get the king to make him a handsome subsidy for it.[12]

It was money well spent, for Richard never again posed a threat to his brother's rule. On the other hand, Gilbert Marshal got nothing, in part because his aggressive moves against his Welsh neighbours had already earned him disfavour at court. He took it out on Eleanor de Montfort by withholding the first instalment of her dower payment for that year of 1238. Henry paid it, but warned Gilbert to make good the money before he distrained his property.[13]

There may have been a personal reason as well to Richard's rapid reconciliation. Sometime after the Christmas court, Joan was overcome by illness. Her condition worsened until finally, on 21 February, it looked like the end was near and she drew up her will.[14] She was at Havering in Essex when she died on 4 March 1238. The Melrose chronicler records that Henry and Richard were at her side, holding her in their arms. 'With great grief, they buried her with magnificence at the convent in Tarrant', he adds.

This church in Dorset was under the patronage of Queen Eleanor. Choosing it as Joan's final resting place was likely a reflection of the friendship that had arisen between these two queens and sisters-in-law in the past several months.[15] Alexander himself expressed no interest in the arrangements. He quickly forgot all about Joan and went to work on finding a new wife.

The secrecy and speed of the Montfort marriage may have generated comment that Eleanor was pregnant, but none of the chroniclers made any mention of seduction or scandal as the reason for it. Henry himself gave no indication at that time that the marriage had been forced upon him, nor did he hold it against his sister and her new husband for all the trouble their nuptials had caused him. On 3 February, the very day the king was warning his subjects against the designs of his brother, he had a loan of £120 made over to the Montforts. The money was probably part of the funds Simon needed to collect for his journey to Rome to obtain the dispensation to release Eleanor from her vow. Furnished with letters of credence, Simon crossed over to the Continent in late March 1238.[16]

Assassination attempt, both Eleanors give birth, the churching affair

These were difficult months for the queen. First the outrage over the Montfort marriage, which she may or may not have had prior knowledge of, then her brother-in-law's rebellion and death of her sister-in-law Joan. Her week at the Tower of London, her first-known residence there, had been cold and uncomfortable. As she and Henry were leaving again for Westminster on 2 March, orders were sent to have the work on their chambers at the Tower completed, as well as the chimney for her fireplace.

Further home improvements were made as the court got underway that spring. Her chamber at Marlborough was painted and an herb garden planted there between her chapel and the king's. At Tewkesbury it was the privy chambers that received a makeover. In September 1238, the court went to Woodstock and stayed there for the most part until the end of November. The main renovation of the palace during their stay involved barring the windows of both royal chambers with iron and wood.[17] This was in response to an event that occurred there on 9 September.

Matthew Paris describes how 'a certain learned esquire' appeared at court, raving that he was the real king and demanding Henry abdicate in favour of him. Believing the man insane, Henry took pity on him and ordered his attendants not to beat or otherwise molest him. That night, the man crawled through an open window into the king's chamber and drew a knife. He found only an empty bed because Henry and Eleanor were spending the night together in her chamber. The would-be assassin began searching other rooms until he was spotted by one of Eleanor's damsels, who was just then quietly singing psalms by the candlelight. The sleeping attendants were alerted to her cries and apprehended the intruder after breaking down a door he had barred.[18]

The man eventually confessed that an outlawed gang had sent him there to kill the king. Paris does not say whether the royal couple was awakened by the disturbance, just that Henry did not take pity on the man twice. He ordered him taken to Coventry and torn apart by horses for attempting to 'murder the king's majesty'. This singular lack of mercy is probably better explained in a letter dispatched to his officials in Dover, where Henry said the 'scoundrel' (*ribaldum*) had also confessed his intention to kill the queen as well.[19]

On 14 October, Simon de Montfort arrived from the Continent with a declaration from Pope Gregory IX stating that 'nothing is to be presumed against the marriage contracted between (Eleanor) and S de Montfort'. Three copies were drawn up: one for her, one for Simon, and one for Otto to make sure the English clergy understood that the marriage was valid in the eyes of the papacy. The grumbling nevertheless persisted. A friar named William of Abingdon insisted that because Eleanor had accepted the ring, her action had 'roused Christ to jealousy'. He then fell back on a treatise that declared 'virgins or widows, bound by a vow of continence, whether they had taken the veil or not, can in nowise be married'. Paris seems to agree, but only with words to the effect that the Holy Father works in mysterious ways.[20]

Eleanor had become pregnant sometime before Simon left and was already in confinement at Kenilworth. On 26 November 1238, she gave birth to a son they called Henry. The king was touched by the honour and also the occasion. This was the third nephew named after him and he himself was the third Henry to rule England. Kenilworth being just a little over fifty kilometres from Woodstock, he decided to rush there in one day to be present at the baptism of the baby and serve as godfather.[21]

Henry had already made a short visit to his sister at Kenilworth before Simon's return, just days after the assassination attempt, and throughout the summer he made sure Eleanor had plenty of deer and wine. Since she could not be at his Christmas court in Winchester that year, he had her presents sent to her. They included a robe made from gold-elaborated silk trimmed with miniver, a quilt for her bed made out of the same material, and a coverlet lined with scarlet cloth.[22]

The robe was meant for her churching, the ceremony of purification and blessing for a woman following childbirth. She could have also worn it for the feast of Candlemas on 2 February 1239, when her brother, in the Great Hall of Winchester, invested her husband with the title of Earl of Leicester. As Henry did with Hubert and Margaret de Burgh, he wanted Simon to have a title more becoming to the rank of his princess wife. But the ceremony was more of a formality, for Simon had been using the title for a couple of years and even the papal letters he procured for his marriage referred to him as earl.

To believe Paris, there had been a sigh of relief at the birth of Henry de Montfort because 'it was feared that the queen might be barren'. If such fear really existed, it was quickly dispelled, for Eleanor by then would have been about ten weeks pregnant. After Christmas, the location of the court reflected her condition. Since arriving in England, the queen had been on the move, averaging just under ten changes of venue a month. Four of the first six months of 1239, however, were spent at Windsor or Westminster, the latter mostly. Henry was eager for the child to be born at Westminster because it was the home of the abbey church built by Edward the Confessor. It is, however, a question of where the queen would have had her lying-in because her chamber underwent painting after Easter.[23]

The painting works were still going on when on the night of 17-18 June 1239, just a little over nine months after the assassination attempt, Eleanor gave birth to a boy they called Edward, again in devotion to the Confessor. Henry, already 31-years old, was overjoyed at becoming a father for the first time. He had the clerks of the king's chapel sing *Christus vincit* before him and gave an annual pension of £10 to Sybil Giffard for the care she had given the queen during her confinement.

London was also jubilant. The child was not only born in their midst, but would be the first king since the Norman Conquest to bear a distinctly English name. They celebrated by dancing to drums and tambourines and lighting up the streets with lanterns.[24]

The baby was baptised four days later. Richard of Cornwall and Simon de Montfort were among the dignitaries chosen to serve as godfathers. The *Flores Historiarum* chronicler at St Albans says the Countess of Pembroke also assisted at the font. She would have been Margery Marshal, whose brother Alexander II of Scotland had just been re-married to Marie de Coucy, the daughter of a French nobleman. Normally the Archbishop of Canterbury would have presided at the font, but Edmund of Abingdon had not succeeded in having the legate recalled, and since Otto outranked him by virtue of his office, he had to forgo the honour of baptising the baby.[25]

Eleanor and Simon remained high in the king's favour. For their residence in London that summer, Henry had just the place for them. Peter des Roches had died the previous year, but the bishopric of Winchester was still vacant because the king and monks could not agree on his replacement. Henry wanted another urbane, warrior diplomat like Peter in the post and William of Savoy fit that bill. But the chapter in Winchester considered him a 'man of blood' and preferred chief jurist William Raleigh instead.[26] Until the dispute was resolved, the king was free to dispose of the deceased bishop's property and so lent his magnificent palace across the Thames in Southwark to the Montforts for their use.

Naturally Henry's top priority just then was his wife's churching and re-entry into public life. Orders went out to purchase enough wax to make 500 candles and to procure thirty-four oxen, salted venison and 'swans and other sorts of birds' to be served up at the feast.[27] Noble ladies arrived in London to accompany the queen to church on 9 August 1239, including her sister-in-law Eleanor de Montfort. It was going to be magnificent.

Suddenly, without warning, Henry barred his sister and her husband from attending the ceremony. Simon, he declared, was an excommunicated man and therefore had no business being in church, while Eleanor also had no business being there because she had been 'defiled' by him before their marriage. After describing this outburst, Paris says Simon 'left in disgrace' and hurried, with Eleanor, to the bishop's palace. Henry, however, had sent orders ahead to evict them the minute they arrived.

Although the king had humiliated them in public, for all their friends to see, the Montforts decided to go back and plead 'with tears and lamentations' for his forgiveness. If anything, it only made the situation worse. Completely unmindful that it was his wife's day and not his, Henry accused Simon of seducing his sister. He had allowed them to marry only to avoid a scandal, which of course it was now. Simon had, he went on, bribed the pope into overcoming the objections to the marriage raised by Archbishop Edmund, who was present at the spectacle and doubtless pleased at the king's outburst. Finally, Henry got to what was really bothering him.[28]

It involved Thomas of Savoy, William's brother. He too had been destined for a career in the Church, but found better prospects in marrying Joanna, the Countess of Flanders, not long after her rejection of Simon. Thomas had come to England that summer to undertake the traditional homage of the Counts of Flanders to the English Crown in return for £333. This Henry was willing to give him, but not the £1,333 Thomas also asked for. Apparently Simon owed him that money and had named the king surety for it.

The origin of the debt was Simon's acquisition of Leicester. It cost him at least £700 to secure the rights of all other claimants. In time, this and his other debts grew so large that a suit was brought against him at the papal court, where Thomas of Savoy and his family were influential. Somehow much of the debt was transferred to Thomas, who told Henry that Simon, perhaps during his trip to Rome, had said the king would cover it for him. The Montfort marriage had so far cost Henry the huge sum of £5,500. Another thousand pounds more or less would have been an imposition, but what set Henry off was learning that his brother-in-law had him mixed up in it on his own authority. That was his 'crowning wretchedness' in his eyes.[29]

In recalling the event many years later, Simon said that the king grew so angry that he ordered his arrest and confinement in the Tower of London. Richard of Cornwall, however, refused to allow it. Fearing for their safety, Simon and Eleanor quickly sailed for France, presumably to stay with his relatives in Montfort l'Amaury, some fifty kilometres west of Paris. The speed of their flight meant leaving their 9-month old son behind. He was probably taken from the bishop's palace to the royal nursery at Windsor, although when and by whom is unknown.

It could not have been an easy decision for them, but Eleanor probably could not bear to be seen in public after the way her brother had accused her of breaking her vow of celibacy before marriage. It only confirmed the innuendo surrounding them. Indeed, the monk writing in the Dunstable annals refers to Simon and Eleanor in this incident as 'the Earl of Leicester and Countess of Pembroke', as if they were two unmarried lovers on the run.[30]

More children, more uncles, the Montforts go to Italy

The episode had to be mortifying for the queen as well. Her churching was supposed to be a day of blessing and thanks, and she had much to be grateful for in bringing forth an heir. She had fulfilled the one duty expected of her. The two Eleanors had probably become closer following Joan's death eighteen months earlier and the queen may have found guidance and support from her sister-in-law, also a new mother, during her pregnancy. Seeing her humiliated and cast off on this of all days, in a dispute between her uncle Thomas and her brother-in-law Simon, revealed an unseemly side of family loyalty, not to mention her husband's temper.

The churching affair also exposed the uncomfortable political climate in Europe at that time. The strained relations between the papacy and empire had ruptured on 20 March 1239 when Pope Gregory excommunicated Emperor Frederick. The Savoyards backed the papal camp and to this end Thomas of Savoy worked to have his brother William named the Bishop of Liege in opposition to Frederick's candidate. Since Henry still wanted William to be his Bishop of Winchester, he balked at covering Montfort's debt because he knew Thomas would only use the money to put William in Liege. The brothers were successful, but William suddenly died while on his way to Rome to be confirmed. He was barely 40 at the time, rumoured to have been poisoned, and Paris names an Englishman suspected of carrying it out, but the man was later exonerated.[31]

Eleanor of Provence grieved over the loss of her uncle, but had her duties and newborn to look after. It had been decided to raise Edward and the other children sure to follow him at Windsor. He and his infant cousin Henry de Montfort soon had an older playmate in their 4-year-old cousin Henry. His mother Isabel had recently died in childbirth, on 17 January 1240, and his father Richard of Cornwall was planning to depart on crusade. Meanwhile at Westminster, work began that same month to raise the chimney in the queen's chamber and have the mantle above the fireplace painted with the sad and miserable face of winter. Probably despairing of another cold and wet season, it was about this time that Eleanor found out that she was pregnant again.[32]

Eleanor de Montfort was also pregnant, having conceived around the time she and Simon left for voluntary exile. She was already in confinement when Simon returned to England on 1 April 1240 and was received with great honour. Henry was known to cool down as quickly as he wound up, but Simon probably growled every time the king looked his way. Previously in December, Henry had written to the papal court to seek favour for Thomas of Savoy against a certain 'S de Montfort'. He backed up his words by levying £1,000 against Simon's estates to meet his debt to Thomas.[33]

The queen was eager to restore good relations with the Montforts and made a gift to Simon while he was there of a pot and two cups made of silver, costing £14 for the set. But he did not come to see the royal pair in any case. Simon had taken the cross and was there to raise funds for his crusade. Another, more personal reason for his visit was to fetch his young son Henry and bring him to Eleanor. Sometime later that month, she gave birth to their second child, another son, who was named Simon after his father.[34]

In late May, an English crusading contingent under Richard of Cornwall departed for Marseilles, where they took ship for the Holy Land. Simon was not with them. He decided to take Eleanor and their two boys with him for part of the way. Their plan was to journey with a large number of knights from Henry's household overland through Italy. This may have been the king's idea. By taking this route Simon and Eleanor could visit Frederick and Isabella and offer the emperor Henry's assurances of support in his quarrel with the pope despite the continuing presence of the legate in England.[35] Frederick offered the Montforts the use of his palace in Brindisi on the Adriatic shore across from Albania. Eleanor would stay there with toddlers Henry and Simon after her husband left for Jerusalem.

Henry's rapprochement with the Montforts and Frederick received a setback when Thomas of Savoy, who was leading the papal fight against the empire, visited England again in the summer of 1240 and was received in state. He went to Windsor to see his niece the queen, now in the late stages of her second pregnancy, and 1-year-old Edward.[36] As Eleanor's confinement approached, Henry had hundreds of paupers fed in the Great Hall of Westminster Palace to elicit a mass prayer for his wife at this dangerous time.

On 29 September 1240, she gave birth to a girl. She was named Margaret after Eleanor's sister, but Paris adds that Eleanor had also invoked St Margaret, the patron saint of childbirth, during labour pains. Henry was ecstatic and made gifts to his wife and daughter of twelve ounces of gold. Across the Channel, Margaret too finally had her first child, also a girl, but was so worried that it was not a boy that she asked the Bishop of Paris to break the news to her husband Louis and his mother, who were sure to be disappointed.[37]

Another very disappointed man, the Archbishop of Canterbury, left England at this time to make another appeal to Rome against his monks. The Lanercost chronicler adds an apocryphal story to his departure: 'Standing on a hill near the city of London, and casting his eyes over the land, he stretched forth his consecrated hand, and conferred his blessing on his fatherland, while adding his malediction on the woman and her future offspring.' The woman was Eleanor de Montfort, whom he apparently never forgave for breaking her vow of celibacy. If he had indeed stopped on his way abroad to curse her and her children, it was one of his final acts. After arriving in France, he took ill and died on 16 November 1240 in Soissy.[38]

Had Edmund waited a little longer, he would have seen Cardinal Otto leave the kingdom after a three-year legateship. The pope had summoned him and other clerics to a council, possibly to depose the emperor. Paris was glad to be rid of Otto, but noticed with disquiet a new face at the Christmas court in Westminster. It was another of Queen Eleanor's uncles, Peter of Savoy. Like Thomas, he too gave up a career in the Church to make war and marry well. For Henry, he arrived at just the right time, for retirement, death and crusading had deprived his council of leading figures. He was also still plotting to recover English lordships on the Continent and saw someone of Peter's ability and experience essential for it.[39]

There was a fourth Savoyard uncle who had arrived in England even before Peter, but in name only. Boniface of Savoy was the Bishop-elect of Belley, a small diocese in Burgundy. The death of his brother William in November 1239 opened up the possibility of him becoming the Bishop of Winchester, or at least that was the way Henry saw it. The chapter voted Boniface down and refused to budge despite the king's threats. It was just as well, for the recent death of Edmund of Abingdon made an even better prize available to him.

Henry informed the monks of Canterbury of his desire to see this Boniface become their next archbishop, even though none of them, not even the king, had met him before. The monks had just been absolved of the penalties placed on them by Edmund, but their late, quarrelsome archbishop had an equally ferocious deputy in Archdeacon Simon Langton, brother of former Archbishop Stephen. They were worried he would continue to make their life hell and so sought protection from the king. Henry warned Langton to back off or else, and so the monks duly elected Boniface on 1 February 1241.[40]

Boniface, however, would not be coming to England any time soon. Gregory IX died in August 1241, aged almost 100, and not until a new pope was elected could the archbishop-elect be confirmed in the post. The raised profile of these two new foreign uncles, Peter and Boniface of Savoy, left Eleanor exposed to monastic criticism. Paris insinuates that Henry lobbied for Boniface 'at the instigation of the queen'. She was certainly busy behind the scenes acquiring extra security for herself and her family. In the same month of the Canterbury election, Henry ordered that, in the event of his death, various castles in and around Chester were to be handed over to Eleanor to maintain for Edward 'or another heir begotten or to be begotten by the king and queen'.[41]

Mirroring the rise of the Savoyards in Henry's eyes was the fall of the Marshals. Gilbert Marshal had finally become reconciled to the king, but then risked another break by accepting Peter of Savoy's challenge to a tournament. Henry frowned on tournaments for their violence and intrigue and so had it banned, but Gilbert organised another one, also contrary to royal prohibition. He was thrown while showing off on an unfamiliar horse and dragged to his death on 27 June 1241. Since he and Margery had no children, his brother Walter was in line to succeed him. Henry was angered by Walter's presence at the same, banned tournament and refused his entreaties. Eleanor and her doctor Nicholas Farnham, now the Bishop of Durham, interceded for Walter, and in October, the king belted him the Earl of Pembroke.[42]

By then the crusade was over for the English. Richard of Cornwall's group arrived after a peace treaty had been sealed, so instead of campaigning, he helped rebuild fortifications and repatriate prisoners. Richard stopped in Sicily to meet Frederick and visit his sister Isabella, who was pregnant again. It is unknown but most likely that Eleanor de Montfort was also able to visit her sister the empress during their stay in Italy. There would be no more chance afterward, for Isabella died on 1 December 1241 after giving birth to a daughter. She was 27-years old and her loss was deeply mourned. 'Her beauty and manners had procured the favour of all', says Paris.[43]

4

Flowers Among Women 1242–1246

The king and queen go to Gascony,
the Montforts return from the east

Charity was an essential part of Henry III's piety and kingship. It became the practice of his reign to feed at least 150 paupers every day. The number dropped to 100 whenever Eleanor was absent from court because she fed paupers daily wherever her household was. The king and queen also undertook massive feedings to mark holidays and special occasions. For one All Soul's Day, before Eleanor arrived in England, he ordered 10,000 poor folk fed throughout the villages and countryside. When his officials claimed there simply were not that many, Henry offered the example of the Abbot of Osney. All the cleric had to do was nod his head, said the king, and 15,000 paupers would show up.[1]

Then as today, there was a certain amount of self-interest in almsgiving and doing good works. Feeding a huge horde of hungry people was a sure way of eliciting thousands of prayers all at once for both the dead and living. Now, in April 1242, Henry ordered 102,000 poor folk fed for his sister Isabella's soul in the afterlife. Inasmuch as she died in childbirth, and Eleanor was seven months pregnant with her third child, doubtless they were encouraged to think well of the queen too during the meal.[2]

There was a flurry of diplomatic activity going on at court at this time. It began the previous summer when King Louis IX invested his brother Alphonse as the Count of Poitou. Richard of Cornwall had borne that title since 1225, and since he was on crusade at the time, Louis's action, spurred on by his mother Blanche, was deemed an affront to the English. To check this ongoing French expansionism, Henry's court sought a marriage contract between widower Richard and Eleanor of Provence's sister Sanchia. As the oldest unmarried child of Count Raymond Berenger, it was hoped Sanchia would inherit Provence and

Richard would rule it as count in right of his wife. Until such time, she would live in England and together the two sisters could delight in each other's company, talking in Occitan of home, youth and courtly matters.[3]

The Poitevin lords viewed Alphonse as an intruder out to curtail their independence. Led by Henry and Richard's mother Isabella of Angoulême and her husband Hugh Lusignan, they put together a patchwork alliance to oppose the Capetians. Henry was unable to convince Parliament to fund an expedition in support of their revolt. He somehow found the money and prepared to set sail in May. Prior to that, he made arrangements for the succession in the event he did not come back. The keepers of several castles, Dover and Kenilworth among them, were instructed to hand them over to Eleanor to hold as regent to his heir. She herself received a charter on 5 April stating that her dower from all her husband's lands, castles and tenements were to be 'reasonable'.[4]

Although heavily pregnant, the queen joined the expedition. After their arrival in Gascony on 13 May, she retired upriver to the castle of La Réole while Henry went north. She fell ill during that time and was moved to the capital Bordeaux. There on 25 June 1242 she gave birth to a daughter, named after her mother Beatrice. Not for a month would Henry get a chance to see mother and child and then not in the best of circumstances.

The expedition had been a rout. Louis steamrolled through Poitou with his army, forcing one Poitevin lord after another to surrender, including Hugh Lusignan. Henry wanted to make a stand at Saintes, but one of the six English earls with him thought it was madness. He even wondered aloud if he and his compatriots should not lock up the king somewhere for his own safety, preferably in a place with iron bars on the windows.[5]

It was Simon de Montfort. Like Richard of Cornwall, Simon had also had an unwarlike crusade. He dove into the politics of the Christian states and was nominated by rival factions to become the governor of Jerusalem. There is no record of what became of his nomination or how he and his family went homeward. They had a new addition, another boy they named after Simon's brother Amaury de Montfort, who died in Italy on his way home from the crusade. Simon received a summons from Henry to join his expeditionary force, which he agreed to do only after the king promised to compensate him for the losses he incurred in his dispute with Thomas of Savoy.[6]

The rout had begun when the English force failed to secure the bridge at Taillebourg. They needed a truce to avoid becoming trapped and taken prisoner, and for this they had Richard of Cornwall. He picked up a pilgrim's staff, walked into the enemy camp, and asked Louis for the truce in person. Richard had ransomed dozens of French prisoners from the sultan while on crusade. Surely Louis would not deny him. The King of France obliged, but gave them only one day and only then because it was a Sunday.[7]

In undertaking the truce, Richard had demanded that his brother give him Gascony as his reward. It was only right since he deserved compensation for the loss of Poitou. With no other options available, Henry agreed. Eleanor was alarmed to hear this. The whole point of retaining Gascony was to give it to Edward someday. Once he grew up, he would have his own principality to lord over while waiting to succeed his father. The grant had to be revoked. Henry, of course, knew all this but, being in the jam that he was, was prepared to promise anything. Now he was probably telling Eleanor something like, 'Don't worry, I'll fix it'.

According to Paris, the brothers quarrelled after they reached safety. Henry took Gascony off the table, and Richard may have demanded the earldom of Chester instead. Henry had acquired the earldom by buying out the heirs of John the Scot after his death five years earlier. Richard did not get that prize either and he suspected that it was Eleanor behind him walking away empty-handed in both cases. He expressed some heat about it to the queen and demanded permission to leave the court.

Henry hoped he would remain. His marriage to Sanchia had been formalised on 17 July 1242 and she would be arriving in Bordeaux, but Richard departed in October 'without the king's indignation'. Around Christmas, Eleanor received word from home that Richard had since cooled down. A smaller landed settlement and £2,000 in cash from Henry in respect of his forthcoming marriage helped.[8]

The king and queen stayed on for a whole year because pacifying Gascony, which had been in tumult for most of the past decade, was also on the agenda for the expedition. Most of the nobility followed Richard to England, even obtaining Louis's permission to go home through France. One who stayed behind was Simon de Montfort. Henry needed his military expertise and Simon needed full restoration. There is no record to confirm it, but the two Eleanors, sisters-in-law and both young mothers with growing families, likely spent some of that time in each other's company.

In April 1243, Henry concluded a five-year truce with Louis. The next month Queen Eleanor had the joy of seeing her mother and sister again after more than seven years. Henry ordered several of the Channel ports to organise a fleet to retrieve the English court from the Continent, but their actual homecoming was delayed on account of Eleanor. She was unwell and may have had a miscarriage. It was at that time, on 17 August 1243, that Henry reshuffled her dower to replace certain manors and cities assigned to her with the whole county of Chester.[9]

They did not leave until late September. Beatrice and Sanchia set sail a month after them so they could be received in state. At 34, Richard was much older than the 15-year-old Sanchia, who was said to be even more beautiful than Eleanor. Their wedding took place on 23 November 1243. According to Paris, the food and entertainment were so magnificent and splendid that it was too tedious to describe it all, so he declined to do so.[10]

The Montforts are restored,
the queen and church affairs, the royal children

The Montforts also arrived that autumn, Eleanor's first time home in more than four years. There was still some coolness between her and Henry. Her financial situation with Simon was woeful but apparently she felt she could not approach her brother about it the way she so often did in the past. Seeing how enamoured Henry was of his mother-in-law, and the gifts he made to her, Eleanor and Simon turned to Beatrice of Savoy for help. She was astounded to learn that Henry had done so many nice things for her brothers William, Thomas, Peter and Boniface, and yet he heartlessly ignored his own sister. Beatrice took the king to task about his lack of generosity to his own kin, basically telling him, 'Now, now, my lord king, this won't do at all'.[11]

Whether Henry was shamed into acting or he was planning to act anyway, because he was going to need Simon's help for some upcoming battles, the Montforts were completely restored to favour. Henry granted his sister a late dowry for her second marriage in the form of a £333 annual fee, he pardoned £1,834 of her and Simon's debts to the Crown, and in February 1244 gave them the stately castle of Kenilworth. In June, Henry sold the Umfraville wardship to the Montforts for £6,667, to be paid in annual instalments of £333. Since that figure cancelled the payment of their fee, the wardship in a sense became Eleanor's marriage portion. In the following month, Henry pardoned the £110 they owed the Jewish moneylender David of Oxford. They were also given protection from any suit brought against them for the money by David's widow Licoricia.[12]

The battles Henry had in front of him in 1244 were numerous. He needed a tax from Parliament to cover his own debts, which Simon faithfully lobbied for on his behalf. He had to mobilise for trouble with Scotland and Wales, costing him more money. He had managed to pay most of his way by taxing the Jews mercilessly and from exploiting several wardships and bishoprics that had come into his hands. But the revenue from the last source dried up after the newly elected pope, Innocent IV, confirmed Boniface as the Archbishop of Canterbury and William Raleigh as the Bishop of Winchester. The Crown had earned almost £20,000 from Winchester alone in the six years since the death of Peter des Roches.[13]

Henry was sorry to see Winchester go for other reasons. He did not want Raleigh as the bishop there and furiously appealed to the pope to reconsider. He began to harass Raleigh, even denying him entry to the city. The ecclesiastical community was dismayed by the king's rough treatment of one of their own. When Raleigh fled to France, Innocent wrote a letter to Henry asking him to lighten up. The pope wrote to the queen as well, telling her that it was within her power to soften her husband's severe rancour because the Latin word for 'woman' (*mulier*) is derived from the expression meaning 'softening the man' (*molliens herum*).[14]

Eleanor received another letter from a high church official at this time. Robert Grosseteste, the Bishop of Lincoln, deplored how the king interfered in Church affairs and elections. He approached the queen for support. 'Now is the place and time for your beauty, as we have said, to disclose its brilliance to the lord king, if it please, persuading him, as befits royal majesty, to cut off the new causes of disturbance that have arisen and not permit them to sprout elsewhere.'[15]

Grosseteste made her job that much harder when it came time to postulate a new Bishop of Chichester. Henry wanted the office for his faithful servant Robert Passelewe and the chapter duly elected him. Passelewe still needed to be examined by the Archbishop of Canterbury, but since Boniface had only recently arrived in the country, he asked a group of bishops to do it for him. Led by Grosseteste, they found Passelewe's knowledge of scripture wanting and advised the archbishop to reject him. Boniface not only concurred with their decision, but blindly accepted their own candidate Richard Wyche for Chichester. None of the bishops advised him to consult the king first.[16]

Henry had to wonder whether Boniface was naïve or stupid and no doubt did so out loud for Eleanor to hear. Realising the delicate position he had put his niece in, the archbishop sent messengers to the queen asking her not to be angry with him. He was told not to be surprised if that was the case. He had offended her husband, the same man who had helped him obtain his distinguished position. She relayed this in a letter to Henry and assured him that it was up to her uncle to make things right again:

> Having heard and understood these things, he came to us in person, telling us that he would satisfy your will over these matters and all others, as far as he could. We persuaded him that he must satisfy your will if he wished to quiet our indignation; since while discord lasted between you and him, our wrath or indignation against him would not in any way abate.[17]

Doubtless pleased that his wife took his side, Henry was determined to teach the bishops a lesson and appealed to Rome against the postulation of Wyche at Chichester. Eleanor did her best, regardless, to soften his attitude. According to Paris, she told her husband that he should be thankful for what Boniface did, because Passelewe, a forest justice, kept money flowing into the exchequer from the fines he imposed. Henry eventually lost his appeal and Passelewe had to settle with becoming an archdeacon instead, but Eleanor gained a new friend in Bishop Wyche.[18]

Eleanor was pregnant through most of these controversies and entered confinement as 1244 drew to a close. Henry was mindful of the difficulties of her last birth. On 15 November, he ordered a thousand candles made, each from half a pound of wax, and had them placed around the shrine of Thomas Becket at Canterbury, with a like number going to the nearby church of St Augustine, 'for the health and delivery of the queen, who is with child'.[19]

The entire realm was hoping it would be a boy, the necessary 'spare' for the succession. If indeed it was, Henry planned to name him after St Edmund, the Anglo-Saxon king martyred at the hands of the Vikings. When Eleanor went into labour, he decided he needed to invoke another more immediate Edmund, his former archbishop who had died four years earlier. Supposedly the cloak worn by Edmund of Abingdon worked miracles at Catesby Priory, where Edmund's two sisters were nuns. The cloak was brought to Westminster to offer spiritual support.

Finally, after two days of what must have been an ordeal, Eleanor gave birth to a boy on 16 January 1245. The joy and relief were profound. The queen seemed to recover well, for on 24 February, Master Walter de Elenches and his fellows received 25 shillings for singing *Christus Vincit* to her on the day of her purification.[20]

Henry and Eleanor now had four children—Edward (5), Margaret (4), Beatrice (2) and baby Edmund. They grew up mostly at Windsor in a household managed by an English couple, Hugh and Sybil Giffard, assisted by a Savoyard clerk Walter de Dya and two nursemaids, Alice and Sarah. Their parents kept close tabs on their well-being while they were abroad in Gascony. Hugh was told by letter to retain the services of one Richard the Harper to keep the children amused with song, dance and games. Then, having heard complaints about the wine at Windsor, Henry ordered the constable to give the children the best stuff available in the cellar. It is unclear in what form the toddlers were consuming wine. It may have been served to them for medicinal purposes or used to flavour their drinking water. Certainly they would have preferred the sweeter wines of Gascony to the metallic-tasting varieties produced at home.[21]

The king and queen were already making plans for their futures. Edward was to receive Gascony and Edmund the earldom of Chester. The recent showdown with Scotland concluded peacefully with an agreement that Margaret should one day marry Alexander's namesake heir, who was a year younger than her.[22] Beatrice was the only one of their children who was born overseas and would go to live overseas in adulthood.

Eleanor and Simon's piety, marital insubordination and financial insecurity

Simon and Eleanor de Montfort also had four children at this time, all boys—Henry (6), Simon (4), Amaury (2) and a new addition Guy. Their 1-year-old ward Gilbert de Umfraville also joined their household. Their combined property consisted of roughly two dozen manors that formed

Simon's Leicester inheritance and Eleanor's English dower and marriage portion, scattered from the Midlands to Kent in the southeast and Dorset in the southwest.

The man in charge of the reeves and officials who ran the individual manors was Richard de Havering, who was employed by Eleanor as early as 1234 and rose to become the couple's steward. A typical manor was Eleanor's at Luton, between Dunstable and St Albans. It compromised just over ninety-seven acres and earned them close to £15 in rent every year from tenants who farmed just under half of the acreage. At her death it was worth not quite £86, about £65,000 in today's money, enough back then to buy a herd of 250 cows.[23]

The main residences for the Montforts were two gifts from Henry, Kenilworth Castle in the Midlands and Odiham 125 kilometres southeast in Hampshire. Odiham is not far from Waverley Abbey and it is there that we get one of the few glimpses of the Montforts on a family outing. It was 1 April 1245, Palm Sunday, and the couple arrived at the abbey with their two oldest sons and three handmaidens.

As a woman, Eleanor needed and acquired permission from the pope to enter this man's world. She made a great impression on the monks with her timing, having stepped inside the church just as the host was elevated during mass. The moment was ascribed to 'divine appointment'. She gave the monks a precious cloth to be used on the days when the relics were presented at the high altar. The family then heard a sermon in the chapter house, attended high mass, and Eleanor 'having kissed the wood of the Lord, retired from the abbey greatly edified'.[24]

Her circle of friends among men were the ones she shared with her husband, in particular Grosseteste, the Bishop of Lincoln. It was through him that she and Simon got to know Adam Marsh, a Franciscan friar famed for his lectures at Oxford. Born around 1200, Marsh became a close friend and spiritual guide of the Montforts. The surviving collection of his letters offers snippets of the more personal side of their characters and relationships.

In one story often recounted, Eleanor sent her cook John of Leicester to attend Grosseteste after his own cook had died. The bishop was so pleased with John that he told Marsh he wished to hold on to him. When Marsh mentioned this to Eleanor, she replied she would be happy to make the best of her servants, however good and indispensable they might be, available to him at any time.[25]

It was this intimacy and familiarity that allowed Marsh to also chide the Montforts over their shortcomings. He tended to be deferential in Simon's case, but with Eleanor he did not hold back. What bothered him in one missive was her temper and lack of submissiveness to her husband.

> (Scripture) clearly teaches us that a wife is most strictly bound to her husband by her strength and constancy, her prudence and her meekness and kindness ... For this reason the soul of any spouse who does not make the effort to perform this in every way is guilty of damnably breaking the bond of their lifelong association, which she swore to keep inviolate according to the law of matrimony ... Those whose minds do not fear to disturb the love and peace of their married life by demonic fits of anger are proved to be guilty of a violation of this duty.[26]

Eleanor was also censured for her vanity and extravagance. Gone were the days of the cheap fabric she wore as a sign of her chaste widowhood. She was too much into the regal look now, wearing costly finery and jewels as if to remind everyone she was the sister of the king. Marsh rhetorically asked her, 'Is there no difference between the face of a whore and the face of chastity?' Given the controversy of Eleanor's second marriage, he was being more than a little insensitive, but he seems not to have noticed. For her part, Eleanor does not seem to have heeded his advice as he rounded on her in another letter for failing to conduct herself properly:

> For several days now it has pained my heart and made me blush to have heard an increasing number of unpleasant and vexatious reports of improprieties that are soiling your reputation not a little, something that I continually lament with bitterness of spirit. ... I admonish you, I adjure you to multiply your good deeds for the future and both to make a zealous effort to make your conscience clear before the Most High, and to repair your reputation with men ... (by) following the example of praiseworthy matrons.[27]

There was in fact one praiseworthy matron who may have also been disappointed with the way Eleanor had turned out. A few years after these letters were sent, her former governess Cecily de Sandford lay dying. Her confessor, Brother Walter, noticed how she was still wearing the gold ring she had received when she and Eleanor took their vows of celibacy together in 1234. Walter thought it was most unbecoming for her to be ornamented on her deathbed and told the servants to remove the ring. With what strength she had left, Cecily fought them off, telling Walter she had given up 'noble embraces and wealth' that she might present the ring in heaven as the testament of her virtue.[28] Her underlying rebuke was that some people might easily slip off their rings, but she was not one of them.

Eleanor de Montfort may have been able to brush aside any lingering derision about the circumstances of her secret, second marriage, but evidently her husband could not. As the son of a crusading family, Simon was naturally drawn to the friars and their fundamental approach to religion, especially the use of confession in the development of conscience and introspection. He began looking inwardly at this time and found he still had a lot to answer for in leading Eleanor astray from her vow.[29] Even if he had not seduced her as Henry claimed, she was a woman sworn to celibacy who now had four children and he was the father of them. The Montforts would go on to have three more children, but not the next one for another six years.

Another likely source of tension in their marriage was money. Their estates gave them an income of £1,530 a year, supplemented occasionally by feudal windfalls and their combined 130 knights' fees. While far less than the £6,000 earned by her brother Richard of Cornwall or Walter Marshal's £3,500, they were among the wealthiest baronial families. The problem was Eleanor's £930 formed approximately two-thirds of it. As dower lands, they could not be sold, exploited or inherited. They were only for her lifetime. After she died, they went back to the Marshals, leaving the Montfort children with only their father's £600 half-an-earldom to divide up between them. The Umfraville wardship and other smaller grants brought their income up to £1,950, but again, they would lose that land and money when young Gilbert came of age in 1265.[30]

What the Montforts wanted more than anything was land in fee, something they could pass down to their heirs. Henry took a step towards it with regards to her Marshal dower. Walter Marshal had taken advantage of her absence from England to renege on his payments to her. Henry now threatened to seize the lands that constituted her dower and give them to the Montforts. That woke the Earl of Pembroke up and he finally made good his payments, but then he died in November 1245.[31] His brother Anselm quickly followed him to the grave, also without an heir. The huge Marshal estate, and her dower payment, would have to be divided among the heirs of the five sisters.

Meanwhile, Walter's widow Margaret, previously the widow of John de Lacy, received a dower of £572 for the Marshal lands in Ireland alone, nearly a third more than Eleanor's £400 for both Ireland and Wales. Perhaps recognising her feeling of injustice and the part he played in it, Henry took over her dower payments until the partition of the estate was complete, and in August 1246, he gave her a lifetime pardon for the fee farm she owed for her Marshal manor at Wexcombe.

There was no question of Simon standing by her through the litigation ahead, and not just because most of their income came from her dower. But in the enrolment for Wexcombe, Eleanor is referred to as the Countess of Pembroke and Leicester, in that order. If she had been going around talking like that, and issuing charters in her own name as seems to have been the case, then Simon may have had reason to feel his wife undercut his authority as her lord and husband and so had complained about it to people like Marsh.[32]

Queenship by example, losing Provence to the Capetians

Adam Marsh was also a friend of Eleanor of Provence. She valued his advice in both spiritual and practical matters and made demands on his time that could leave him exasperated, but he never chastised the queen in the way he did Eleanor de Montfort, partly because he asked favours of her as well. His correspondence indicates that the two Eleanors were in regular touch with him through letters that they dictated to clerks.

In one of Eleanor de Montfort's letters about her family, Marsh commends her for her carefully crafted words. Marsh himself used a difficult and elaborate style of Latin that suggests both the queen and countess must have had some facility in the language, even if his letters were read to them. Very rarely did he use French, as in the case of the postscript at the end of one letter to the queen. It is a sign of the informality and friendship that existed between him and both Eleanors.

Lady, if at this Easter you wish to have a serious discussion
with the Countess of Leicester about the salvation of souls
for whom, inasmuch as it is in your hands, you have so
piously offered support, I hope in the blessed Son of God
that by the power of his glorious resurrection, he will give
you counsel for the occasion to the glory of his name, that
may lead you into the way of eternal salvation. Amen.[33]

Matthew Paris had a livelier, unaffected Latin, but he undertook to
translate *The Story of St Edward the King* into French at this time because
he intended it to be passed around and read aloud in court circles.[34]
The cult of Edward the Confessor was flourishing, and in 1245 Henry
commenced reconstructing Westminster Abbey to include a shrine in
honour of the saint. Paris presented his version of the *Story* to Eleanor
of Provence and inscribed it with a dedication to her that may be aptly
described as flowery.

Noble, well-born lady, Eleanor, rich queen of England, flower
among ladies by virtue of your qualities and honours, I who
have prepared this book for you put it in your care. There
is no man who does not love and esteem your goodness,
wisdom, and nobility. Were I not to be called a flatterer,
I will praise you briefly, as is fitting and as I dare: like a
carbuncle among gems, you are a flower among women.

The effusive praise seems at odds with the harsh treatment Paris normally
gives the queen in his chronicle, but it is part of his agenda. The *Story* can
be seen as a guide for queenship in England as Edward the Confessor's
wife Edith is beautiful, intelligent and cultured. Judging by the dedication,
Eleanor was all these things too, but she was only halfway there. The
Edith of the *Story* is a submissive partner, a wife devoted to her husband
and his rule. She even accepts her childless marriage with Edward
because he desires celibacy and she supports whatever he wants, however
unwillingly. Her passivity and understanding make her the role model for
good queenship. Become the whole Edith, Paris was telling Eleanor for
all the court to hear, and you will be the perfect queen of England.

The primary duty of any queen consort was to produce children, but
here Paris could afford to mention Edith's lack of progeny. It was the

reason Henry and the whole Norman line were in England in the first place. Besides, Eleanor already had four children. But the chronicler suppressed much of the historical Edith who was also wilful, wealthy and well-connected. She had been very much a part of her husband's rule, not subordinate to it.[35]

This was what worried Paris. He felt Henry was too preoccupied with foreigners and the Continent and blamed it on the increasing influence of Eleanor and her relations. When Paris learned of the marriage contracted between Richard of Cornwall and Sanchia, he bemoaned, 'The whole community in England were much excited, and began to fear that the whole business of the kingdom would be disposed of at the will of the queen and her sister ... a second queen'.[36] He hoped that Eleanor would have been so flattered by the dedication and encouragement to emulate the fictional Edith that she would accept a more diminished role in her adopted land.

It was wishful thinking. In August 1245, Eleanor's father Raymond Berenger died. Henry was on campaign in Wales when he received the news and forbade any announcement of it until he could tell Eleanor himself. In his will Raymond had designated his youngest daughter Beatrice as his sole heir. Whoever married her received Provence.

As the suitors lined up, some of them with aggressive intentions, Countess Beatrice asked the pope to choose. That made it a done deal, because Innocent IV had just deposed Frederick II as the Holy Roman Emperor, then fled to Lyon for safety. Innocent told Blanche that if France guaranteed his protection, she could have young Beatrice for her youngest son Charles of Anjou. Louis knew that meant cutting his wife Margaret, the oldest sister, out of the will, but he agreed. Charles marched in and took Provence for himself even before he and Beatrice were married in January 1246.[37]

Henry and Eleanor were dismayed. They had taken steps to secure Provence by loaning Raymond money in return for the possession of certain castles. They also made a treaty with Count Amadeus that gave Henry the overlordship of Savoy in return for a pension for him and marriage for his granddaughter to an English earl. But the fact remained they were far away and Charles was in Provence doing what he wanted. Raymond had left dowries to his other daughters in his will, £6,667 each to Margaret and Eleanor and half that to Sanchia, but Charles felt no obligation to pay up. Henry and Richard of Cornwall complained to the pope about the injustice of the whole affair, but Innocent basically told them to live with it.[38]

Eleanor had to be mortified, not just because of the part her mother played in it, but because of her uncle Boniface's role as well. He had gone to the pope to be consecrated as the Archbishop of Canterbury but got roped into the Franco-papal alliance. Perhaps afraid of the frosty reception awaiting him in England, Boniface remained in Innocent's service at Lyon for the next couple of years. Eleanor had no such place to hide if pressed by Henry to explain the actions of her family. He had shown at her purification in 1239, when he all but chased the Montforts out of the country, that he had the explosive Angevin temper of his forebears, but he was also the type to cool down quickly.[39] He had been king since the age of 9, nearly three decades now, overcoming endless threats, betrayals and disappointment. He got over this one as well.

Their union was doubtless strengthened by Edward's illness in the summer of 1246. The family was gathered at the time in Hampshire for the dedication of Beaulieu Abbey, which had been founded by Henry's father John. Whatever seized the heir to the throne, it was decided that he could not be moved. Eleanor stayed with her son the whole three weeks he needed to recover, causing something of a scandal because women were not allowed within the confines of the abbey.[40] She and Henry were devoted parents and the thought of leaving the 7-year-old boy alone with the monks and whatever doctors were available was unthinkable. The monks could put down her presence among them as a test of the Lord.

Isabella of Angoulême died around this time, confined to a nunnery after being implicated in a plot to poison Louis and his brothers. She had of course abandoned her own children to start a new life and family elsewhere and had hurt Henry more than helped him in his quest to recover his Continental patrimony. He never held any of that against her and had masses said for her soul.[41]

It is unknown whether Eleanor of Provence ever got to meet her mother-in-law during her year in Gascony. Eleanor de Montfort probably did meet her mother at some point during her years away from England, but nothing is definite. What is known is that Isabella ignored her and her other two surviving children with John in her will. She gave everything to her second crop.

5

Seriously Aroused Displeasure
1247–1252

The Lusignans arrive, the queen's unease

Henry III ruled for forty-five years after his minority ended in 1227. Throughout that time he was constantly accused of favouring foreigners at court. It seemed strange since he was the first king since the Norman Conquest to be born and entirely raised in England, who exalted Saxon king Edward the Confessor. Henry went out of his way to make Edward the patron saint of the land even though St George, who had no connection whatsoever to England, was already well known during his reign.[1] And yet there they were, foreigners like George at court.

Some of it could not be helped. Unlike his Norman predecessors, Henry had a deep appreciation for art, fashion, design and architecture. He naturally would have looked to people on the Continent for different ideas and inspiration. There were also economic considerations. The kingdom was prospering thanks to the export of wool, which in turn fuelled imports of commodities like wine. All this business brought not just foreign merchants and moneyers to England, but also clergymen and papal collection agents, because much of that wool came from land owned by religious houses. The mother church in Rome demanded a cut of their wealth to support the huge multinational corporation it had become.

In terms of politics, the only foreigner at court that had to be there was the queen. Dynastic diplomacy and the awkwardness of marrying one's own subject precluded the thought of an English gal as consort for the king. The queen might have a lady or two from her homeland waiting on her, but that was it. Paris felt Louis and Frederick did it right. After their respective weddings, each sent his wife's bridal party packing.[2]

74

Henry was a far more sensitive and caring husband, but it also suited his nature to have a cosmopolitan court and household. He was moreover determined to settle things with France and was counting on Eleanor's relatives and their retainers helping him to pull it off.

Now, ten years later, Henry was ready to renew that confidence. In May 1247, he confirmed his alliance with Amadeus of Savoy by marrying the count's granddaughter Alice to Edmund de Lacy, soon to be the Earl of Lincoln. She was escorted to England by Peter of Savoy, who brought along another Alice to marry a leading nobleman based in Ireland.

These marriages were followed by two more within a few short months, only they had nothing to do with the queen and her family. The relatives this time were the king's own, a son and daughter from the nine children of Isabella of Angoulême and Hugh Lusignan. On 13 August, Henry married his half-brother William de Valence to Joan Munchensi, the Marshal heiress to Pembroke, while his half-sister, another Alice, he made the wife of John de Warenne, the heir to the earldom of Surrey.[3]

Taken together, these three marriages involving English earldoms and foreign beneficiaries might seem like a complete reversal from a quarter of a century earlier, when Henry married his sister Eleanor to William Marshal II to keep him from marrying a foreigner. In fact, it was a continuation of another policy borne out of the rebellion against King John by the barons, then the later one against Henry by Richard Marshal. In both cases, the ancestral nobility had drawn on their mutual ties for strength, intrigue and defiance.

Now, by marrying the heirs and heiresses of these families to his and Eleanor's foreign relations, the king was out to bind the leading baronial clans closer to the Crown than to each other. Court observers like Paris found this mingling of 'foreign scum', as he called them, with the local aristocracy disgusting. He and other chroniclers took aim at the queen for promoting this invasive element and at the king for bowing to her wishes or else being hopelessly infatuated with smart-talking, smartly dressed foreigners. What they could not see or did not want to admit is that Henry was pursuing this strategy with a council that was dominated by Englishmen from humble backgrounds.

Eleanor of Provence herself turned to these same Englishmen for advice. Some of them like John Mansel and William Kilkenny became friends and trusted confidants.[4] Doubtless she understood through them why her husband had to seek closer cooperation with his overseas siblings. He needed to strengthen his ties to the Lusignans because the situation in Gascony was again deteriorating. His half-brothers were well positioned from their lordships in Poitou to intervene in force there when necessary.

She would have had misgivings just the same because they had landed in force in England in the meantime. William de Valence and Alice had been accompanied by two brothers, Guy and Aymer, and another brother, Geoffrey, was said to be on his way. By contrast, the Savoyards had managed to establish themselves in England because they did not come over all at once and had maintained discreet profiles since their arrivals. Boniface was the only exception, but he was mostly absent anyway.

If the Lusignans were off to a noisy start, it was thanks to Henry. He not only pushed them to the head of the patronage queue, but devised an elaborate introduction for them during his favourite holiday of the year, St Edward's Day on 13 October. For that occasion in 1247, he had been given a vial of Holy Blood from the Patriarch of Jerusalem as an inducement to go on crusade. Henry carried the vial barefoot from St Paul's Cathedral to Westminster Abbey in a lavish spectacle for all to see. At the close of the festivities, he knighted his brother William and some other youths, also for all to see.[5] Showing off the Lusignans in this manner was probably deliberate. Henry wanted to inform the Savoyards, and by extension his wife, that they were no longer the only game in town.

The arrival of the newcomers was bound to stir up resentment and focus unwanted attention on foreigners at court. It was therefore remarkable that the queen should choose this time to get involved in a scandal. In 1248, the Prior of Thetford was stabbed to death by one of the monks of his house. According to Paris, the prior was a debauched individual who brought it on himself by too much partying. Ordinarily the Church would have handled the matter, but because the dead man was a Savoyard, a relation of the queen's no less, Eleanor felt obliged to demand action on behalf of their community. That action, of course, was through the king, who ordered the homicidal monk to be blinded and tossed in a dungeon. Perhaps her anger over the murder was justified, but it gave monastic commentators more reason to bemoan her influence.[6]

More crusading, the Montforts in Gascony, tensions rise at court

Eleanor de Montfort would have greeted the Lusignans with at least the same trepidation as her sister-in-law the queen. They were her kinfolk, but she saw them only as competition for her brother's favours. Her relations with William de Valence in particular were fraught from the outset on account of her Marshal dower. In the spring of 1247, before Valence and his siblings had arrived, the Montforts brought suit against John Munchensi and other Marshal heirs for lands in Pembroke that should have formed Eleanor's dower. Apparently it was Henry's idea. He was surety for her £400 payment but finding it hard to collect the money from all eighteen heirs. Both he and the Montforts would benefit from a favourable ruling.

The case was suspended, however, when Munchensi died that summer. By the time it resumed in the fall, his lands were in the hands of his sister Joan and her new husband William de Valence. These two joined other Marshal heirs like the Earls of Gloucester and Norfolk and the Countess of Surrey in dismissing Eleanor's argument that her agreement with Richard Marshal was invalid because she had been a minor at the time and had only accepted it at her brother's urging. Her real argument, they claimed, was that she was stuck with a bad deal, but whether that was true or not was neither the issue nor their problem.[7]

In December, while the verdict was still pending, Simon de Montfort took the cross. Crusading fervour had again swept through Europe following the fall of Jerusalem in 1244. King Louis vowed to recover it and many English nobles were planning to join his crusade. It was natural that Simon should be one of them. He was friends with Louis, came from a crusading family, and his spiritual adviser Robert Grosseteste was in charge of the fundraising for it. Paris adds that Simon was also still torn about the circumstances of his marriage and felt the need to atone for them. Moved by his doubts and commitment, Eleanor took the cross right after him. They would go on crusade together to make amends for their sins.

Cynical observers might have seen it differently. Other nobles such as William Longespee and Simon's own good friend Walter Cantilupe, the Bishop of Worcester, had already taken the cross more than six months earlier, just as the Montforts were launching their lawsuit.[8] Eleanor and

Simon may have been sincere as everyone else in wanting to become warriors for the faith, but they were not opposed to any leverage it might gain them for their own personal crusade against the Marshal heirs. It would be one thing for their clan to deny them redress, quite another to deny it to two people signed with the cross.

The verdict was supposed to be delivered by 10 February 1248, but for reasons that remain a mystery to this day, none was ever given. The case simply disappeared. Henry may have thought better of it as it dragged on. He was preparing one of the largest parliaments of his reign to ask for a tax to offset his enormous debts. Since so many of his magnates were Marshal heirs, he risked losing their support if the court ordered them to disgorge a chunk of land for the Montforts. Henry may have also made promises to his sister and brother-in-law to forget about it. Already in January he gave Eleanor eighty barrels of wine, more deer for her park (thirty does and ten bucks to be exact) and forgave her the £50 annual rent for Odiham along with three years' worth of arrears.[9]

Another party who may have convinced the Montforts to let the matter drop was Queen Eleanor's mother Beatrice. In recalling the case many years later, Simon said she was visiting England at the time when the verdict should have been given. During her previous visit four years earlier, Beatrice had won concessions for the Montforts from Henry. She had shown she was a friend with their best interests at heart.[10] Whatever arrangements were made now, with or without Beatrice's involvement, the case was history and so, it turns out, were their plans to go on crusade.

In the spring of 1248, there was real concern that Gascony might be lost for good. The truce with France was set to expire and the Spanish kingdoms to the south were hinting at their own claims to the region. Losing the duchy would be a disaster for Henry and Eleanor. Not only would the prestige of the Crown suffer, but they would have to rethink the whole inheritance scheme for their sons. Gascony was also a major trading partner and might even become a prime source of revenue if the seneschals appointed to run it could find a way to quell the disturbances and petty warfare of the local barons. Since they lacked the authority and iron will necessary to restore order there, Henry and his councillors turned to Simon, who noted he was also approached by 'my lady the queen'.[11]

Because he was pledged to the crusade, Montfort was able to dictate the terms. He wanted the governorship for seven years, meaning until

Edward was 16 and able to assume control himself, and plenty of men and money to support him. The agreement was reached on 1 May but he did not leave until autumn. His wife Eleanor probably went with him. As the sister of the king, she naturally enhanced Simon's authority. They returned at Christmas having worked a miracle. The truce with France was renewed, the Spanish kings appeased, and the various factions were at peace.

In the spring of 1249, they prepared to go back. They arranged for their eldest son Henry, then 10-years old, to continue the education he had begun under Grosseteste the previous year. In June, they crossed over. The Montforts were in the party of Longespee and other knights on their way to the crusade.[12] When they exchanged farewells, Simon and Eleanor doubtless expressed their hope to join up with them later on.

They were less than a month in Bordeaux, however, when the mayoral election there turned into a deadly riot. Simon managed to suppress it and took the crackdown into the countryside. A French chaplain visiting him and Eleanor at La Réole on business noted how well he had the situation in Gascony under control. Henry himself felt reasonably assured to make the official grant of the duchy to Edward on 30 September 1249.[13]

Simon then scored his biggest success by capturing the most notorious of the troublemakers, Gaston de Bearn, and shipping him off to England for trial. But he was a first cousin of the queen, his mother being a sister of Raymond Berenger. Eleanor of Provence felt duty-bound to intercede on his behalf. On 28 December, Henry notified Simon that he had given the prisoner a full pardon in return for his homage and allegiance.[14] Gaston went back to Gascony, but began fomenting discord immediately. Years later, Simon bitterly recalled what a colossal mistake it had been to release him.

In truth, he should have dealt with Gaston by himself or not at all. It was Henry's nature to work for reconciliation first and foremost and there was just no helping Gaston's connection to the royal family. There was also the added consideration that locking him up and seizing his lands might have inflamed the other Gascon robber barons. In any case, Simon wrote to the king in late March 1250 that he now had a full-scale guerrilla war on his hands. It may have been at this time, although we cannot be sure, that Eleanor de Montfort gave birth to a daughter in Bordeaux. The infant died shortly afterwards and was buried at the Dominican convent. The Montforts gave the convent money to build an infirmary in her memory.[15]

Back in England, on 6 March, Henry took the cross from the hands of Boniface of Savoy, the Archbishop of Canterbury, in an elaborate ceremony in Westminster Hall. He was spurred on to do it by the wondrous news from the Continent that Louis had conquered Damietta in Egypt in just one day. Inasmuch as Eleanor's sister Margaret of Provence was with her husband on the crusade, the Waverley annalist was probably right in saying that the queen also took the cross on this occasion.[16]

None of them could know it, but the crusading army was by then close to destruction. Their march to Cairo had ended with the advance guard being cut to pieces at Mansurah and the remaining troops overwhelmed on the banks of the Nile. On 6 April 1250, Louis and his brothers Alphonse of Poitiers and Charles of Anjou were captured and imprisoned. Some ungodly fate may have awaited them had it not been for Queen Margaret. Although days away from giving birth, she managed to secure Damietta as a bargaining counter for the freedom of her husband and surviving crusaders. They did not include Longespee and other members of the English contingent, who had been entrapped and slaughtered.[17]

Word of the catastrophe had not reached England when, on 17 May, Henry ordered the Master of the Temple to lend the queen a book of romances written in French. It contained the story of the siege of Antioch during the First Crusade. Even after the full narrative of the defeat in Egypt became known at the end of summer, Henry and Eleanor threw themselves into the crusading spirit. They cut back on household expenditures to save money for the expedition, but at the same time commissioned wall scenes of Antioch reproduced at Winchester, Clarendon and Westminster.[18]

The Montforts had arrived from Gascony on 3 May 1250. They made arrangements for their third son Amaury, who was destined for a career in the Church, to join his oldest brother for tutorship under the Bishop of Lincoln.[19] Simon made a full report to Henry about the increasing uncertainty of his mission. It all came down to money, he told him. The king took out a loan from Italian bankers to help meet his costs, but Simon continued to demand and receive more funds after he left again before the end of the month.[20] We know that Eleanor went with him because Marsh wrote to tell her to expect the arrival of a friar in their household and ask her to reply by courier about 'your ladyship's following'. Marsh himself was supposed to set off for the papal court, but 'the lady queen strongly resisted it and strove hard to retain me'.[21]

On 10 June, Henry conveyed intelligence to Simon that another leading Gascon noble was preparing a full-scale insurrection. It was probably then that Eleanor returned to England, for in July she received another gift of deer from Henry. The uprising of the Gascon nobles had started to take its toll on Simon. Marsh advised him to turn to Scripture for solace, particularly the book of Job, and assured him that the royal couple still had full confidence in his administration. 'I have spoken earnestly to the lady queen about your proposals, and she replied reasonably and kindly to everything, being very hopeful of your receiving (funds).' And then in mid-October, Marsh was banished from court, permitted not to see anyone, not even the queen. He had incurred Henry's displeasure, but would only say it had something to do with him preaching 'the words of life'.[22]

The real reason may have been Henry's nomination of his half-brother Aymer de Valence to succeed the recently deceased William Raleigh as the Bishop of Winchester. Aymer had been studying theology in Oxford since arriving in England, but was still in his early 20s, well below the age of episcopal consecration. During the previous election at Winchester, Henry had caused a scandal when he tried to thwart Raleigh's postulation. Queen Eleanor was recruited by the clergy at that time to exert her influence on the king. Knowing her husband was determined not to lose this one, Eleanor stayed out of it and Marsh may have been caught in an unguarded moment trying to enlist her help again. Aymer was elected in November 1250.[23]

The next time Eleanor de Montfort saw her husband was sometime after 6 January 1251, the day before what would be their thirteenth wedding anniversary. It is unlikely he brought any gift with him from Gascony to mark the occasion. He was accompanied by only three retainers and the poor condition of their horses suggested they had made homeward with all due speed. Simon told Henry the situation was critical. Without more money and troops, the duchy was lost. He reminded him what kind of people they were dealing with, how they refused to help the queen before and after she gave birth to Beatrice back in 1242. That was true, Henry said, but he had nevertheless received reports that his viceroy was acting like a tyrant and that was getting everybody all worked up. Simon replied that the king's own experience rendered these complaints 'unworthy of belief'.[24]

Simon left again in March, picking up some mercenaries along the way to thrash the Gascons. His clampdown worked insofar as it allowed

Eleanor to join him again that year, but the harshness of Simon's methods began to cause alarm at court. Marsh encouraged Eleanor to work on her husband: 'Use your sweetness and good advice to conduct himself more cautiously in the future.' Such was the growing tenseness that he urged the Montforts not to rush in their desire to set off for England. 'In this business a prudent delay ought not to be harmful', he warned Eleanor.[25]

They left in November 1251. Paris has the Montforts crossing the Channel in the company of Guy Lusignan, who was returning from the crusade that saw his father and brother, both named Hugh, killed in Egypt. Apparently their sailing party was in sight of the English coast when the winds drove them all the way back to France. When they finally did make it, Henry was supposedly glad to see his half-brother, but was otherwise indifferent to his sister and brother-in-law.[26]

Daughter Margaret gets married, Henry sacks Simon

There were five big royal weddings in England during the course of Henry's long reign. The first took place in York in 1221 between his sister Joan and Alexander II of Scotland. Henry was then 13-years old, Simon roughly the same age. Eleanor de Montfort was about 6 and the birth of Queen Eleanor was still two years away. It was now 1251, thirty years later, and the fourth of those big weddings (following Henry's to Eleanor and Richard of Cornwall's to Sanchia) was about to take place in York again. The Scottish king had died suddenly in 1249 and was succeeded by his 8-year-old son Alexander by his second wife Marie. Since Henry and Eleanor were planning to go on crusade, which meant they could be gone for years, it was decided to go ahead with the marriage that had been contracted between young Alexander and their daughter Margaret as part of the peace treaty between Scotland and England in 1244.

Henry and Eleanor would settle for it being nothing less than the grandest of occasions. Before the nuptials, the King of England knighted the King of Scotland and presented him with a silver-handled sword in a scabbard of silk along with a pair of silver-gilt spurs. Twenty other youths were knighted alongside Alexander, although it is unlikely they received similar gifts. The bride was escorted to the altar by her brother

Lord Edward and three of his companions, all of them wearing costly garments of gold cloth embroidered with the three leopards of the arms of England.[27]

The wedding was actually a secret affair. Walter Gray, the elderly Archbishop of York who presided over the earlier wedding in 1221, had done a splendid job with organising the festivities, but various brawls broke out among the thousands of guests from England, Scotland and France crammed inside the city walls. To play it safe, the nuptials were held on the day after Christmas, 26 December 1251, early in the morning, when most of the merrymakers were likely asleep or dealing with hangovers. Any disappointment over missing the wedding would have been made up for by the feast afterwards. The size of the crowd can be guessed from the requisitions: 170 boar, 1,400 deer, 7,000 chickens, 10,000 haddock, 25,000 gallons of wine and nearly 70,000 loaves of bread.[28]

Margaret was the first of Eleanor of Provence's children to be married. She was only 11, but then Eleanor had only been a year older when she married Henry. Since Alexander was a year younger than his new queen, there was no fear about Margaret having to deal with early sexual activity. In any case, Matilda Cantilupe, the widow of Henry's former household steward, would go with her to Scotland, and two powerful Anglo-Scottish barons, John Balliol and Robert de Ros, would be responsible for her treatment under Alexander's minority council.[29] If they did not have a clue then that Henry and Eleanor would be the most famous doting parents in English royal history, they would soon enough.

Learning that Margaret and Alexander's wedding was to be conducted in secret must have made the Montforts smile, but they could consider themselves lucky that Henry did not bar them from attending it as he had done to them at the queen's churching in 1239. He had received another report that Gascony was again in turmoil and it was all the fault of his military overseer, who was just then standing in front of him with the bill for all the castles he was building in the duchy. Fed up, Henry refused to reimburse Simon for the costs.

At this point, the queen was drawn into their argument and had Henry give way on the castles. They would after all go to Edward someday. Henry nevertheless refused to let Simon go back and quell the latest outbreak of violence. He would send a commission instead to get to the bottom of the situation. When Simon took that amiss, Henry told him he should be happy for it. If all is what you say, your glory will be greater still, he told him.[30]

Henry by then was way beyond sarcasm. He was seething over the mess in his last overseas province. For more than three years, Simon had assured him he was on the right track, but all Henry could see was no end in sight to the costs and vehement dissatisfaction with his viceroy. The two Eleanors attempted to restore the king's faith and support, but not even his wife and sister together could make any headway. To a fellow friar, Adam Marsh reported:

> Both the queen and the Countess of Leicester are making efforts with blessed and tireless solicitude to appease the wrath of his royal majesty, seriously aroused by reason of (Gascony), although up until now they have made poor progress, as I hear, with assuaging his highnesses' renewed displeasure.[31]

Queen Eleanor enlisted Marsh to help them hammer out a new agreement they could present to the king. After talking with her in Reading, Marsh set off to meet the Montforts at Odiham thirty kilometres away. He found the business 'exceedingly troublesome' but stayed the whole weekend with them. He then went back to Reading, travelled another twenty-six kilometres to consult the Montforts at Bromhall Priory, and finally accompanied Simon and Peter of Savoy to talk with the queen at Windsor twelve kilometres away. Between 25 February and 7 March, Marsh covered nearly a hundred kilometres and summed up his efforts to Grosseteste by saying, 'I am weary of life'.[32]

Apparently the discussions were meant to come up with a figure for castles and expenses that both Henry and Simon could live with. Marsh may have retired from the scene worn out, but Simon, who received permission to return before the talks got underway, set off to have his revenge in Gascony. Sometime after that Henry received the report of his commissioners. They found Simon's seneschal there barely holding on, thanks in part to aid brought to him from Poitou by Geoffrey Lusignan, and they spoke of a league ready to take on Montfort the minute he got there. That could only mean more war. Henry decided the only way to settle the problem was to have both parties appear before him. On 23 March 1252, he ordered Simon to return to England immediately to face his accusers.[33]

In the showdown that followed, Henry was inclined to believe the worst about the man he now addressed as the 'Earl of Leicester', a far cry from the 'beloved and faithful brother-in-law' Simon had been when he undertook the assignment four years earlier. The passions in the refectory of Westminster Abbey, where his trial was held in May and June, reached the point of king and subject trading insults with each other. Henry was forced to accept the verdict of the baronial panel, which came out fully behind their fellow peer. Both sides were ordered to return and observe a truce, but the Gascons ambushed Simon's troop and the war was on again. In the end, Henry was forced to buy him out of their agreement for £4,667.[34]

Marsh described the events of the trial in a letter to Grosseteste written at Eleanor's manor in Sutton. She was then five months pregnant and naturally feeling anxious about the whole situation. In the letter Marsh tells the Bishop of Lincoln that she commends her husband, children, household and herself to him for spiritual protection 'in this time of fear and danger'. She went to Kenilworth for her confinement and apparently the friar was close at hand. There, in another letter, he informed Simon that she had contractions on 9 October, but they turned out to be false. Marsh then spent the rest of his letter taking Simon to task for forcing a priest to join him abroad. Indiscreetly, Marsh mentioned he received that information from Eleanor.[35]

The queen sent her messenger to Kenilworth to see how her sister-in-law was doing. Simon's barber then brought 'rumours' of the birth to Windsor, an indication that Eleanor's labour was protracted and difficult. The child was born safely, another boy, her fifth son. He was named Richard, presumably after his uncle Richard of Cornwall. Receiving the news, the queen sent one of her own nurses to care for Eleanor. They remained in touch by messenger in the months following, and on 1 December the queen sent a gift of jewellery to the countess.[36]

Henry and Eleanor of Provence quarrel, the Lusignans and Savoyards brawl

By then, the king and queen were not on speaking terms. The fallout over Gascony coincided with their own personal dispute, and Eleanor's support for Simon only exacerbated it. The roots of it began a decade earlier when Henry granted the wardship of the heir to Roger de Tony to his wife. The grant did not include the advowsons, the right to fill church offices in the gift of the wardship. Nevertheless, when the church at Flamstead fell vacant at Easter of 1251, the queen gave it to her chaplain William of London. In December, just before Margaret's wedding, Henry bestowed several benefices of the wardship. Flamstead he gave to his wardrobe clerk Artaud de St Romain. At an income of £67, it was a benefice worth having.[37]

When Henry learned that his wife had beaten him to it, he flew into a rage. According to Paris, he snapped that 'a woman's pride knows no bounds unless properly restrained'. The king probably thought she was being singularly greedy and ungrateful in this instance. He used wardships to give Eleanor financial independence and to use as her own source of patronage. In both cases, it enhanced her position as queen. Then she had to go and pull a stunt like this.

His response was to dismiss William of London from her service and have him tossed out of Flamstead. In March 1252, the king ordered Grosseteste to admit St Romain to the church, but the bishop refused. Henry's clerk came from Burgundy and Grosseteste was against the presence of foreign clergy like him on English soil. His grounds were their inability to speak the local language endangered the souls of parishioners. He excommunicated St Romain and placed Flamstead under interdict, surprising since that definitely harmed the souls of these particular parishioners. The ones who died in the meantime had to be left unburied nearby.[38]

Queen Eleanor was humiliated by what she felt was her husband's overreaction and highhandedness. He therefore deserved the inconvenience and embarrassment of having to name proctors to argue his side of the case in court, which dragged on into autumn. By late October, Henry was sufficiently peeved by it all to order the arrest of Robert del Ho, a clerk at the exchequer of the Jews, on charges of corruption. It was an unrelated matter and the charges against him were murky, but since Ho conducted business for Eleanor, his arrest may have been a warning to her about overstepping her authority. Ho was released on bail on 2 November. It might have been meant as a gesture for reconciliation between the pair, but the events of the next day ruined any immediate chance of it.[39]

The issue was again patronage. The post of prior at the hospital of St Thomas in Southwark had fallen vacant. The advowson belonged to Winchester and Henry's brother Aymer, the bishop-elect, duly named one of his clerks to the post. An official of the Archbishop of Canterbury took offence at not being asked about it first. When the official found he could not eject the new prior, he had him imprisoned. Aymer put together a posse to free the prior, but not finding him, they kidnapped the offending official. They let him go, but the indignity of his treatment caused much excitement.[40]

The court was at Windsor when word of the confrontation arrived. Eleanor was outraged at this attack against her uncle's men, even though Boniface was out of the country. She was already on edge in the aftermath of the murder of another distant relative of hers, Bernard of Champagne, in Hereford during the summer. Whatever the queen said against Aymer now, it clearly set Henry off. First Montfort, then Flamstead, now this. The next day on 4 November 1252, he seized custody of her lands and income and sent her off to Guildford to think things over.[41] Just so she knew where things stood, Christmas court would be spent in Winchester as guests of Aymer.

In the meantime, Boniface returned from the papal court. He denounced the raid and excommunicated Aymer and his lot, but they ignored him. The archbishop enticed two of his suffragans to join him in pronouncing sentence, or perhaps these two bishops knew Queen Eleanor would want them to offer him their support. One was her friend Richard Wyche of Chichester and the other Peter d'Aigueblanche of Hereford. The latter was a Savoyard in that he came to England as a clerk of William of Savoy and had so impressed Henry with his diplomatic abilities that the king arranged his election as Bishop of Hereford in 1240 to add clout to his forthcoming missions. Henry was displeased that the court took sides like this. He ordered his magnates to stay out of the quarrel, and just to get the message across, he stopped payments to Aymer's brother William de Valence and Boniface's brother Peter of Savoy.[42]

The queen got her land and money back within a few weeks but she spent most of December at Marlborough while Henry was elsewhere. He expected her to use that time to work on reconciliation between both sides. By the end of the year, Eleanor and her Lusignan brothers-in-law were exchanging gifts. She gave William and Geoffrey costly belts and she received some plate from Aymer. She gave her husband a crystal goblet on a stand and received her own belt from him. Later, in front of a gathering of nobles and clergy, Aymer swore an oath that he had never intended any violence in freeing his clerk. Boniface nullified the sentence of excommunication against him, the case was referred to arbitration, and the two clerics made up. It was over for now.[43]

From the sidelines, there was a certain malicious joy in watching the two leading groups of foreigners, the king's men and the queen's men as Paris called them, getting into a major scrap over one benefice. They were sneered at not just for being scroungers, but violent and ill-bred ones to boot. It was, as ever, a superficial argument. Their behaviour was typical for that era. There was a lot of talk about honour and chivalry, but the real action, when it came down to it, was the pursuit of rights and payback for slights.

The nasty competitiveness was not just limited to the aristocrats and churchmen, either. Henry's court had a poet laureate, Master Henry of Avaranches. Sometime in the early 1250s, a poetry contest was held between him and one Michael of Cornwall. Although Master Henry by then was an old man with poor vision and failing memory, the contest quickly became personal. Among other things, Michael accused the respected poet of taking a fine robe given to him by the queen and passing it along to a red-headed whore. Doubtless many private jokes were made at Eleanor's expense on account of this. For what it is worth, one of the judges of the contest was Aymer.[44]

6

Historic Undertakings 1253–1255

Henry goes to Gascony, he names the queen regent,
she has her last child

The first of January was the feast of the Circumcision, the gift-giving time of the Christmas season. In 1253, Queen Eleanor presented several brooches to the various nurses at Windsor taking care of the royal brood. There was Lady Agnes, in charge of 10-year-old Beatrice, and Lady Alice, who had Edward under her care. He was now 13, an eager hunter who often scrapped with his companions. Edmund turned 8 on 16 January. He seems to have been ill a lot at this time. His mother called in three different physicians who prescribed him syrups and whatever else fit the diagnosis. Other children in and out of Windsor included Sanchia's 2-year-old son Edmund and Alice de Lacy's infant boy Henry. Their nurses also received brooches. In all, Eleanor passed out over sixty jewels that month, worth around £260.[1]

Her relations with Henry had fully mended, and with the coming of spring she found herself pregnant. There was likely some concern because, after having four children in less than six years, she had not given birth for more than eight years. This was not unusual. Eleanor de Montfort had also had four children in a row, then the next one after six years, and she had been 35 at the time compared to the queen now being 30.[2] The most famous example of intervals in childbearing was Countess Eleanor's mother Isabella of Angoulême. She had no children after seven years of marriage to King John. She then had three children in a row, none for four years after that, then two children, none again for six years, then nine in a row with Hugh Lusignan. She was well into her 40s when she bore her last child.

Certainly external events created extra anxiety. In early April, the queen's dear friend Richard Wyche died while preaching the crusade. He showed his devotion to her by remembering her in his will. Henry, who had tried to prevent Wyche's election as the Bishop of Chichester, hired his clerk to serve in Eleanor's chapel.[3]

The biggest worry again, though, was Gascony. Henry had gambled that sacrificing his viceroy would quiet the province at last. Instead, it left a vacuum open to exploitation by the new King of Castile, Alfonso X. When Alfonso put it out that he planned to make Gascony his, Gaston de Bearn and other disaffected nobles switched their allegiances to him. Henry would have to go there himself with an expeditionary force and muzzle them as Simon did before him.

He summoned Parliament to ask for a tax. He secured £7,000 as a feudal aid for the knighting of his eldest son, scrambled for the rest, and moved down to Portsmouth to set off. Before that Henry drew up his will. Eleanor was to get custody of their children and all his territories until Edward came of age. She was also to pay his debts and make sure his servants were remembered.[4] An even greater mark of his trust and confidence in her can be found in a letter patent issued on 7 July 1253 from Portsmouth:

> Appointment of Queen Eleanor to keep and govern the realm of England and the lands of Wales and Ireland with the counsel of Richard, Earl of Cornwall, the king's brother, until the king's return from Gascony : and mandate to all to be intendant to her.[5]

In naming Eleanor sole regent, Henry did not necessarily give her the keys to the kingdom. She was in possession of the Great Seal, but only to keep it safely stored away. All business of the realm was to go out under the seal of the exchequer, which the chancellor William Kilkenny was to receive from the queen. Eleanor and Richard of Cornwall, her counsel, were allowed to dismiss sheriffs and bailiffs who 'fall short of their offices', but the king was to be consulted about major ecclesiastical elections and the removal of castellans. Only Richard and the chancellor, however, were empowered to confer benefices. It could have been a vindictive move on Henry's part over the Flamstead incident or he wanted to make sure the queen did not become entangled in a similar controversy with a child to bear and realm to run.[6]

Not until 6 August were the winds right for sailing. Among the letters Henry dispatched from Portsmouth was one to his son-in-law

Alexander III in Scotland. While informing him of his plans to leave the country, he asked if Margaret might not visit England for a while. It would give Eleanor much joy and solace to have her daughter at hand for her upcoming confinement. He promised they would send Margaret right back after her mother's purification. The other bit of touching family togetherness from this time has Henry and Edward weeping long over their farewell and the boy still shedding tears as the sails dipped below the horizon.[7]

Prior to his departure, Henry had considered resuming Simon's trial in Gascony. Once he got there, he forgot about it as he could see for himself what his lieutenant had been up against. On 4 October, Henry wrote to him to come and discuss the situation. It was not just out of guilt or the need for his military expertise that Henry reached out to his brother-in-law. He knew the French government was making offers to him to join their council. So far Simon had wisely declined, but clearly the two of them had to put their ill feelings behind them.[8]

Grosseteste, who died five days after the letter was sent, had been urging his friend toward reconciliation with the king. He told Simon not to forget the good things Henry had done for him, like giving him his marriage, earldom and wardship. Chastened, Simon came to the English camp and brought a body of troops with him. Paris says he was also moved to do it by charity and humility, but he acquired something for himself and Eleanor as well. In the ensuing bargaining, the Montforts were forgiven their annual payments for the wardship, and their fee at the exchequer (which had offset the wardship) was increased by £67 to £400. Formerly Eleanor had held Kenilworth for life and Odiham during pleasure. The Montforts were now to get both castles together for life.[9]

These arrangements did not just come out of nowhere. Eleanor had done her part behind the scenes. Earlier that year she had gone to Marsh to ask him to cross over to France and meet Simon. There was also her friendship with the queen, who had remembered Eleanor's damsels and knights in the New Year's brooches she passed out. In the summer the countess paid a visit to her sister-in-law at Windsor, arriving in such state that her entourage required twenty-eight horses.[10] Otherwise Eleanor de Montfort had plenty to keep her busy. While wet nurses would have looked after her baby, she had five boys, a large household and their extensive estates to manage.

Eleanor of Provence's regency, her historic Parliaments

Henry had asked his wife not to forget to put on a grand feast for St Edward's Day on 13 October. A huge menu of peacocks, cranes, swans and swine was ordered. The queen was then close to her confinement, but the company of her daughter Margaret was expected in vain. Safe-conducts had been issued, but the Scottish minority council were apprehensive about letting their young queen go and refused to give their permission for her departure.

Even from her bed at Westminster, if indeed she was lying in, Eleanor tended to governmental affairs. There were several elections to license and approve. A new bishop, new prioress, new mayors of London and Winchester. The recent deaths of major bishops and lords like Grosseteste, Countess Clemence of Chester, and William de Vescy, the Lord of Alnwick who died in Gascony soon after the expedition went inland, required lots of administrative action.[11]

On 25 November 1253, Eleanor gave birth to a daughter Katherine. Paris writes that the queen rose 'safely from childbed' and indeed a writ was issued in her name on that very day. Henry's yeoman William de Valers brought him the news of his 'fair daughter' and was rewarded with a fee of £15. On 14 December, still technically in confinement, the queen authorised the bi-annual payment of £200 to her sister-in-law Eleanor for her dower. She celebrated her purification on the other St Edward's Day (5 January, marking the death of the Confessor) in the company of Boniface, who baptised Katherine, Richard of Cornwall, and we may presume Eleanor de Montfort. For her gift to the king that New Year's, the queen sent him £333.[12]

The military expedition had done remarkably well. Gaston was put to flight and all but a couple of castles were reclaimed. They knew, however, that peace in the region depended on Alfonso withdrawing his claim to Gascony and support for the rebels. Well before setting off from England, Henry had decided to pursue a diplomatic solution and seek an alliance by marrying Edward or Beatrice to a member of the Castilian royal family. As Henry wrote to Alfonso in May 1253, 'Friendship between princes can be obtained in no more fitting manner than by the link of the conjugal troth'.[13]

Henry and Eleanor had first floated a marriage for Edward in 1247 to the daughter of the Duke of Brabant, which lies within today's Holland.

Paris says that 'secret impediments' scuttled the negotiations. Perhaps some questions had been raised about Edward's legitimacy on account of Henry's earlier marriage to Joan of Ponthieu, which was not far from Brabant. Although Pope Gregory IX had long ago issued letters annulling that marriage on the grounds of consanguinity, Henry undertook to secure a more detailed annulment. In 1249, the Bishop of Hereford oversaw the process of summoning witnesses and taking statements for a report to send to Rome. Five years later, Innocent IV confirmed his findings that Henry and Joan were indeed related four degrees back to Louis VI of France and so could not be wed under canon law.[14]

At first, Alfonso responded favourably to the marriage offer, but then during the summer of 1253, while Henry was outfitting the expedition, King Theobald I of neighbouring Navarre died and was succeeded by his underage son Theobald II. Alfonso had a claim to Navarre as well and preferred a marriage in that direction as a way of enforcing it. The dowager Queen of Navarre met his proposal by entering an alliance with Aragon to her east. Alfonso decided to show her by mobilising his army, but at the time Henry could not be sure whether Gascony was not his real target. With his treasure running low, he instructed Eleanor and Richard to summon Parliament to ask for men and money.

They did not know it, but the assembly that convened on 27 January 1254 was an historic occasion. For the first time a woman, as the acting head of state, summoned and presided over Parliament. Queen Eleanor certainly had help from her brother-in-law Richard in making the king's case and together they reported that the outcome was mixed. The prelates were ready to come to his aid, but the lower clergy was already paying a crusade tax and wanted better conditions for it. The barons who owed the king service would go overseas in the event of an attack by Castile, but those who did not were more worried about the situation at home. They complained that the sheriffs and bailiffs were doing what they wanted and taking little heed of the charter of liberties.

Parliament adjourned around 11 February. On that date a writ was dispatched to the sheriffs instructing them to convene their local knights, have them discuss how much of a tax they might be willing to offer, and elect two of them to go to Westminster after Easter to discuss it. This assembly was equally historic.[15] For the first time on record Parliament met with a democratic mandate and it was Eleanor of Provence's name on the writ that summoned it.[16]

On 24 March, Henry sent a letter meant to be read out loud at the gathering. In bombastic style, he thanked his subjects from the bottom of his heart, he assured them he was making every effort to secure a treaty, but he had reasons to believe that Alfonso and the rebels were preparing for war. He ordered that Magna Carta be proclaimed throughout the counties and enforced by the sheriffs, adding that he expected the bishops and barons to make sure their own officials observed it as well.[17]

By the time Parliament met, it was all over. After being rebuffed by his neighbours, Alfonso had resumed negotiations with Henry in earnest, but made stiff demands. He wanted both Edward and Beatrice for marriages. He wanted Edward endowed with lands worth £10,000 a year and the honour of knighting him. He also wanted Henry to go crusading with him in North Africa. Henry had very little land to spare, he had probably dreamt of knighting his son on St Edward's Day, and he was vowed to go on crusade to the Holy Land. He said yes to everything. On 1 April 1254, the treaty was sealed and the King of Castile abandoned his claim to Gascony.[18]

Queen Eleanor had as big a role as anybody in formulating the instruments of the treaty. She had to preside over the huge transfer of lordships to her son to meet the endowment required by Alfonso, which included the county of Chester. It had been removed from Eleanor's dower back when Henry was drawing up his will, but she had received compensation for it and more in a new agreement drawn up on 23 July 1253. Because Chester had been intended for Edmund, it was thought best not to confer the title of Earl of Chester on Edward as well.[19]

There was still the problem of an endowment for Edmund. What to give their second son was behind another decision taken by Henry just as he was finalising the treaty with Alfonso. It was a huge gamble, but if everything panned out, it would enhance the glory and prestige of England not seen since Richard the Lionheart performed his legendary feats in the Mediterranean more than six decades earlier. And if it did not, they would just have to find something else for Edmund.

The Sicilian business, Edward gets married, Henry and Eleanor meet Louis and Margaret

The success of Eleanor of Provence's regency ultimately came down to paying the bills that came in from abroad, like paying the balance due

Simon de Montfort for buying him out of his contract. Her task now was to scrape together all the cash she could to bring with her to the duchy. The crown jewels and treasure were valued and retrieved from the New Temple and Westminster Abbey. Some she was to take with her, the rest were pledged to Richard of Cornwall in return for a loan of £6,667. Richard also procured the regency after Walter Gray, the Archbishop of York, declined to take it for reasons of age and health.[20]

Leaving her younger children at Windsor, Eleanor moved to Portsmouth with Edward and their retinue of more than 130 people. They included her devoted companion Willelma, set to retire in a couple of years, Matthias Bezill, a native of Touraine who had risen in royal service to become her steward, the queen's cook Master William, and also Edmund's cook, another Master William. Paris says Edmund went with them, but the rolls show the opposite, suggesting it was a last-minute decision to leave him home.[21]

Their plans to sail were nearly scuttled, however, when another feud broke out. The men who outfitted Eleanor's ship in Winchelsea got wind that the ship prepared for Edward at Yarmouth was much bigger and grander than theirs. Enraged by jealousy, they attacked the rival vessel like a band of pirates, killing several of the crew and carrying off the mast to present to the queen like a trophy. She was appalled by their lawlessness and violence, and if that were not enough, she received an urgent message from Henry not to sail. It came out of nowhere and provided no reason. Paris has her 'concealing her annoyance' and confronting the crisis head on: 'Troubles arise on all sides; everything is ready for setting sail; I have bade farewell to all; the wind blows most favourably; and shall I go back? No.'[22]

The flotilla left on 29 May 1254 and arrived in Bordeaux just under two weeks later. Henry was not there to meet them. He still had one castle to capture and a succession dispute to settle, both apparently behind his message to the queen to delay her departure. The family was together by August, when they welcomed a very special visitor. She was Joan of Ponthieu, the woman Henry had married while negotiating for Eleanor's hand, and the mother of Edward's intended. Perhaps curious to meet nineteen years after their proxy wedding, Henry issued her a safe-conduct to pass through Gascony on her way to Ponthieu. Their marriage had been officially nullified, so Henry, Eleanor and Joan were able to sit together with goblets of wine in good cheer and easy reminiscing.

Edward was also there and could learn more from Joan about his future wife. Like the women of our story, she too was Eleanor. Born to Joan and King Ferdinand III in 1241, Eleanor of Castile was two years younger than Edward. Like Eleanor of Provence, she grew up in a fluid society of books, romance, gardens and sunshine. She seems to have got on well with her half-brother Alfonso and was probably closer to him than her own mother. In any event, Joan did not bother to stay for her daughter's wedding. She was in Ponthieu by October and remained there until her death in 1279.[23]

The ten months Henry and Eleanor had spent apart was the longest of their married life so far. There was much to catch up on, especially Henry's big news about Edmund. He was going to be the King of Sicily. Henry had been offered the throne for him and he formally accepted it in March. The offer had been around for years, since the death of Frederick II in 1250. Pope Innocent IV wanted to strip his heirs of the kingdom of Sicily, which included southern Italy, and give it to a royal prince instead.

At the end of 1252, a papal notary named Albert of Parma came to England to offer the throne to Richard of Cornwall. He had the vanity and money to negotiate hard for the project, too hard in the end, because Pope Innocent IV refused to provide the security and cash Richard demanded up front. Albert would have to move on to the next candidate, Charles of Anjou, but while in England he met the king and queen and received an expensive goblet from Eleanor as a New Year's gift. It is possible they suggested that Albert might want to add Edmund to his shortlist.[24]

Edmund was not even 9 at the time, but the implication was that the Crown of England would be behind the project. Charles of Anjou was approached just the same. He wanted it, but Louis, still biding his time in the crusader states, ordered him not to get involved. Charles went north and got involved in a civil war in Holland instead. So Edmund got the nod.

Innocent dispatched Albert to Gascony to find out how soon they might expect Henry to send his son and an army. They should have thought about that before making the offer. The King of England, Albert learned, was totally broke. He had spent everything on his Gascon expedition, including the gold treasure he had been saving up for his crusade. He was supposed to sail for the Holy Land in two years, but even with the crusade tax he had no chance of raising all the funds needed to get there.

Henry clearly used the offer as a way out of his dilemma. He had counted on Innocent switching his crusade vow and the tax associated with it to Sicily. He would not even lead the army there himself, just have the Savoyards conquer the island with a mercenary force and pay off the debts with the spoils. He had expected the whole thing to just fall into his lap. The flustered pope decided to act as if the offer had never been made to him.[25]

While Edward went south to be married, his parents prepared to return home. They had hoped to go overland through France, where they could avoid the perils of a sea voyage, make some pilgrimages, and see the great cities and cathedrals of the kingdom. The French royal couple had returned a few months earlier after an absence of six years. A first-time meeting between the two kings and their sister queens would be a social and political event unparallel in that age.[26]

The royal couples met up at Orleans. The two queens had the joy of seeing each other for the first time in eighteen years. Eleanor was now 31 with five children and Margaret 33 with seven, three of them born overseas. The crusade had been a long, harrowing experience for Margaret, but it gave her a certain parity with Eleanor, whose regency had made her the more accomplished of the two.

Margaret's whole time as the Queen of France had been something of an ordeal because of her mother-in-law. She was wrong, however, if she had hoped Blanche's death two years earlier in 1252 would change things. Louis was just like his mother and did not trust his wife to run her own household, much less the kingdom. Her heart probably sank further when she saw how attentive and affectionate Henry was towards Eleanor. Louis had been difficult enough to live with before the crusade. Now he was full of gloom and self-pity and talked about hanging it all up and retiring to a monastery.

He stood in contrast to Henry, who long ago learned to take defeat in stride. At 47, Henry was seven years older than Louis and probably a bit shorter and stouter. Both were former boy kings who were devoted sons and faithful husbands. They liked each other off the bat. The English pair hurriedly made a pilgrimage to Pontigny and the tomb of St Edmund of Abingdon, the man who married them, and on 9 December the Anglo-French royal cortege entered Paris.

Eleanor and Margaret's mother Beatrice and their sister Beatrice were with them, as was Sanchia, whom Richard of Cornwall sent to join them in grand style. The significance of the occasion was not lost on anyone. Hordes of Parisians and students alike turned out to greet them in rapturous awe. The two kings who had been technically at war with each other for three decades were sitting side by side, smiling and chatting away. They also wanted a glimpse at the fabled beautiful daughters of Provence, the eldest two queens, the youngest two countesses. Rarely would Europe see a family reunion of this rank, elegance and splendour again.

Henry tended to get carried away by big moments and none were bigger than this one. Visiting St Chapelle, he achingly wished he could lift it up off its foundations, put it on a cart, and roll it back to England. He announced to the poor of Paris that he would feed them all and the next day he did. The feasting and company at the official banquet later on was so ravenous and distinguished that Matthew Paris felt it outrivaled the days of King Arthur. For Louis, it was a much needed boost and made him hopeful for peace between their nations. 'Have we not married two sisters', he told Henry, 'and our brothers the other two? All that shall be born of them, both sons and daughters, will be brothers and sisters.'

With his eye ever on the main chance, Henry asked him to return his Continental patrimony. Louis said he would like to, but his peers would not hear of it. There was probably some truth in that. The King of France had hoped to redeem himself with another crusade and knew he needed to have his spiritual house in order first, including the burden of his legacy. His father had tried to take the throne from Henry, did take Poitou from him, and died a gruelling death from dysentery. Clearly amends needed to be made.

For now, Henry had to settle with two parting gifts, both magnificent. Margaret gave him a richly jewelled basin shaped like peacock, and from Louis he received an elephant. It had been a gift from one of the sultans, a very dubious one considering it was all Louis had to show from a crusade begun with such high hopes. A special sanctuary was built for the animal at the Tower of London, where Henry kept a varying collection of exotic animals. A few years earlier a polar bear arrived from the King of Norway and amazed spectators who saw it diving for fish in the Thames while tethered with a collar and chain. Although the bear was a tough act to follow, the elephant was the first ever seen in England and naturally bedazzled the crowds, who knew of such creatures only from fables and biblical stories.[27]

Bigorre and Eleanor de Montfort's estate management

The Montforts missed out on the lavish meeting of kings and queens in Paris. It was not for want of status, as Eleanor was the sister of one king and Simon a good friend of the other. She had been abroad with the court earlier that year, because on 30 May 1254 she was able to get Henry to pardon a certain John Hykedun, who was charged with clipping coins. John had fled the realm, presumably to France where he approached the countess. She made the appeal together with William de Valence, the only record where Eleanor is working in harmony with one of her Lusignan half-siblings.[28]

Simon himself was in England at the time, making one of his flash appearances at the Easter Parliament and picking up his wife's bi-annual payment for her dower at the exchequer. He was in Bordeaux on 25 August 1254 when Henry dispatched him on a secret mission to Scotland. It was literally the case, for the letters of credence only say that the king 'put certain secrets in his mouth'. We may presume that Eleanor went with him as far as England. On 28 September, Simon was in Warwickshire attending the funeral of William Cantilupe. Since he was a nephew of family friend Walter Cantilupe, Eleanor was probably one of the mourners graveside.[29]

In February 1255, Eleanor went to see her brother in Westminster. She asked him to exempt an import merchant from prise duties for three years and to pardon another man for manslaughter. Next came family business, namely a new payment plan for the Montforts. This one had nothing to do with her dower, rather Simon's tenure as viceroy in Gascony. It concerned the county of Bigorre, which was almost as complicated a story as Sicily.

The county was run by an aged countess named Perronelle, who was actually Simon's sister-in-law. During the Albigensian Crusade, she had been married to his brother Guy and gave him two daughters before Guy's death in 1220. When Perronelle died in 1251, she willed her county to a grandson named Esquivat. But she had five husbands in total, and another daughter from her last marriage was the wife of Gaston de Bearn. They figured they had just as much right to the county as Esquivat. When Gaston started making his life miserable, Esquivat turned to his great-uncle Simon for protection. This left him deeply in debt to him.

Bigorre was strategically important because it bordered Navarre in the south. Upon arriving in Gascony, Henry undertook to ensure Esquivat's loyalty by offering him £1,000 for his castles. Since Esquivat was still in debt to Simon for beating off Gaston, he told Henry, with Eleanor de Montfort as witness, that the king could pay the money directly to the Montforts. The agreement was enrolled in the chancery on 19 February 1255. On that same day Henry also gave permission to Simon to make his will. It seems almost like an afterthought, as if Eleanor were walking out the door, then turned around and said, 'Oh, and one more thing, my husband needs a will'.[30]

If the Montforts were indeed apart for much of the year, we can get an idea of Eleanor's estate management from a surviving roll of her household accounts. They are the oldest records of this type in existence, and although they date to a period ten years in the future, that was also a time when Simon was mostly absent. In showing her expenditures for food, clothing and other household articles, these accounts offer a rare glimpse into their daily lives.

To start with, her household would have numbered around 200, including clerks, officers, servants and the poor. That was a lot of people to feed, so like all baronial families, they made the rounds of their estates in search of their next meal. Usually everything was planned out in advance based on the harvests. Once everything was in and the totals calculated, the local reeve or bailiff, working under a steward who answered to the countess, would convey that information by messengers. In Eleanor's accounts, these messengers bear decidedly English names like Truebody and Slingaway. From their main residence at Kenilworth, her household might proceed south to Berkshire, Wiltshire and Dorset, where they had eleven manors total, and end up at their other main residence of Odiham in Hampshire.

Eleanor still had a special affection for nearby Waverley Abbey and made various donations to the monks, including money to buy 150 acres of land. She and the abbot, Ralph, were good friends and we can see from her accounts what kind of meal was prepared when he came to visit. A quarter and a half of dry grain was used to make roughly 270 loaves of bread, enough to feed her household, his entourage, and the poor lingering outside. Thirty-eight litres of wine were served, but just to the wellborn. Grooms and servants always drank beer, which was made from any type of cereal and flavoured with spices like fennel or pepper. The beer was either brewed at home or bought locally, in either case a lot was needed, for typically about 750 litres were consumed every week.

The actual meal itself consisted of fish and 400 herring, peas and onions boiled into a thick gruel, and apples for dessert. The grain and alcohol came from the castle stores, the rest had to be purchased. Including accessories like napkins and hay for the visiting horses, thirty-two of them, the extra cost of his visit was 16 shillings, 5½ pence, or £600 in today's money.[31]

Rescuing Margaret in Scotland, blood money

Following their Parisian triumph, poor winds forced the king and queen to spend Christmas of 1254 in Boulogne. The giddy experience of Paris behind them, they came to London on 4 January in a feisty mood. It had to do with the murder of Bernard of Champagne, another of Eleanor's kinfolk who had come to Hereford to serve as prior under the Savoyard bishop, Peter d'Aigueblanche. Bernard's various disputes with local ecclesiastics and worshippers led a group of them to beat him to death during mass in the summer of 1252. A clerk named John of Fromme had been arrested as the ringleader but he escaped from Newgate prison in London and fled abroad just before the royal couple returned. Henry was furious and had the two sheriffs for London put in the Tower for a month, then deposed.[32]

Henry and Eleanor's biggest concern upon returning was their daughter Margaret. The Scottish minority council for Alexander III had split into factions soon after the wedding in York. Simon's secret mission to Scotland was probably related to the situation there. The queen's physician Reginald of Bath was dispatched to ascertain about the wellbeing of Margaret and Alexander, whom Eleanor 'loved as an adopted child'. Finding Margaret sad and pale, Reginald flew into a rage and warned the Scots that somebody was going to pay for her ill treatment. He then fell sick and died, convinced the Scots had poisoned him.[33]

Alarmed by the letter Reginald was able to write before expiring, the king decided on another secret mission and entrusted it to John Mansel and Richard de Clare, the Earl of Gloucester and a rising star at court. They bluffed their way into Edinburgh Castle and secured it with troops supplied by the sympathetic Earl of Dunbar. They found Margaret indeed miserable. She complained of being locked up all day long in a gloomy stone fortress with wretched air and no nice views. She was stuck with unfamiliar handmaidens and denied the warm embraces of her husband. Mansel and Clare were able to fix the last problem immediately by putting the young couple, aged 14 and 13 respectively, in the same bed.

After hearing Mansel and Clare's report, Henry came down hard on John Balliol and Robert de Ros, Margaret's Anglo-Scottish custodians. Ros was forced to surrender the castle of Wark near the border and Margaret and Alexander were conveyed there to meet her parents in early September. Eleanor had taken seriously ill, so Margaret was allowed to stay with her while Henry and his son-in-law went north to sort out the minority council.[34]

Happy to have her daughter in her company again, Eleanor seemed in no hurry to recover. Henry wrapped things up on 21 September and headed south, leaving behind the queen and £100 for her expenses. He was in a hurry as he expected special guests for this year's feast of St Edward in Westminster, including their soon-to-arrive daughter-in-law Eleanor of Castile, but he had to stop in Lincoln along the way to resolve a very delicate matter.[35]

The special guests included an Italian cardinal and papal nuncio. They were connected to the offer of Sicily, which Henry had accepted eighteen months previously on behalf of Edmund but had since done nothing to pursue. Innocent IV had died on 7 December 1254, two days before Henry and Eleanor entered Paris, and his successor Alexander IV had no clue what to do with the Sicilian business except to get on with it. He renewed the offer of the throne to Edmund on condition that Henry assume the debt of £90,000 so far spent on the project, plus raise an army. Since saving Gascony had robbed Henry of any chance of sailing for the Holy Land, and the pope was ready to commute his vow that he might pursue this more political crusade, Henry accepted.[36]

The cardinal had come to present Edmund with a ring designating him the King of Sicily, and the nuncio, a Gascon named Rostand, was commissioned with re-directing Henry's crusade vow and the money underpinning it to the island. For what it was worth, Henry convened his council at Windsor on 21 November 1255 and got their approval for the business, but it received a fatal blow four days later when Thomas of Savoy was imprisoned in Turin in an unrelated action. He had been

Henry's original driving force behind the project. The resources that could have gone into making Sicily a success now had to be shifted towards winning his freedom.[37]

Eleanor of Provence's illness prevented her from witnessing her son's virtual enthronement at Westminster. Not until late October was she ready to journey homeward from Scotland. After she arrived, £300 was sent to the Bishop of Durham to cover the balance of her stay in the north. Henry also undertook to settle her queen's gold, the money owed to her as a ten per cent surcharge on the fines paid to the Crown.[38]

On 26 November 1255, Henry ordered that the £172 of queen's gold owed by the Jews of Lincoln be paid out of the property that was confiscated from those who had been hanged or imprisoned or fled in the aftermath of a case of blood libel in the city that summer. A young boy named Hugh had gone missing and when his body was discovered in a well, his mother and others charged the Jews with kidnapping him to perform a ritual crucifixion. This was the delicate matter Henry had to address on his way home from Scotland. By the time he got to Lincoln on 3 October, his steward had secured a confession that had terrible consequences for their community. At this distance of time, it is impossible to know how the boy died, just that a lot of lives were destroyed and blood money changed hands afterward. Some of it went to the queen.[39]

7

An Arduous and Difficult Matter
1256–1258

Simon and Eleanor's land transactions,
her soul and final childbirth

Simon de Montfort should have been the one magnate for Henry to count on to support the Sicilian business. He had an adventurous, warlike spirit, and would have seen nothing wrong with using the king's crusade for political purposes. All crusades had conquest and enrichment on the agenda and his father's brutal campaign against the Albigensian heretics had been no different. But there is no indication Simon supported the king's request for a tax at the recent Parliament, nor was he among the councillors who afterward gave Sicily their approval.

He had various reasons for not wanting the kingdom to go in that direction, all of them personal. His closest friends were churchmen furious at how the king and pope constantly fleeced them of their wealth and Sicily was the most outrageous example of it yet. There was also the fiasco in Gascony. That experience had embittered him against Henry to such a degree that we can imagine he plotted to have his revenge someday.

His greatest concern, however, was the realisation that any new strain on royal revenue, as Sicily was sure to be, would make it harder for the king to honour his debts to the Montforts. This had plainly become the case in July 1256 when Henry admitted he owed 'his beloved sister' a great deal of money as the surety for her dower. He told his treasurer Philip Lovel to find the money somehow so that she 'not remain unsatisfied'.

The problem was the Marshal heirs had continued to shirk their obligation to pay their share of her annual £400 dower payment. The most notorious among them was Margaret de Lacy, whose husband John, the Earl of Lincoln, had been Simon's closet ally during his early years in government. Her husband's death in July 1240 left Margaret with four children and a dower of £315. Eighteen months later she married Walter Marshal, now the Earl of Pembroke, but they were childless when he died in late 1245. Two years later his lands in Ireland and Wales were valued at £2,310, giving her a one-third dower of £770.

That was nearly twice the £400 fobbed off on Eleanor a decade before that, which was bad enough, but Margaret had defaulted on all her payments to Eleanor for the seven years since the partition of the estate. On 22 August 1256, Henry ordered Margaret to pay the £1,066 she owed directly to Simon and Eleanor, which she had done by October. Henry also promised that all money coming in from the Marshal heirs would go directly to the Montforts, an indication that that had not always been the case.[1]

Margaret de Lacy had been able to get away with defaulting because she was a friend of the queen. Her two younger daughters had been raised at Windsor with the royal children and her son and heir Edmund had a Savoyard wife. Her settlement with the Montforts, moreover, may have been a ruse to get Simon to join her team of negotiators to contract the marriage of her 5-year-old grandson Henry de Lacy to another Margaret, the daughter of William Longespee, whose father was killed on crusade in Egypt. The covenant was reached on 23 December 1256. Four days later, Henry authorised a writ of allocate (payment) to Margaret de Lacy for the entire £1,066 she had paid the Montforts two months earlier.[2]

In the midst of these transactions, 17-year-old Henry de Montfort went to France with a member of his father's affinity. The reason for the journey may have had something to do with the county of Bigorre again. Esquivat had been unable to defend it against Gaston de Bearn and so gave it outright to his great-uncle Simon. Simon and Eleanor were happy to receive the county as a future lordship for one of their five sons, but realised it was going to take effort to make the deal stick. Indeed, it was soon apparent the charter had been another ruse. Esquivat had used the threat of the Montforts taking over Bigorre to get Gaston to agree to arbitration. Once that had been accomplished, Esquivat went on ruling as if the county was still his. He could have easily answered any particular inquiry about who the Lord of Bigorre was with, 'Simon who?'[3]

The Montforts received another acquisition at this time in the form of the Embleton barony in Northumbria. The owners swapped it for two of their manors in the south of England. At £300, Embleton was worth at least twice the two manors and its proximity to the Umfraville estate allowed them to exploit the commercial potential of this area. There were also the political considerations. Having one son set up in Bigorre and another in Embleton would extend Simon and Eleanor's clout from the Pyrenees to the border of Scotland.[4]

Eleanor de Montfort was now in her 40s, Simon just shy of his 50s. In November 1257, the couple received confraternity letters from the abbey of St Albans, the home of Matthew Paris, detailing the prayers and masses to be said for their souls in the afterlife and for the feeding of the poor on their behalf. The letters were issued from Eleanor's manor at Luton and were probably thanks from the monks for a donation made by the Montforts at Luton the previous year.

It is nevertheless significant that Eleanor's final child, a daughter named after her, was born at this time, probably the next year. She and Simon may have asked for the confraternity when they learned she was pregnant. Given her age and the dangers of childbirth, which had claimed her sister Isabella, these provisions for her soul doubtless provided comfort as her term approached.[5]

The queen's motherly worries, her shady business

The queen's greatest concern during these years was her children. The likelihood of Edmund becoming the King of Sicily grew ever remoter as the efforts to free her uncle Thomas from captivity met no success. The Sicilian business did, however, increase the marriage prospects of Henry and Eleanor's younger children. In April 1256, 20-year-old Plaisance of Antioch, who ruled the island of Cyprus as queen regent, suggested a marriage between herself and Edmund and one between Beatrice and her infant son Hugh, the future king. Another proposal made at this time called for Edmund to marry Constance, the 7-year-old daughter of Manfred, his rival for Sicily. This way the kingdom would come to Edmund more or less as a wedding gift.

Pope Alexander IV would not hear of it. Like his predecessors, he had become obsessed with ridding the world of Frederick's Hohenstaufen dynasty. That was all that mattered. Henry needed to stop all this talk about marriage and get on with paying the bill.[6]

Losing both her younger children to far-off Mediterranean kingdoms would have been a terrible blow to Eleanor. She and Henry were already trying to fend off another marriage proposal for Beatrice, who turned 14 that year. Alfonso of Castile insisted that she marry his brother Emanuel as part of their treaty arrangements, but Henry's council was opposed because they understood that in Castile, the king had the authority to dispossess anyone, even his brother, by his will and pleasure, without due process. As Richard of Cornwall pointed out, it was unacceptable to marry Beatrice into a kingdom that operated like that.[7]

Richard had his own reasons for not doing Alfonso any favours. In January 1256, the King of Germany had been killed and the search for a successor was underway. It was a title with very little power but a lot of prestige and Richard figured he could afford to buy four of the seven electors and the coronation to follow. His only contender was Alfonso, who might have expected Henry to remain neutral. They were allies, after all. But Henry saw Richard's enthronement in Germany, Edmund's in Sicily, and his own in England as three kings from the same family, something that brought to mind the three kings of the Nativity.[8]

In June, Edward turned 17-years old. His tall, blonde, finely chiselled features and passion for feats of arms made him the ideal prince of the age. In this month Henry relaxed his opposition to tournaments to allow one to go forward at Blyth in Nottinghamshire. It probably was not as much a birthday present to his son as it was justification for his decision to lower the distraint of knighthood (conscription) to an income of £15 a year. While officially seen as a boost to chivalry in England, it was clearly a money-making scheme. Anyone eschewing knighthood, because it was terribly expensive, was invited to purchase an exemption.

There was actually little chivalry in the thirteenth-century tournament. It was a melee between two teams on horseback trying to pound each other into submission, using whatever tactics and deceit were available. Deaths were not uncommon and it was no different at Blyth. Among those crushed and trampled or otherwise receiving mortal injuries were Robert de Quincy, whose wife Helena had died a few years earlier, and William Longespee, hence the rush to marry off his daughter Margaret before he died.[9]

Henry and Eleanor must have been tense waiting for news on the outcome at Blyth. Perhaps as prearranged, everybody went easy on Edward, or at least he emerged without a scratch. From there, he and his entourage continued north to Scotland, possibly with his wife Eleanor of Castile joining them, to visit his sister Margaret and King Alexander.

It was more than just a social call between two young royal couples, all in their teens. Tensions in Scotland were again high between the warring factions and Edward's parents doubtless encouraged him to make the journey to check up on their daughter and son-in-law.[10]

One of Margaret's former custodians in Scotland was an official named Geoffrey Langley. Born around 1200, he was like many men in Henry's administration self-made. After a stint as a household knight, he rose to become a justice of the forest. According to Paris, he came down hard on anybody who committed the slightest offense in the royal wilderness and that made him a scoundrel, but Henry and Eleanor liked men of his stamp. They got things done because they were not afraid to step on toes.

Langley had been sent up north to join Alexander's regency council, but the Scots found him an insufferable jerk and threw him out. That should have made it obvious to the king and queen that he was not the man to appoint as Edward's steward for his new lands in Wales, but that is what Henry did in 1254.[11] The queen certainly was not blind to Langley's faults. She knew all about his unscrupulous ways, especially when there was easy money to be made. This included the most notorious trafficking of the day, the trade in Jewish bonds denoting the debts of their Christian borrowers.

During the previous decade, Henry had imposed stiff taxation on the Jews as a way of getting the money that Parliament denied him. Forced to raise cash to pay the taxes, the Jews sold their bonds to Christians, who might then put pressure on the debtor to pay up, by selling their land if necessary. An example was Robert de Willoughby. In November 1256, he relinquished his manor of Ashover in Derbyshire after his debts to the Jews were pardoned by the king. His manor went to Langley under a twenty-year lease for £214. That money, as the wardrobe accounts show, went to the queen. Transactions of this sort naturally created a lot of anger in the newly emerging gentry class, who might suddenly find themselves bereft of credit and disenfranchised by a racket that had the full connivance and participation of the court.[12]

Losing Katherine, nervous breakdown

These days Eleanor of Provence was mostly in residence at Windsor. Typically she might spend thirty weeks out of the year there on average.

In March 1257, Henry ordered his bailiffs at Southampton to deliver twenty tuns of wine (160 barrels) to Windsor 'seeing that the queen, who is lying ill, and her children there with her, are greatly in want of wine'. One of her children, 12-year-old Edmund, was about to leave for Westminster, where he had a big show in front of him. Parliament was meeting to discuss a tax for Sicily, and Henry, the first truly gifted event organiser in English history, had decided to go all out.

The venue was the newly opened, wondrous chapter house of Westminster Abbey and the king presented the boy to the gathering dressed in the Apulian fashion of southern Italy. Edmund now had a set of clothes to match the ring on his finger. Henry hoped the sight of the little King of Sicily would remind his barons and clergy that the Mediterranean had also been part of their glorious Norman past. Richard of Cornwall probably resented this bit of theatre. He had been elected the King of Germany and was there to say goodbye. He had spent a lot of money for this moment, upwards of £20,000, and could not have appreciated Henry stealing his thunder like this.[13]

The outcome of the Parliament was moderately successful, but it was unlikely to have improved the queen's spirits. Her illness at this time may have been related to her sorrow over her 3-year-old daughter Katherine. She seems to have suffered from a degenerative disorder early on. By the time she was 18-months old, she was already being cared for apart from the other children at Swallowfield in Berkshire. This can be surmised from Henry's request in August 1255 that the warden there catch a roe deer (*capriolus*) to give to her as a pet of sorts.

She was back at Windsor early the next year and in March of 1256 Henry had a silver image made of a woman, presumably St Katherine, to be offered at the shrine of St Edward 'for Katherine the king's daughter who has recently been ill'. When a messenger arrived from the queen three days later with news that Katherine was better, Henry rewarded him with a robe.[14]

The little girl died on 3 May 1257. Paris, who describes her as 'speechless and helpless, but very beautiful in appearance', suggests her mother suffered a nervous breakdown. 'The queen was so overcome with grief that it brought on a disease, which was thought to be incurable, as she could obtain no relief either from medical skill or human consolation.'

At the end of May, Henry also collapsed with a fever and was bedridden for a time in London. In rebuilding Westminster Abbey, he intended it to become a royal mausoleum. Katherine would be the first member of the family buried there. He had an elaborate tomb built for her with a silver effigy on top and adorned with gold and 180 precious stones.[15]

Not even Westminster Abbey was safe from the religious vandalism of later centuries and her tomb has since disappeared, but the short life of their youngest daughter is further testament to the strong emotional bond between Henry and Eleanor and their children. Losing Katherine may have been particularly agonising due to the special circumstances. She was a toddler, born after the most difficult period of their marriage, and she was afflicted with a disorder that none of their prayers could arrest. They doubtless loved the little girl for herself, beyond the dynastic value she might have brought to the realm.

In justifying the marriage of his sister Eleanor to William Marshal II in 1224, Henry had famously described her as his 'greatest treasure'. The children of Henry and Eleanor of Provence were similarly viewed as treasure. The marriages of the two oldest children had been political matches first and foremost and nothing would change for the two youngest. But they were also treasures of the heart and the king and queen endured many anxious moments worrying about their wellbeing.[16] Their anguish over Katherine coincided with uncertainty about Margaret in Scotland, Edmund's aspiration to the throne of Sicily, and Beatrice's marriage prospects to faraway kingdoms. Edward, however, was about to cause Eleanor her greatest distress of all. His actions and behaviour would come close to costing her and Henry everything, including their crowns.

A restless heir, Eleanor of Castile, uprising in Wales, courting the Earl of Gloucester

Already as a teenager, it was clear that Edward was going to be nothing like his father. He grew to be tall, 188 cm opposed to 174 for Henry. He had a drooping eyelid, which a later chronicler claimed he inherited from Henry, but Paris, who met Henry on many occasions, made no mention of it in his physical descriptions or drawings of the king. It is possible Edward got it from an accident, for unlike Henry, he loved being in the saddle on the hunt or exchanging blows in tournaments. Two traits father and son did share were an intense piety and faithfulness to their wives.[17]

Apart from levelling an unpopular tax, Edward had acquitted himself well in ruling Gascony, especially as he had just turned 16. In August, Henry ordered him to move on to his other newly-acquired lordships, specifically Ireland. He was instructed to go there without his young wife, whom the king and queen would look after in England. Eleanor of Provence's convalescence in the north was coming to an end when Henry received their daughter-in-law in state on 17 October 1255. He gave her quarters at Westminster Palace decked out with tapestries in the Castilian fashion, even on the floor, thus introducing carpeting to England but arousing more indignation in the xenophobic Paris.[18]

It is our misfortune that there is no record of the first meeting of these two Eleanors, mother and daughter-in-law. Both had come to England as young girls from the sunny, cultured south of Europe, where a love of romances, gardens and good plumbing came naturally to them. Each woman shared the same passions of their husbands. Eleanor of Provence enjoyed fashion and pageantry while Eleanor of Castile preferred hunting and outdoor pursuits. Although both were devoted to their families, the younger Eleanor was to spend a lot of time apart from her own children while they were growing up, something unthinkable in her mother-in-law. Neither Henry nor Edward (or Simon for that matter) are known to have strayed from their Eleanors, suggesting an exceptional quality somewhere that contributed to stability in their marriages and in the kingdom overall.[19]

As queens, both Eleanors were demanding and acquisitive lords, conduct that drew harsh rebuke from commentators. Where they differed was in their role as consort. Eleanor of Provence had the beauty, elegance, manners and heirs that would make any other medieval queen successful, but Matthew Paris for one expected her to keep a low profile and that she refused to do. She was completely on top of the affairs of her day, culminating in a regency that showed she was more than capable of running the realm. Eleanor of Castile probably would have made a good regent as well, but it is unlikely that Edward, given his sensibilities, would have appointed her had there been an occasion for it. She did not, moreover, establish any foreign relatives in England and was far more discreet in exercising influence on her husband. She was, in short, the queen Paris and plenty of others had hoped her mother-in-law would be.

That was all in the future. What kept the two women from forming a close relationship from the beginning was simple rivalry. Excluding the fact that Eleanor of Castile was the daughter of the first woman whom Henry married and that she would one day succeed to Eleanor of Provence's position as queen, there was Edward. His mother had been the impresario of his life so far, whether nursing him through the worst of his illnesses or making sure he received a rich endowment. Now he was married and a lord in his own right. As with her daughter Margaret, Eleanor of Provence was going to find letting him go another tough lesson in motherhood and queenship.[20]

And Edward did not make it easy for his parents. He blatantly ignored Henry's order to go to Ireland, rather followed his wife to England. He then got into a row with Henry during Christmas court in Winchester over which of them was going to call the shots in Gascony. In the summer of 1256, he visited his lordships in Wales. He departed almost as soon as he arrived, without addressing the rising tide of complaints against Langley's administration there. Fed up, Llywelyn ap Gruffudd, the leading Welsh prince, overran the region in November.[21]

Edward wanted to give Llywelyn and his followers a beating they would never forget, but complained he lacked the money for it. His father told him that now was his time to shine, not whine. He procured a loan from his uncle Richard of Cornwall, but the best his mother could do was offer him, together with Peter of Savoy, £4,000 for his Ferrers wardship. He was not with his troops when they set out against the Welsh, which was his good fortune, because they were slaughtered. In August, Henry was forced to call out the feudal host to march on Wales. They set out from Chester in September, but neither he nor Edward had any stomach for it and the offensive was quickly called off. They would try again in the spring.[22]

The only progress was made in the south under the men led by Richard de Clare, the Earl of Gloucester. Then inexplicably Clare left the front for a meeting with the queen. Henry had originally sent Eleanor to stay at Nottingham while he was on campaign, but the smoky atmosphere there created by outdoor coal-burning pits forced her to flee forty kilometres west to Tutbury Castle, which she held as part of the Ferrers wardship she received from Edward. How Eleanor arranged to meet Clare there is unknown, only that it was all very secretive, according to the Dunstable annalist.[23]

The queen had had her eye on the 35-year-old Clare for some time. He was a good friend of her rivals the Lusignans and in 1252, at Henry's urging, he agreed to marry his son and heir Gilbert to Alice, the daughter of Count Hugh Lusignan of Angoulême, who had been killed on Louis's crusade. Gloucester was one of the richest earldoms and Clare one of the most unpredictable earls. Eleanor had hoped to lure him away from the Lusignans with a marriage for his eldest daughter Isabel to her kinsman William, the Marquis of Montferrat. On 8 October 1257, the proctors for both sides drew up the terms. The men of the marquis would choose one of Clare's three daughters, who would bring a dowry with her to the marriage of £2,667.[24]

On that same day the queen arrived at St Albans in the company of her daughter-in-law Eleanor of Castile and several other ladies. She wanted to give thanks for recovering from what Paris describes as 'a very serious illness'. He probably meant her earlier collapse following the death of her daughter, for she had left for Nottingham in mid-summer and was then deal-making with Clare at Tutbury. She made an offering at the tomb of the martyr St Albans and the gift of a costly cloak at the altar.[25] While undertaking her devotions, it is possible she slipped in a prayer for a successful outcome to the Clare-Montferrat negotiations. The covenant was ratified on 18 December 1257 in the queen's chamber at Westminster in front of her, the king, Edward and Simon de Montfort among others. In the event, Clare's oldest daughter Isabel was chosen.

Edward's poor choice of friends, a confederacy comes together

The queen's confidant Geoffrey Langley was made the scapegoat for the debacle in Wales and cashiered. Eleanor thought it was unfair and by 14 February 1258 had succeeded in winning a pardon for Langley, but there was no way Edward was taking him back.[26] Up until this point, his household and staff had been chosen by his parents and Savoyard handlers. All that he gained from that was humiliation in Wales.

The conflict introduced him to a breed of men he felt were better able to deal with the situation. These were the Marcher lords whose clans had lived along the borderlands for generations, battling the Welsh and each other. Edward started in August 1257 by having the constable of Montgomery, a Savoyard retainer, replaced with a Marcher called Hamo Lestrange, who would later be singled out for his acts of plunder. The queen was appalled by her son throwing over a member of her circle to associate with this violent, unruly lot.[27]

She also did not think much of his renewed contact with his cousin Henry, the son of Richard of Cornwall. Henry had returned from his father's coronation in Aachen in May 1257 and was now referred to as 'of Almain' (Germany) as if to suggest he was a German prince. Eleanor's reservation about Henry of Almain had to do with his close relations to his Lusignan uncles.

The same could be said about Edward's other new friend John de Warenne, the Earl of Surrey, who had also been at the coronation. Warenne had been married to Alice Lusignan until her death the previous year. He was broken-hearted and remained close to her brothers. On the other hand, he had only contempt for Eleanor's uncle Peter of Savoy, who had exploited his wardship of Warenne to the hilt.[28]

But it was Edward's own relations with his Lusignan uncles that worried her most. Like the Marchers, they too had a reputation for aggressive, arrogant behaviour. Henry had established them in England a decade earlier because their support was essential in retaining Gascony. There was the risk that their presence would create factionalism at court, but apart from the incident between Boniface and Aymer, it had worked for the most part.

Now, ten years later, the queue for Henry's beneficence was as long as ever but his store of patronage was dwindling, his revenue was at an all-time low, and Wales put an unexpected burden on what resources he had left. He was even running a shortfall of £700 to maintain the queen's household. As relative newcomers with a personal connection to the king, the Lusignans were the focus of the resentment that arises when the well runs dry.[29]

Edward too had wrangled with them over conflicting grants and this must have reassured his mother. But in the spring of 1258, word came that he had mortgaged several of his manors and towns to William and Aymer and he had borrowed money from Geoffrey Lusignan. The queen could only interpret this as their attempt to seduce Edward away from his parents. It was not hard to do. They not only offered him money, but an escape from their tutelage, which was intolerable now that he was going on 19. In terms of temperament and personality, he had more in common with them anyway than with his stuffy Savoyard handlers.[30]

Fortunately for Eleanor, she did not have to look far for allies to thwart this development. There were her uncles, Peter and Boniface of Savoy. Richard de Clare turned against his former friends the Lusignans after William de Valence suggested he was in league with the Welsh, a clear reference to his disappearance from the front to meet the queen. Another magnate behind the queen was John Fitz-Geoffrey, who was Edward's chief councillor. As the justiciar of Ireland, Fitz-Geoffrey had helped fight off an attempt by Geoffrey Lusignan to gain lands there at Edward's expense.[31]

She could also count on Simon de Montfort. His resentment against William de Valence went all the way back to the younger man's first appearance in England. It was not just that Valence had acquired property through marriage that should have gone to Eleanor de Montfort in dower. Henry also gave him various grants that by this point had raised his income to £2,800, compared to £2,500 for the Montforts, and he had converted more than £500 of his fees into land, whereas no action had been taken on Eleanor and Simon's £400 fee.[32]

Here Henry tried his best, but he had had a run of bad luck. The 1240s had been a decade of plenty after the deaths of various magnates had provided him with windfalls of patronage to dispense. Now nobody was dying, and to make matters worse, several of the wardships created then were coming to an end.[33] The only way Henry could meet all the claims for land was by going out and conquering it.

He had a chance to do so in Wales in 1246, but preferred a peaceful solution. Now that was in tatters. There was always Sicily, and he doubtless tried to drum up enthusiasm in his barons with tales of all the riches enjoyed by their Norman ancestors when they ruled the island. They probably did not even blink before telling him, 'Pass'.

Land was only part of the issue for Eleanor and Simon. There was still the matter of all the money Henry owed them. On 18 December 1257, the same day Simon stood witness for the Clare-Montferrat marriage covenant, the exchequer did the books and found a figure of £1,198, 14 shillings and 10½ pence was outstanding, worth about £900,000 in today's money. It was a huge sum, but in recent years they had also received substantial payments in spite of the king's poverty, all told nearly £7,000, including the money from Margaret de Lacy.[34] Henry had, moreover, authorised Simon to apply any claims for land in France that might result from the peace treaty with Louis he was just then helping to negotiate. But the little gifts to Eleanor had become little indeed during these years. In July 1257, we find Henry giving his sister three bucks from the royal forest.[35] Nothing more.

More deer and any wine probably would not have detracted from the antagonism the Montforts felt for the Lusignans in any case. Henry's favouritism for William was especially obscene because William continued to default on his payments to Eleanor for her dower despite all the money and gifts he received from the Crown. A clash was inevitable and it occurred when Simon accused William of trespassing and stealing some of his property. In front of the king and nobles, William replied by calling the Earl of Leicester a liar and traitor to boot. Although he was fifteen to twenty years older than his impetuous rival, Montfort rushed at him. According to Paris, who attributed this anger to 'short madness', Simon would have killed him had Henry not physically restrained him.[36]

It was one of the Lusignans themselves who provided the opening for a conspiracy against them. On 1 April 1258, there was a huge brawl at a church in Surrey where the advowson was claimed by John Fitz-Geoffrey, the Lord of Shere. When it was over, the priest was dead and several members of his household badly beaten up. The perpetrators were fifty-odd peasants sent there by Aymer de Valence, the Bishop-elect of Winchester, to eject the priest because the advowson for the church was his to give, not Fitz-Geoffrey's. It had only been five years since a similar confrontation took place between him and Boniface. Clearly Aymer thought the best way of handling disputes of this sort was through physical intimidation. Fitz-Geoffrey went to Henry to complain, but according to Paris, the king asked him to drop the case. So Fitz-Geoffrey went to others.[37]

The nobles were gathered in Westminster for the convening of Parliament. Wales was the dominant issue and an order to muster the feudal host in June had already gone out. They had to move quickly because the Comyn faction had once again seized control in Scotland and sought an alliance with Llywelyn. Also, since he had his nobility in assembly, the king would make another appeal for the thing that would not go away, his Sicilian project.[38]

The session opened on or around 9 April. Valence again blamed Llywelyn's success on traitors sitting amongst them, his brother-in-law Simon de Montfort in particular. Simon returned the insult and again had to be restrained by the king from attacking him. It was the last straw. On 12 April, Montfort entered a confederation with Fitz-Geoffrey, Clare and Peter of Savoy to stand together against their enemies, meaning the Lusignans.

They were joined by three other magnates. One was Peter de Montfort, the Lord of Beaudesert in Warwickshire, no relation of Simon but a good friend and ally. The other two were Roger Bigod, the Earl of Norfolk, and his younger brother Hugh. Roger had had a run-in with Aymer over a wardship, but what drew him into the confederacy was simple family loyalty. He and Hugh were brothers-in-law of Fitz-Geoffrey. Hugh was also a rising courtier, and whatever the Lusignans lost would be his to gain.[39]

The reform movement begins, the Lusignans are expelled

We cannot be for sure about what followed next. There seems to have been a confederation because a copy of the original document survived in the Montfort family archives. Paris also speaks of a league being formed at this time involving the Earls of Leicester, Norfolk and Hereford. But as for a confrontation, there is only a single account, contained in the annals of Tewkesbury near southern Wales.

It tells of how the barons responded to the king's request for Sicily by showing up at his chamber on 30 April dressed for battle. After stacking their weapons at the door, they walked in, saluted him and listened as Roger Bigod told Henry they were fed up with the Lusignans and all other foreigners and wanted them out. They were also fed up with the way he was running the realm and wanted him to reform. He was asked to swear an oath to do this, so was Edward, and to hand over his Great Seal for good measure.[40]

There is plenty of doubt about whether this confrontation actually occurred. For one thing, Peter of Savoy and Simon would have been dumbfounded to hear Bigod demand the expulsion of all aliens. They would have to pack up and leave as well. In his own account, Paris says Henry listened to their complaints in Parliament itself and admitted he needed to mend his ways, but the barons were dubious because it was an 'arduous and difficult matter' holding him to his promises.

Then there are the chancery records. They show that on 2 May 1258, Henry agreed to undertake reforms in return for a promise by the magnates to try and win him a subsidy for Sicily. Edward swore to abide by this decision and is listed as the first witness. After him come four foreigners: two Lusignans, Geoffrey and William, followed by Peter of Savoy and John de Plessis, the Earl of Warwick, who was a Poitevin by birth. If there had indeed been a call for the king to get rid of all foreigners, he ignored it.[41]

A committee of twenty-four, half for the king, half for the barons, was charged with drafting a list of reforms for discussion and ratification at another Parliament the following month in Oxford. The two camps arrived there with their military service, presumably to march on Wales after that, but the baronial side had other ideas. At some point a petition appeared in their ranks with twenty-nine points on how to better organise and run the kingdom. The reforms they intended to push through were clearly going to upset certain people on the king's side. The barons told their men to be on guard for the events about to unfold when Parliament opened on 11 June 1258.[42]

The Provisions of Oxford subsequently enacted undertook an entire sweep of the government. The committee of twenty-four was replaced by a permanent council of fifteen, which worked in unison with the king and not necessarily under him in discharging the affairs of the realm, especially patronage. The chancellor was to seal all writs at the command of the council, not the king alone. Parliament was also no longer the king's prerogative, rather now an institution of state, to meet three times a year at fixed intervals and represented before the king and council by a standing committee. Lastly, the office of justiciar, working with a commission of knights appointed in each county, was revived to go out and bring justice directly to the people.[43]

Everything, it seemed, depended on who was going to be named to the council. It was decided that each side would select two from the other one and together these four would get the honour. The two Bigod brothers were nominated for the barons, John Mansel and John de Plessis for the king. On 22 June 1258, Henry ordered them to proceed. The fifteen councillors they chose included themselves (except Hugh Bigod, who had already been appointed justiciar), Simon de Montfort, Richard de Clare, John Fitz-Geoffrey, Peter de Montfort and Peter of Savoy. In other words, all the confederates. Not a single Lusignan, nor were any of them named to the parliamentary committee. They were shut out of the new government.

This was the work of Mansel and Plessis, both friends of the queen, and in the case of Mansel a close confidant. Clearly these two had been drawn into the intrigue against the Lusignans. A letter in the chancery rolls suggests that Clare, who counted Mansel a friend and ally, was the point man.[44] The two of them, working closely with the queen and Savoyards behind the scenes, had lulled the Lusignans into a false sense of security.

Their move against them, moreover, did not stop with excluding them from government. Citing the impoverishment of the Crown, the reformers wanted them to hand over all the castles, lands and wardships they had received from Henry. The newly elected council would from now on decide who got what of England's bounty.[45]

Realising they had been had, the Lusignans began obstructing the parliamentary proceedings. When it came time to take an oath to protect these enactments, the king did so but his brothers refused. According to a later complaint of the barons, they tried to turn Henry against the reforms, promising him all kinds of wealth, but the king stood fast. They had more success with Edward and persuaded him to appoint Guy and Geoffrey Lusignan to run his affairs in Gascony and the Isle of Oléron. When their actions came to light, they took fright and fled with Edward to Winchester. The king and barons followed them there and, after intense negotiations, the Lusignans agreed to go into exile.[46]

They crossed over with their households and several thousand pounds in cash on 14 July, but found themselves stuck in Boulogne. By this time word had reached Queen Margaret that the brothers had defamed her sister, apparently blaming Eleanor for their demise, and Margaret convinced Louis to refuse them passage to their homeland in Poitou. Young Henry de Montfort saw this as an opportunity to avenge the insults William de Valence had hurled at his father and gathered up some friends and family to harass him and his brothers there. Eventually Louis granted them safe passage through his kingdom.[47]

It would seem that Eleanor of Provence's gamble had paid off. All four of her brothers-in-law and their retinues were gone, and her son, in view of his deplorable behaviour, was now saddled with four councillors to keep special tabs on him. She probably did not think the conspiracy would result in the realm undergoing a whole new makeover and she might have dreaded the thought of the changes to come as a consequence of purging her enemies. Her queen's gold, for one, was included in the first point of the 'Petition of the Barons' as a problem that needed addressing.[48]

More worrisome was her husband's loss of prerogative when it came to making her grants. No longer could he make her the gift of a wardship by simply telling his clerk, 'Do it'. Now everything had to go through the channel of the king and council together. Henry gave her a taste of what was to come when Edmund de Lacy, the 28-year-old Earl of Lincoln, lay dying and the queen was eager for the wardship of his heir to go to the boy's mother Alice, Eleanor's kinswoman from the Continent. Henry made the grant to Alice on 1 June, but conditioned it on approval coming from the upcoming Parliament.[49]

Looking at the makeup of the council, the queen doubtless felt she had enough support there. Of the fifteen members, two were her uncles, Boniface and Peter of Savoy. Five were good friends: Mansel, Plessis, Fitz-Geoffrey, Clare and Montfort, and three were solid friends and allies of Simon: Peter de Montfort, Richard de Grey and Walter Cantilupe.[50] That gave her a respectable two-thirds majority, and there was of course her husband, who was not just any council member, but the king and it was naturally assumed all efforts should be made to accommodate his wishes. He was, after all, their lord.

The question remains why Henry was willing to give up so much power. His position was strong enough if, at some point, he decided reforms had gone far enough. John de Warenne and Henry of Almain, who was more or less the acting Earl of Cornwall for his father Richard, had also been unwilling to take the oath to the Provisions of Oxford.[51] Together with Edward and the Lusignans, they commanded several large lordships that could have easily come to the king's aid if the baronial reformers decided to renounce their fealty to Henry and attack. The king might have thought this was his last chance to win support for the Sicilian project and therefore to avoid ecclesiastical penalties. Henry's piety was certainly the deciding factor here, but for another reason.

Throughout his reign, Henry had made the feeding of the poor, both daily and for great celebrations, a true manifestation of his majesty. Poor weather over the past couple of years had ruined successive harvests, leading to famine throughout the realm. It became so bad that an appeal had been made to Richard of Cornwall in Germany and he responded by sending fifty ships earlier that spring laden with corn and grain. Hunger forced thousands to the cities, where they died in heaps.

Taking the circuitous route that he did from London to Oxford, Henry could have easily witnessed the toll taken by the famine on his subjects. He did not have to see or read the 'Petition of the Barons' to know something was wrong and needed to be fixed. Sacrificing his brothers,

Family trees of the thirteenth century

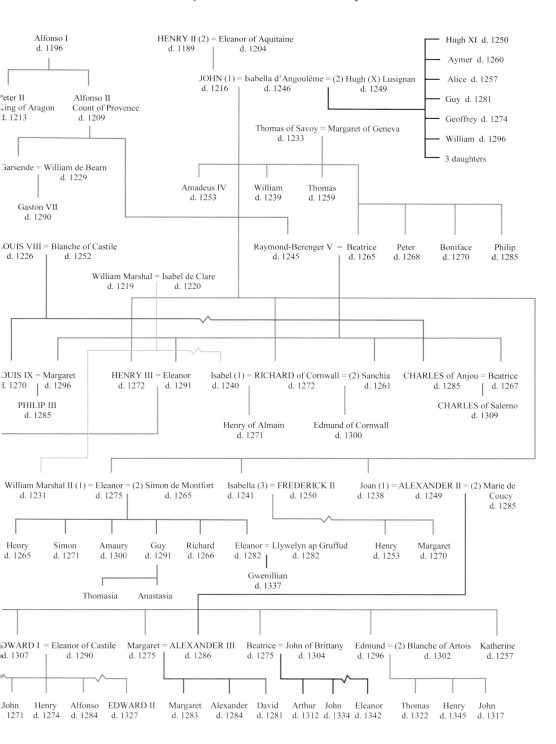

Alfonso I
d. 1196

HENRY II (2) = Eleanor of Aquitaine
d. 1189   d. 1204

Hugh XI d. 1250

Aymer d. 1260

Alice d. 1257

JOHN (1) = Isabella d'Angoulême = (2) Hugh (X) Lusignan
d. 1216   d. 1246   d. 1249

Guy d. 1281

Geoffrey d. 1274

Peter II
King of Aragon
d. 1213

Alfonso II
Count of Provence
d. 1209

William d. 1296

Thomas of Savoy = Margaret of Geneva
d. 1233

3 daughters

Garsende = William de Bearn
d. 1229

Amadeus IV
d. 1253

William
d. 1239

Thomas
d. 1259

Gaston VII
d. 1290

LOUIS VIII = Blanche of Castile
d. 1226   d. 1252

Raymond-Berenger V = Beatrice
d. 1245   d. 1265

Peter
d. 1268

Boniface
d. 1270

Philip
d. 1285

William Marshal = Isabel de Clare
d. 1219   d. 1220

LOUIS IX = Margaret
d. 1270   d. 1296

PHILIP III
d. 1285

HENRY III = Eleanor
d. 1272   d. 1291

Isabel (1) = RICHARD of Cornwall = (2) Sanchia
d. 1240   d. 1272   d. 1261

CHARLES of Anjou = Beatrice
d. 1285   d. 1267

CHARLES of Salerno
d. 1309

Henry of Almain
d. 1271

Edmund of Cornwall
d. 1300

William Marshal II (1) = Eleanor = (2) Simon de Montfort
d. 1231   d. 1275   d. 1265

Isabella (3) = FREDERICK II
d. 1241   d. 1250

Joan (1) = ALEXANDER II = (2) Marie de
d. 1238   d. 1249   Coucy
d. 1285

Henry
d. 1265

Simon
d. 1271

Amaury
d. 1300

Guy
d. 1291

Richard
d. 1266

Eleanor = Llywelyn ap Gruffud
d. 1282   d. 1282

Henry
d. 1253

Margaret
d. 1270

Gwenillian
d. 1337

Thomasia   Anastasia

EDWARD I = Eleanor of Castile
d. 1307   d. 1290

Margaret = ALEXANDER III
d. 1275   d. 1286

Beatrice = John of Brittany
d. 1275   d. 1304

Edmund = (2) Blanche of Artois
d. 1296   d. 1302

Katherine
d. 1257

John
d. 1271

Henry
d. 1274

Alfonso
d. 1284

EDWARD II
d. 1327

Margaret
d. 1283

Alexander
d. 1284

David
d. 1281

Arthur
d. 1312

John
d. 1334

Eleanor
d. 1342

Thomas
d. 1322

Henry
d. 1345

John
d. 1317

The effigies of King John and Isabella of Angoulême. The genealogical line below shows their five children: Henry III; Richard of Cornwall, the King of Germany; Joan, the Queen of Scots; Eleanor, who was the youngest; and Isabella, the Holy Roman Empress. From left to right in the bottom row are Richard's sons Henry of Almain and Edmund of Cornwall, followed by Eleanor's children Henry, Simon, Amaury, Guy, Richard and Eleanor.

Henry III at his second coronation in 1220. First crowned as a boy of nine in 1216, Henry underwent a difficult minority without any older relatives to guide him. Sensitive, pious and very generous, he is not known to have been with any woman prior to Eleanor of Provence, nor was he unfaithful during their thirty-six years together.

The effigies of William Marshal, Henry's first regent, and his namesake son at the New Temple in London. Henry married his sister Eleanor to the younger William in 1224. His untimely death seven years later, when Eleanor was just 16, had far-reaching consequences for them all. Below is the seal of Simon de Montfort, son of the Albigensian crusader, showing him as the tall French adventurer who came to England in 1230. Looking to marry well, he courted two wealthy widows before marrying Eleanor Marshal in secret in 1238.

Matthew Paris drew this picture of Henry and Eleanor of Provence sometime after their wedding and her coronation in January 1236. It clearly shows the age difference between them, his 28 to her 12.

An illustration of the King's Chamber at Westminster Palace made in the eighteenth century. The elaborately decorated 'Painted Chamber' as it was subsequently called was meant to be a centrepiece of Henry's reign. The people who entered it were welcomed with some advice over the doorway that said, 'He who does not give what he has will not get what he wants'.

The reconstructed 'Queen Eleanor' herb garden located outside the Great Hall of Winchester Castle. Eleanor of Provence maintained elaborate gardens at all her stately residences. The hall is all that remains of the castle, which is probably where Eleanor de Montfort was born in 1215. Her brother the king belted her husband Simon the Earl of Leicester inside the hall, below, in 1239.

La Réole Castle in southwest France. It was Eleanor of Provence's first residence during her husband's expedition to Gascony in 1242. Seven years later Eleanor de Montfort called La Réole home when she accompanied Simon to the province for his controversial tenure there as viceroy. The image below shows the royal pair returning from Gascony after eighteen months abroad, and with a new child, Beatrice.

Henry and Eleanor had five children, shown here in this genealogical membrane. From left the future King Edward I; Queen Margaret of Scotland; Edmund, who was actually the fourth child, founded the House of Lancaster; Beatrice, married to John of Brittany, the future Earl of Richmond; and Katherine, whose death at the age of three in 1257 left her parents distraught. It was under Henry's reign that Windsor Castle, below, became a royal residence and where their children and their companions from the nobility were raised.

Eleanor and Simon de Montfort had two principal residences, Kenilworth Castle in Warwickshire and Odiham Castle in Hampshire. They received Kenilworth, above, from the king in 1244 and Simon went about making additions and improvements that made the fortress impregnable when it became the last major holdout of the Disinherited. Below are the ruins of Odiham, which Henry gave to his sister in 1236 as a gift for her 21st birthday. It was here, in April 1265, that Eleanor and Simon saw each other for the last time.

These two illustrations show medieval London Bridge. In July 1263, the city erupted in violence against royalists and foreigners with the approach of Simon de Montfort's army. Worried for the queen's safety, Henry and Eleanor decided she should try to reach Edward at Windsor, but her barge was turned back at the bridge in a hailstorm of stones, debris and insults from the crowd. Eleanor of Provence got the last laugh when Henry gave her control of the bridge following Simon's defeat.

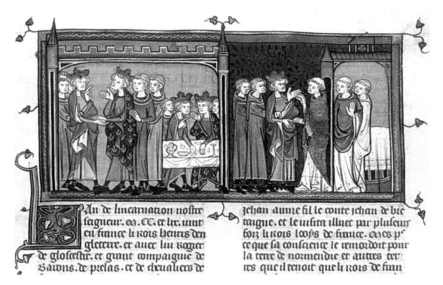

The image above shows Henry III meeting Louis IX. These former boy kings, married to sisters Margaret and Eleanor of Provence, became good friends but Louis and Margaret were also good friends of Simon and Eleanor de Montfort. Forced to take sides, Louis threw his support to Henry, but it helped bring on civil war in England. The scene below shows the Battle of Lewes in 1264, with Henry and his coat of arms of three leopards on the left and Simon with his forked-tail lion on the right.

Above are the ruins of Wallingford Castle in Oxfordshire, where Eleanor de Montfort had custody of the royal hostages. In the summer of 1264, Eleanor of Provence organised a rescue attempt of Edward from her base in France. As Simon's regime began to fall apart early the next year, Eleanor de Montfort secured Dover Castle, below. When her nephew Edward arrived with troops in October 1265, she and her surviving children escaped to the Continent.

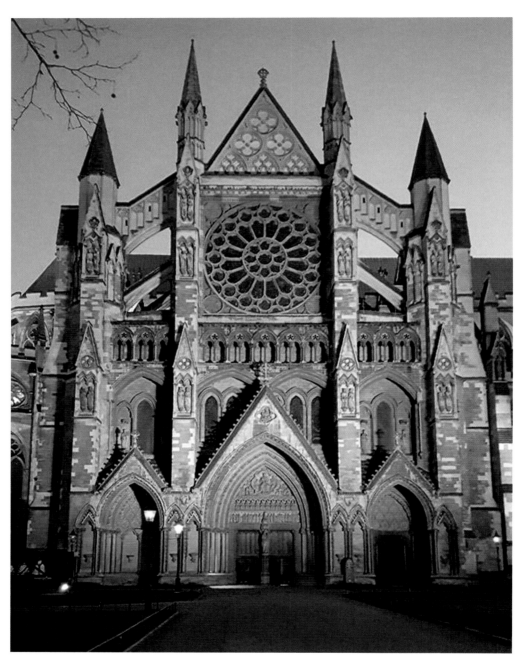

Westminster Abbey, Henry III's greatest achievement, where his tomb is located today. Eleanor of Provence was supposed to be buried next to him near the shrine, but her son Edward I gave her spot to his own wife Eleanor of Castile when she died just before her mother-in-law.

Eleanor of Provence, England's most powerful queen of the Middle Ages, was buried at Amesbury Priory in Wiltshire. Her tomb was later destroyed during the Dissolution of Henry VIII. Today this Cedar of Lebanon stands over the site of her presumed grave, just a short walk from Stonehenge below.

Corbel of Eleanor of Provence in the Muniment room of Westminster Abbey. As the acting head of state in 1254, she summoned Parliament to meet, the first woman to do so, and also the first Parliament ever with a democratic mandate. These achievements meant little to the men who wrote the chronicles, who preferred to see her, both as a woman and foreigner, as the source of all the troubles besetting the realm.

whose divisiveness at court he could not have missed, was a small price to pay.[52]

The king had his doubts about the undertaking, but not so much about the reforms as one man in particular. Paris describes a scene in July 1258, after the first phase of enactment had been completed, when Henry was forced to seek shelter from a thunderstorm on the Thames. The occupant of the house at that time was his brother-in-law Simon, who upon receiving the king told him not to be afraid, the storm had passed.

Henry replied he was not afraid of the storm, but of *him*.[53] His reasons were not unfounded. A man of Simon's pride and temperament could not forget the king banishing him from the queen's churching, putting him on trial over Gascony, and ignoring him and his wife when it came to their grievances. He would definitely use his place on the council to set things right again. Indeed, one of Henry's first acts after agreeing to undertake reforms was to authorise the committee of twenty-four, of which Simon was a member, to make whatever provision they could for converting his fee into land.[54] Unfortunately for the Montforts, the work of reform permitted them no time to do it.

In November, Simon got his chance to get back at the king. The peace treaty with France was ready to be ratified and a meeting was scheduled in Cambrai between Henry, Louis and Richard of Cornwall (as the King of Germany). Henry put great store in the meeting of three kings bringing peace to the world, an allusion to the *Magi* of the Bible, but at the last minute the council decided not to let him go. Somebody had stoked fears that when he came back, he could have the Lusignans with him.

It was humiliating for Henry, being grounded by the council, and they rubbed it in by sending Simon and a delegation to take his place. For all he knew, it was his brother-in-law behind this move to straightjacket him. If so, Simon overplayed his hand. Louis was a good friend, had known him a lot longer than he knew Henry, but he thought the English side was acting in bad faith by not allowing their own sovereign to ratify the treaty. He refused to attend the conference.[55]

Peace with France had become vital to Henry and Eleanor because the Sicilian business was dependent on it. Earlier in May, while Simon, Peter of Savoy and Hugh Bigod were conspiring against the Lusignans, these three joined two of them, Guy and Geoffrey, on an embassy to Louis to finalise the terms for the treaty. It was then that Louis, under pressure from the papacy, agreed to compensate Henry for his lost lands by funding a force of 500 knights for two years. These knights were then to form the core of the army that Henry was supposed to take with him on crusade.[56]

The delay in ratifying the treaty was followed by an even worse setback for Sicily. Back in August, the baronial council wrote a letter to the pope informing him of their promise to help the king obtain a subsidy for the project in return for reforms, but so far they had done nothing. The rest of the letter, which Simon took the lead in drafting, was given over to a vicious attack on the Lusignans.

On 18 December 1258, Pope Alexander responded to it in the most ungrateful terms. He huffed that since Henry had not kept his end of the bargain, he was free to offer the kingdom of Sicily to somebody else. Of course, if Henry still wanted it for Edmund in the meantime, all he had to do was pay the bill. The pope did have some choice words for the barons, however, regarding all this reform business. He exhorted them to show all due fidelity and respect not only to the king as their sovereign, but also to 'our dear daughter in Christ, the illustrious queen of England'.[57]

8

Great Indignation and Fury
1259–1261

The Montfort family enterprise,
obstructing the Treaty of Paris

As Henry feared, Simon de Montfort had emerged as one of the leading baronial reformers, if not the leader. In terms of rank and personality, only Roger Bigod, the Earl of Norfolk, and Richard de Clare, the Earl of Gloucester, could challenge him, but both men were deep-seated royalists at heart. For them, it was fine to purge the court and assume control of Crown patronage and prerogative, but they did not want inquiries made into the way they ran their own fiefdoms.

Roger had gone to Cambrai on an equal footing with Simon, but after the peace conference there failed to materialise, he retired to his estates in Norfolk for the time being. Earlier, Clare had nearly been killed in an epidemic that hit Winchester after Parliament moved there in pursuit of the Lusignans. He was left 'scabby and disfigured', but had sufficiently recovered to receive his stepfather, Richard of Cornwall, as he landed in England at the end of January 1259 after spending eighteen months abroad as the new King of Germany.[1]

Paris describes how there was much apprehension about Richard's visit because he too was a brother of the Lusignans. He adds that Simon de Montfort himself had still not returned from the Continent and this led to suspicions that he was being detained against his will.[2] In fact, Simon was with his two oldest sons taking care of personal business. On 1 January 1259, he dictated his will to 20-year-old Henry de Montfort, who drafted it in the elegant handwriting he learned while a pupil of Robert Grosseteste. Simon's overriding concern was for his debts to be paid and that amends be made to the 'poor people' of his land whom he had ruthlessly exploited as their lord. He names Eleanor his executor, to be replaced by young Henry should something happen to her.

> The responsibility for executing all those matters appertaining to my testament I leave and grant to the countess, my wife, and I appoint her my attorney. I beg, request and command her, by the faith that she owes me, that she carries out my wishes in the way that an honourable lady should, in the interests of her lord and husband who places his trust in her.[3]

His will was an affirmation of the Montforts as a family enterprise, ready to stand together for the controversy that lay ahead. When Simon returned for Parliament in February, he probably travelled with the Dean of Berry, who had been sent by Louis to get the peace treaty back on track. The dean was there to witness the renunciation of rights to Normandy and other English lands on the Continent by the children and certain grandchildren of King John. Richard of Cornwall and his son Henry of Almain were the first to do so, followed by Henry and his son Edmund, but Edward refused.[4] Holding up the treaty seemed his best bet to regain the independence he lost on account of his secret dealings with the Lusignans.

Eleanor de Montfort also refused to renounce until action was finally taken on her and Simon's grievances. There was still the money owed to them by the Crown, still the grant of land in place of their fee, and still her Marshal dower. A council meeting at Windsor on 10 March nominated Clare, Mansel, John Balliol and royal steward Robert Walerand to 'make peace' with the Montforts over their claims. These arbitrators, together with Simon and Peter of Savoy, were delegated on that same day to France to expedite the treaty.[5] According to Paris, the issue of Eleanor's renunciation was the hot topic of discussion among the English negotiators at St Germain:

> For the Countess of Leicester would not on any account give up quiet possession of her portion of Normandy, which the King of England was to resign to the King of France, according to the terms of their agreement. It was in consequence of this that the Earl of Gloucester hurled insulting speeches at the Earl of Leicester, who repaid his offensive speeches by others as sharp and severe.

The other envoys had to intervene to keep the two earls from coming to blows.[6] Simon stayed behind in France while the rest of the party went home to discuss the Montforts with the king and council before a session of Parliament. With the treaty now deemed vitally important to the entire kingdom, a decision was reached to appease Eleanor and Simon. On 15 May, they received the nearly £237 owed to them by the Crown. Nine days later, the envoys were again charged with arbitrating the dispute over their other two grievances. They were to determine whether the king had, as his sister claimed, forced her to accept the agreement with Richard Marshal over her dower, and if yes, then whether their fee was meant as compensation for it or was purely a gift, as Simon and Eleanor insisted. A letter was dispatched to Louis to inform him that every effort was being made to get Eleanor to renounce.

> To the King of France. In the presence of very many prelates and magnates of the realm lately in the court of London, the king offered to his sister Eleanor, Countess of Leicester, that he would submit himself to the award which was lately provided at St Germain in France ... and also offered to give security to the countess according to the form therein provided for the same; in which things however the said countess did not acquiesce.

Louis was also told that if in the end they had to go without her renunciation, he would be indemnified for any claims she brought against him for her father's lands.[7] The council nevertheless pressed on with trying to get the Montforts to quit stalling and granted them the coveted land in place of their fee. They were temporarily given nine manors reckoned to be worth at or around £400 pending another assessment of their value and status.

Since Simon was still in France, wisely keeping out of sight of his colleagues, it was up to Eleanor to take possession of the manors. She wasted no time in sending her officials, probably under guidance from the Montforts' steward Richard de Havering, to evict the occupants. They became overzealous at two of the manors and seized the corn and livestock, forcing Henry to order the return of both assets to their rightful owners.[8]

All this was small potatoes compared to what the Montforts had in store for king and council. On 23 July 1259, three arbitrators were appointed to hear their complaints about Eleanor's dower and to issue an award by 1 November. To begin with, it might be agreed that her original settlement had been unfair. The partition of the Marshal estate in 1247 had shown that the true value of her dower was nearly double what she was stuck with, but the figures they received from the Montforts were absolutely outrageous. They claimed Eleanor should have received in excess of three times more, not £400 but £1,333, and they wanted it not only going forward, but all the way back to her agreement with Marshal. That meant an extra £933 for twenty-six years, or £24,258, which was a whole year's worth of royal revenue.[9]

Nobody had that kind of cash, but Simon knew nobody had that kind of cash as of *yet*. Under the peace treaty, Henry was going to receive enough money to maintain 500 hundred knights for two years, an amount that was eventually fixed at £33,500. Simon was among the envoys who negotiated this concession and it was most likely his work that the treaty contained the stipulation that the money was to be spent pending 'the consent of loyal Englishmen chosen by the King of England and the magnates'. The time was May 1258, with reforms of the kingdom just under a month away, and Simon was already plotting for the council to take control of the government.[10] That way, when the treaty money was paid, it would be up to the council to decide how to spend it, not the king. Instead of throwing it away on an army of knights, it was better to satisfy the Montforts for their claims and use the balance to cover the increase in her dower for the next ten years.

There is no evidence to suggest this was Simon and Eleanor's strategy other than their wildly overstated numbers, but they could afford to pursue it because it was not going to cost the Marshal heirs a thing. Henry's response is unknown, probably more clawing at the air at the mere mention of his sister's dower. He may have even subjected his overly pious soul to a slip of the tongue and swore he would be damned before he let the Montforts have a penny of the treaty money.

On 30 July, his proctors presented the French with a draft of the treaty that omitted Eleanor's renunciation. Henry's promise to indemnify Louis for any suit brought by Eleanor or her children was deemed sufficient, but in late August, as Henry prepared to sail, the deal was suddenly off. Simon at that time was in the company of his good friend Eudes Rigaud, the Archbishop of Rouen, who was Louis's chief negotiator for the treaty.[11] The delay seems to have been Simon's work, a calculated attempt to sabotage his own lord and king in a diplomatic matter where he was supposed to be representing his best interests.

It was testament to the skill of the Montforts as a husband-and-wife team that they were able to coordinate their obstruction of the peace treaty with only messengers going back and forth between England and France. In October, Simon returned for Parliament at Westminster and Eleanor joined him there. She requested a pardon for a man who had killed another man in self-defence and it was granted, not by Henry but by Hugh Bigod, the justiciar.[12] This does not mean the king had refused to see his sister, rather Bigod was personally handling much of the judicial pleas because the second great phase of reform was just then being legislated and Henry already had enough to do with the treaty.

Back in February, Simon had been instrumental in pushing through the enactments that led to these new laws, called the Provisions of Westminster, which among other things provided protection for lesser barons and knights against magnates like him. His only concern now, however, was his and Eleanor's claims. On 15 October, he entered a private agreement with Edward, who had finally renounced his rights to Normandy but was still under the tight tutelage of the council. Under the agreement, Edward swore to go to war with Simon in defence of the reform movement and the award about to be issued by the arbitration panel. Simon expected Marshal heirs like Clare to try to prevent any redistribution of the estate and wanted Edward's support in enforcing the award. What Edward received is not known, probably Simon's promise to win him that coveted release from his probation.[13]

Simon went back to France after that, well before the end of Parliament, but not before infuriating Henry further by telling the French envoys in Westminster that without a satisfactory settlement, Eleanor would activate her claims to Normandy. The threat became real when the first of November arrived, but no arbitral award on her dower was issued. Henry later claimed that the Montforts' good friends had discovered that the award was nothing what they had hoped it to be and so prevailed upon the members of the panel to quash it.

And yet the king continued to seek the cooperation of his sister and brother-in-law. On 6 November, he deprived John Mansel of £20 worth of land in Kent and gave it to Simon. Six days later, as the court stopped in Canterbury on the way to France, Henry took action on the Jewish debts of a local landholder at Eleanor's intercession.[14]

And still they refused to budge. On 24 November, the two courts met at St Denis and next day moved to Paris for a formal reception. Another eight days of wrangling ensued. Louis agreed to give the Montforts a fief-rent of £110 a year, presumably for Simon surrendering his own rights in France, and to withhold £10,000 of the treaty money for two years as an inducement to settle her dower once and for all. At last, Eleanor made her renunciation and on 4 December, the Treaty of Paris was finally ratified.[15]

All the former Plantagenet lordships on the Continent were officially ceded to the King of France, and the King of England agreed to hold Gascony as his liegeman the Duke of Aquitaine. In return, Louis surrendered several smaller outlying territories to Henry and agreed to pay the big windfall of money. The two kingdoms were at peace after more than half a century. There was much rejoicing as the two courts prepared to spend Christmas together in Paris, but the Montforts were excluded. Simon took his leave of Louis so he could join Eleanor, who by then was in Normandy. He did not bother informing his own king that he was leaving.[16]

Break between Simon and the Savoyards, between the two Eleanors

In setting out to hold the treaty hostage to their claims, Eleanor and Simon knew they risked an irreparable breach with her brother. They probably did not care. All the old resentments of the queen's churching, Simon's tenure in Gascony, the king's favouritism for everybody except them had trumped whatever gratitude they might have felt for all the good things Henry had done for them.

Fired with revenge, there was little they could do during his personal rule, but now they could afford to incur the king's displeasure because reform had made him answerable to the council. He could take no punitive action against them on his own authority, and Simon had enough allies on the council to make sure of it. If that meant the end of whatever was left of their friendship and family connection, so be it.

The Montforts also seem to have cared little if they alienated the queen in the process. She had always been a dependable friend and supporter during their troubles with her husband. She could not have approved of the way he humiliated them at her churching in 1239. It was also her mother Beatrice who won Simon and Eleanor full restoration after their return to England in

1243, and the queen risked her own breach with her husband by standing by the Montforts during Simon's trial over Gascony. And of course she and the Savoyards were fully behind the plans of Simon and the other confederates to oust the Lusignans. But such was the determination of the Montforts to get what they saw as justice for themselves that their relationship with the queen was likely to end up as collateral damage before it was over.

The rift had begun when Simon and the council tried to usurp Henry's place at the peace conference in Cambrai in late 1258. The English queen was a strong backer of the treaty with France because it was essential for Sicily and there was also the personal reason that her sister Margaret was the Queen of France. Indeed, with peace seemingly imminent, Margaret proposed a match between Eleanor and Henry's daughter Beatrice and John, the son of the Duke of Brittany.[17] This would restore ancestral relations between England and Brittany that had flourished after the Conquest but were severed when the duke's father defected to the French Crown in 1234.

Next came the Parliament of February 1259. It was here that the Montforts commenced their obstruction of the treaty, and yet Simon at the same time pushed for a radical sweep of feudal oppression. This put him at odds with Richard de Clare, who preferred to slow down the pace of reform.[18] Clare and other conservative magnates like Peter of Savoy were content to leave most laws and customs as they were. Neither man showed any signs of having an epiphany about bringing justice and fairness to all, similar to the one gleaned from Simon's will. It is safe to say that neither did the queen.

Even before the reform movement began, Eleanor's steward was notorious for his management of her estates. He was William of Tarrant, a monk of the Cistercian order who, according to Paris, 'gaped after money like a horseleech after blood'. Supposedly Eleanor was informed many times of his malpractices but always excused them.[19] Brother William died as the movement was taking off, but the queen does not seem to have taken the lesson of estate reforms seriously. Years later another of her stewards, Robert of Pevensey, was also cited for imposing unjust fines and paying off officials. In short, he was a crook, but as with Brother William and Geoffrey Langley, he was that type of unscrupulous man she liked to do business with.[20]

So far the reform programme had been a success for her. The Lusignans were gone, Edward was under firm control, and even her patronage had been largely unaffected. As she wished, her kinswoman Alice de Saluzzo, widow of Edmund de Lacy, was awarded the wardship of their son and heir Henry. Alice was to pay just over £362 yearly for it, with the money going to the building works of Westminster Abbey, which certainly pleased the king.[21]

But Montfort's radicalism took hold of others even if he himself only seemed preoccupied with his own demands. The Provisions of Westminster passed at Parliament in October 1259 not only clamped down on oppressive lords like Eleanor, Clare and Peter of Savoy, but also on her prerogatives as queen. Provision number fourteen, for example, decreed that wardships were to be sold at the discretion of a committee, who were also given control over the payment of her queen's gold. The five men on the committee were mostly friendly, but wardships and queen's gold were major sources of royal income and power.[22] Any attempt to regulate them could only diminish her authority. The infringement of these prerogatives was doubtless the work of that growing breed of militants that adhered to Montfort.

Making matters worse, it was at this time that Edward, now 20-years old and more restless than ever, reappeared on the national scene. At the start of Parliament on 13 October, a group of knights dubbed 'the bachelors' called on him, Clare and other magnates to follow the king's lead and start doing something for the common good. Edward admitted that he had been slow to reform, but was fully on board and ready to stand with the bachelors to impose the new legislation if necessary.[23]

That was the kind of talk Simon liked to hear and so it was during this Parliament that the two hotheads entered their private alliance. Whether the queen knew about it or not, there were signs that Edward, who was not going to France, would make a bid for freedom once his parents were gone. On 7 December, he did it by ejecting Robert Walerand as the castellan of his castle in Bristol and installing his own man, Roger Leybourne, despite his father's explicit instructions not to take such action. Leybourne would have been objectionable in any case on the grounds that, although originally from Kent, he hung out with the Marcher lords and was as violent and aggressive as any of them.[24]

Throughout all of this, the fate of the treaty hung in the balance on account of the obstinacy of Eleanor de Montfort. In subjecting one of the great political achievements of their time to extortion, her conduct had been appalling, but Simon's became downright contemptible when he acted like a sore loser in the wake of the treaty ratification. It was not just that he insulted Henry by not taking his leave of him in Paris, but before then he tried to undermine the wedding of Princess Beatrice to John of Brittany, which was to take place in January.

The marriage negotiations had started in earnest in May 1259, about the time that Henry promised Louis he would indemnify him if his sister did not renounce her claims. In October, as Queen Eleanor was on her way to London to attend the feast of St Edward, she stopped at St Albans, where she caught the monks just as they were finishing dinner. She was accompanied by Mansel, one of the English negotiators for the marriage, and the Bishop of Brienne, who was representing the Duke of Brittany. There was a violent storm the next day and the queen was feeling unwell, but she pressed on to London.[25]

It was during Parliament that the bishop, says the *Flores* chronicler, all but stalked the king and queen in pursuit of what the duke was after from the marriage. The honour of Richmond in the north of England had been held by his ancestors until it was confiscated from the duke's father. He could get it back for his descendents if it formed the marriage portion for Beatrice.[26] Henry agreed, but he had given Richmond eighteen years earlier to Peter of Savoy, who, although one of the marriage negotiators, was determined to hang on to it.

Simon was of the mind that he should give it up, if only because he and Peter were now enemies. The break between them occurred in March 1259, just after Thomas of Savoy died. Peter had arranged a loan of £2,000 from some merchants in Florence to pay the arrears in fees owed to his brother Thomas and their relatives in Savoy. Simon's name appeared among the councillors who were to stand surety for the money, but he ordered his name struck off.[27] Apparently he felt the Savoyards had sponged long enough off the exchequer and he was not going to approve any more money for them while his own claims went unanswered.

To get around the problem of the marriage portion for Beatrice, a deal was worked out to give the revenue of the county of Agenais, which was to revert to Henry under the treaty, to the newlyweds pending a final settlement. This decision was reached in the Queen's Chapel at Westminster on 18 October 1259, suggesting it was a clandestine meeting that excluded certain members of the council. Simon de Montfort was among those shut out because he would see it as the king and queen circumventing the council to protect the interests of her uncle, another

Savoyard scrounger. Simon was fully aware of what had happened by the time he reached France. During the celebrations, he told the duke that all acts of state needed the full consent of the council. No grant of Beatrice's marriage portion was valid without it.[28]

Henry, no doubt speaking for his wife, angrily accused Simon of trying to upset the marriage. It was probably by this point that Eleanor de Montfort had left for Normandy. Any word that now passed between her and the queen was bound to be awkward and fraught with tension. The relations between the two Eleanors, strained for the past year, looked to be broken for good.

Edward in league with Simon, showdown over Parliament

The departure of the Montforts, who were also friends of Louis and Margaret, allowed the two royal couples to enjoy the usual solemnities of the holiday season. Eleanor handed out gifts of rings and jewels to her sister and the Queen of Navarre, as well as to various countesses in attendance along with their damsels and knights. After Christmas, she and Henry went about their separate ways, he playing the tourist and Eleanor probably staying with Margaret. Their sister Beatrice, the Countess of Provence, was then in Paris. Perhaps the three of them were together at some point, with Eleanor mediating between the oldest and youngest sisters in their ongoing dispute about their inheritance in Provence.[29]

Both royal couples were supposed to reunite in Compiègne on 14 January for the wedding of young Beatrice and John of Brittany. Henry was heading in that direction when word arrived that Louis and Margaret's 15-year-old son and heir had suddenly died. His body was brought to the abbey of St Denis for the start of the funeral cortège to the abbey of Royaumont, twenty kilometres northwest. Henry acted as one of the pallbearers for the first stage of the procession.[30]

The wedding was held eight days later. Having just lost their son, Margaret and Louis showed great courage in being there. At 17, three years younger than the groom, Beatrice was going into wedded life with the maturity that her mother and sister lacked at the time of their marriages, but like them, she too married a faithful, loving husband. The young couple was supposed to go to Brittany, but on 9 March 1260, Henry wrote to the duke from St Omer near the French coast that they were still with him and Eleanor and he expressed his desire that they continue with them to England so he could knight his new son-in-law on St Edward's Day.[31]

It goes without saying that the queen had something to do with this development. Having her daughter close by was comfort for her recent anxieties, which included the fear that Aymer was trying to get back into the realm. We can imagine she and her husband had quite a row when she learned that the king had apparently backed a papal attempt during the summer to have him reinstated. While they were still at St Denis, a chastened Henry wrote to the pope to protest against his brother's return, pointing out that Aymer had tried to poison his mind against his wife and son. Clare, Mansel and Peter of Savoy were the usual witnesses to the letter, but the queen was probably not far in the background.[32]

Henry's letter to the duke explained why John and Beatrice had not yet appeared in Brittany, but not why Henry and Eleanor, the King and Queen of England, were still abroad more than four months after their departure and long after the treaty had been sealed. The answer, he might have given, was Simon de Montfort. He and Eleanor had returned from Normandy before the end of the year, likely in a sour mood over the way their scheme to block the treaty had not panned out.

In February, Simon came to London for the first of the three Parliaments to be held that year as stipulated by the Provisions of Oxford. Already before that, on 26 January 1260, Henry wrote to Hugh Bigod, one of the acting regents, to announce that the king had been delayed by the funeral, wedding and treaty implementation, and so no Parliament should be held until he returned. The way Simon saw it, that was not his choice to make. Parliament was no longer a royal prerogative. Henry should come back for it, at the predetermined time, and if he missed it, he was derelict in his duty.[33]

So began a three-month standoff over control of Parliament, with Simon and his supporters arrayed against moderates like the Bigods and conservatives like Clare, who backed the king. Simon had enough strength on the council to have Peter of Savoy sacked when he returned from France in February, and his threat to force Parliament to convene was bolstered by the arrival in London of Edward and his Marcher retinue. Clare then appeared with his own men and arms and for a while it looked as if war might erupt at any time. Richard of Cornwall was brought in and together with Hugh Bigod and Philip Basset, whose family was among the most distinguished in the land, they maintained an uneasy peace between the two camps.[34]

Everybody waited for the king, but he was broke and going nowhere in St Omer. Hugh Bigod had been intimidated by Montfort's threats and sent Henry only a quarter of the money he requested. The royal couple had already pawned part of their crown jewels as security for a loan of £1,260. Margaret of Provence had arranged one loan of £622 from the Temple in Paris and Eleanor another one for £500 from the merchants of Ypres.

It was Louis who came to the rescue, with £2,778 as the first instalment of the treaty money. As much as he liked Henry, he did not like any foreign king hanging around too long and came to give him the cash in person along with advice to go home. Eleanor was also required to seal the documents for the remittance. Henry promised to use the money 'in the service of God and the Church, and to the advantage of the realm of England' as per the treaty. He then went out and hired a mercenary force and landed at Dover towards the end of April.[35]

The king marched into London unopposed and convened Parliament at the chapter house in St Paul's. According to the Dunstable annalist, Henry was 'angry beyond measure' when rumours reached him that his son had joined up with Simon to depose him. Fearful that his paternal instincts would nevertheless lead him to forgive and embrace his son on the spot, he kept him locked outside the city. Eleanor may have been behind this stern approach, for the annalist notes other rumours that she was 'the cause of all the trouble'. When finally admitted, Edward swore he meant no disobedience and was welcomed back by his parents. It cost his Marcher companions their positions as his castellans, but otherwise they could remain friends for now.[36]

The royal couple were probably inclined to see it all as Montfort's fault anyway. As Henry later complained, Edward had been 'seduced from his father's friendship and obedience by a certain man', who could only have been Simon. For the queen, he was now a bigger threat than the Lusignans. Making matters worse, Simon had even become their ally. While in Paris, he had sought out William de Valence to make peace between them so that they might assist him in bringing men and arms into England. The situation was all the more dangerous because Edward had lost none of his fondness for his banished uncles. When Esquivat moved to take the county of Bigorre back from the Montforts, it was

Edward who persuaded Geoffrey, Guy and William to intervene on Simon's behalf from their base in Poitou.[37]

Such was Henry's fury against his brother-in-law that he ordered articles of indictment prepared against him. There were thirty-nine in all, but Simon answered them so convincingly that the proctors were stumped. His cavalier tone owed something to the arrival on 7 July 1260 of two friends from Normandy, one of them Eudes Rigaud, the Archbishop of Rouen. Their presence was a signal from Louis that the court in France was very much interested in the outcome of the proceedings. They also had business to conduct with Simon, and here Eleanor de Montfort likely handled the arrangements of their stay. When Eudes left two weeks later, he took the third Montfort son, 17-year-old Amaury, with him to Rouen to install him in a new benefice at the cathedral.[38]

Edward still defiant, Eleanor de Montfort sues, Margaret gives birth

The second trial of Simon de Montfort was supposed to be held during the July Parliament, but word came of a new Welsh offensive. His trial was postponed and he was even appointed one of the commanders of the army to be mustered because he was 'a prudent and mighty warrior of England'.[39] A truce was in place by the end of August and Henry intended for the trial to be heard at the next Parliament, but Edward, defiant as ever, was the more immediate problem. He was keen to not only thwart his parents where he could, but embarrass them in the process. He saw a good opportunity for it when Walter Kirkham, the Bishop of Durham, died on 9 August 1260.

Henry and Eleanor wanted their faithful adviser John Mansel to be the next bishop and elaborated a plan to win him the election. When the delegation of monks from the chapter visited the king at Winchester to ask for the license to elect, he invited them to dinner. Just after the meal, a messenger arrived from the queen, who was staying at Marlborough, with a letter urging the election of Mansel. It was read aloud in front of the monks and at the end Henry chimed in that Mansel would indeed make a great bishop. The king and queen then wrote separate letters to the chapter itself. In hers, Eleanor stated her belief that Mansel was the man to make Durham an even greater church than it already was.

A little over a week later, the monks received a third letter, this one from Edward, advising them to forget that scoundrel Mansel. Instead, he urged them to elect the nephew of Walter Cantilupe, one of the closest friends of the Montforts. Striking an elitist tone, Edward reminded the monks that the Cantilupes were of high birth, not lowlife stock like Mansel and his breed. (Kirkham had been somewhere in between.) An aggravated Henry told his son he would do well to show more interest in Gascony than Durham. In the end, the chapter decided to play it safe and elected one of their own.[40]

Eleanor's heartache over her son's taunting attitude was mitigated by the arrival of her 20-year-old daughter Margaret. The Queen of Scotland was pregnant with her first child and desired to spend her confinement in the company of her mother. The Scottish council opposed it on the grounds that the heir to the throne they hoped for should be born within his future kingdom. Alexander III, now 19 and very much a king, insisted on the trip but procured strict pledges to ensure the return of mother and child after her purification.

Their presence at the feast of St Edward on 13 October made the occasion especially eventful because it marked the gathering of three kings. Henry and Alexander were joined by Richard of Cornwall, who had just returned from Germany after making a last, unsuccessful bid to become Holy Roman Emperor. There were only two queens at the celebrations, however, as Sanchia lay ill at Berkhamsted Castle.[41]

Henry as usual went all out and had a boat decked out with banners row by on the Thames with a band playing trumpets and all manner of instruments. During the ceremonies, he knighted John of Brittany and twenty-four other youths, but Edward had already preceded him by knighting his two Montfort cousins, Henry and Simon. It was as if their father had wanted him to do it and not the king. Edward also helped Simon arrange to have the council deputise Henry of Almain to serve in his place as the steward of the feast.[42]

It had been nearly a quarter of a century since Simon eagerly assumed the role of steward so he could serve the king and his new bride Eleanor of Provence at their wedding feast. They had all been young people then, soon to be great friends but with the first estrangement just around the corner. Now Henry was 53, Eleanor of Provence 37, Simon 52 and Eleanor de Montfort 45. Both couples had been through a lot together and had grown children who were cousins. Despite all that, the one thing the arrangements of this feast said about their relationship was that they just as soon kept their distance from one other.

Distracted by the three-kings setting he so admired and having all his children together, Henry was probably unaware of the machinations his rebellious heir was undertaking with Montfort. The two of them put aside their feud with Clare and allowed him to undercut the principal provisions of reform at this Parliament. The sheriffs were not replaced, no special eyre into local abuses was launched, and the magnates were given the power to rectify their officials at their own discretion.

In return, Edward acquired the lucrative Forz wardship and Simon had his trial called off. More importantly, the two of them were ceded the main say in the appointment of the chief officers of state. Hugh Bigod was now considered too much the king's man and was ousted. His position as justiciar was filled by Simon's devoted disciple Hugh Despenser. Edward's supporter John de Caux, the Abbot of Peterborough, was named treasurer, and Nicholas of Ely replaced loyal royal clerk Henry Wengham as chancellor.[43] For Simon, reform was first and foremost about controlling the king. Justice for the rest of the realm would naturally follow.

Henry deplored their presumption to straightjacket him with ministers not of his choosing, with his son's connivance no less, but as the king's attempt to interfere in the Durham election showed, the power of the council was on the wane. It had not even met in the two months leading up to Parliament.[44] The inability or unwillingness of the councillors to hold Montfort to account for his nefarious and seditious behaviour had wrecked their credibility as a governing body. As the lord king, Henry now presumed to step in and set things right. Just as the council had allowed Simon, Edward and Clare to gut reform, so he would gut the council.

The first step was to get rid of his son, which was made easy by Edward leading his Montfort cousins and all the new knights to the Continent in November to try their luck on the tournament circuit. But much to his mother's distress, he continued to associate with his Lusignan uncles while in Paris. He even appointed Guy his seneschal in Gascony.[45] This may have created alarming suspicions, because at this same time Simon de Montfort also went abroad. His rapprochement with the Lusignans the year before had already caused concerns. A firm alliance between Simon, Edward and the Lusignans could only spell trouble. In fact,

Simon did not travel alone. Eleanor went with him, and they were not there to make common cause with her half-brothers, rather to sue them.

It went back to the 1242 Poitevin expedition. At some point, sensing the disaster that the Lusignans had brought on themselves by their defiance of the French Crown, Isabella of Angoulême prevailed upon her son Henry to renounce any claims to her land and castles and to have her other children with King John, Richard of Cornwall and Eleanor, to do the same. Neither had renounced by the time Isabella died in 1246 and she left them out of her will.

Eleanor decided to launch a lawsuit for a share of her mother's estate in Angoulême as another hopeful means of increasing her and Simon's landed wealth for their family of five sons and one daughter. Naturally an arbitration panel was set up and in November 1260, Guy and Geoffrey Lusignan and William de Valence found surety for their oaths to observe whatever award came of it. Eleanor was to go to Poitiers in January to present her case.[46]

Aymer was left out of the suit because he was a churchman and still committed to reclaiming his diocese of Winchester. He had spent much of the two years of his exile at the papal court and won favour there. Earlier in May, Pope Alexander IV decided to speed up his return to England by consecrating him bishop. The move was seen as a threat. Unless Aymer was allowed to come back and put on his pontificals, England would face interdict, something Henry would never stand for. Queen Eleanor was just going to have to accept the fact that her hated enemy would soon be in her midst again.

And then, out of nowhere, came word that on 4 December 1260, Aymer died suddenly in Paris. Henry mourned the loss of his brother and had 10,000 of the poor fed at Winchester and Oxford in his memory, but otherwise he saw it as his chance to end the feud between his wife and half-brothers. Peter of Savoy had just arrived from the Continent, perhaps timed so he would not have to face John of Brittany, and was also told to get over it. Peace between the Lusignans and Savoyards was essential if they were going to get Edward to drop his rebelliousness and infatuation with Montfort. Eleanor nevertheless demanded that each Lusignan give assurances of good faith to her sister Margaret in France before proceeding to England. William de Valence balked at what he saw as a degrading submission, but he and his brothers eventually undertook it.[47]

It was going to be a fine Christmas that year for the queen, with both her daughters and youngest son at court. The weather, moreover, had been its most agreeable in years. Says *Flores*, 'there was such softness in the air that you would have said it was the pleasant time of summer rather than winter'. The family moved to Windsor for Margaret's confinement and there in February 1261, she gave birth to a daughter named after herself. Henry and Eleanor's elation in becoming grandparents for the first time can be seen in his grant of a pension to the man who brought the king the news.[48]

Henry resurgent, Simon and Eleanor go into exile, the queen asserts her authority

Edward was not expected for the Candlemas Parliament in February, but Simon and Clare were and they would surely seek to resurrect the council, which had ceased to function before Christmas. Henry and his circle of advisers—Richard of Cornwall, Peter of Savoy, Mansel, Walerand and, of course, the queen—devised a plan where the king would do it for them, but only for the purpose of accusing the council of misconduct. This would keep the barons on the defensive until the masterstroke of their plan was ready.

In late January, Mansel's nephew, also named John, left for Rome. His mission was to have the pope nullify the Provisions of Oxford and absolve everyone from the king downward of their oaths to protect and maintain them. Since outrage was sure to ensue when that happened, possibly even violence if Simon got his way, Henry moved to the Tower for most of the negotiations. By the end of March, Parliament was at an impasse over how to make reform work while at the same time respecting and maintaining the king's dignity and authority.[49]

In April, Edward returned from the Continent with William de Valence, who was restored to favour upon his oath to observe the Provisions of Oxford. He probably enjoyed the irony that, less than a month later, papal bulls arrived from Alexander IV absolving him, the queen and the rest of the realm of their oaths. By this point Henry had a body of foreign knights with him in case of trouble and in early June he went to Winchester to publish the bulls. It would be the city of his birth and rebirth. His wife followed and reached Sutton on 4 June for a social call. Eleanor de Montfort had a manor there, but the queen arrived to meet the Count of St Pol, who commanded the knightly force.[50]

The success of Henry's recovery of power depended on Edward, and the king's complaints against the barons in Parliament suggest he still could not be sure of his son's loyalty. The very confused account given by *Flores* says Edward renewed his oath and joined up again with Montfort and Clare to oppose his parents. Whether any of that was true, he was in Winchester when the bulls were published. The *Annals of London* credit Eleanor with having turned him around through 'flattery', which hints that she finally said something nice about his Lusignan uncles, but what certainly helped was a bailout.

Edward had returned from France broke and heavily in debt. He needed large injections of cash and Henry was willing to provide them, but only on the understanding that he became the dutiful and obedient heir expected of him. Edward took the deal and headed back to the Continent the next month, presumably so he would not have to look his uncle Simon in the face. His wife Eleanor of Castile was with him and gave birth abroad to the queen's second granddaughter. She was named Katherine, possibly in memory of Edward's sister.[51]

Simon de Montfort was by all accounts in a furious mood that summer. As early as May, he suspected what Henry was up to and made provisions to bring in his own mercenaries. He had been the main target of the king's wrath when Henry assailed his barons in Parliament and Simon had been sufficiently unnerved by it to accept an offer, already two months old, to let Louis mediate the dispute between him and Eleanor on one side and her brother on the other.

He naturally viewed the publication of the papal absolution on 12 June 1261 as a betrayal and he was not alone. The Earls of Gloucester, Norfolk and Surrey, all grandsons of William Marshal it should be noted, joined their fellow Earl of Leicester, along with others, in a new confederacy of resistance, but Henry outflanked them by retreating to the Tower. They would have to go to war to get him to come out and talk and that they were loath to do. To attack him in the Tower, or anywhere, meant disinheritance and forfeiture of title.[52]

Henry had not done away with the popular aspects of reform in any event. He did not abolish the offices of state, he just demanded the right to appoint the men who filled them. But even here his first appointees, Philip Basset as justiciar and Walter Merton as chancellor, were wholly acceptable to the barons. It was only Simon pushing for militant action, again because he was a disgruntled sort who was after some glittering prize for himself and his wife.

To pacify him and Eleanor, if that was even possible, Henry agreed that a new arbitration panel might settle their personal quarrels by 1 November. Where it differed from the earlier attempts is that two French mediators were to be brought in, and one of them, the Duke of Burgundy, was another good friend of the Montforts. Failing that, Queen Margaret might ultimately decide.[53]

Meanwhile, the queen busied herself with preparations to send Beatrice to her husband in Brittany, where John had gone after winding up his tournament exploits. Eleanor gave her daughter some seventy rings to distribute as gifts to the new household she was about to enter, and she may have also given her a book of hours (illuminated prayer book) made special for Beatrice that survives to this day. The princess was accompanied across the Channel in late July by Ebulo de Montibus, a Savoyard protégé of the queen, and in a sign of the new unity between the former antagonists at court, their party was met by Geoffrey Lusignan in Nantes. In a letter to Henry, Geoffrey noted that Montibus arrived with a fever and that he caught it from him, but otherwise the visit went very well.[54]

Back in England, the situation was now as close to war as it had been since Richard Marshal's uprising nearly three decades earlier. The king controlled Dover, but Montfort and Clare secured the other Channel ports, and Henry suspected that Simon had gone abroad to recruit mercenaries. When the king appointed his own sheriffs, the barons responded by naming anti-sheriffs, or 'keepers' of the counties. Only one local confrontation occurred between these opposing factions, in Gloucester, where another member of the queen's household, her steward Matthias Bezill, was serving as sheriff. When Bezill learned that the baronial keeper was holding court there, he and his deputies broke in, grabbed the keeper, and flung him into the mud outside.[55]

Simon's boldest move was to summon Parliament without the king. Together with Clare and Walter Cantilupe, he had the keepers invite three knights from each county to come to St Albans on 21 September to discuss the situation. Henry put a stop to it by inviting the knights to meet him at Parliament in Windsor instead. Then, for the regular October Parliament, he summoned loyalist barons to come armed and ready for action.

Behind the scenes, Eleanor lobbied those in the middle with help from Mansel, 'who would do his utmost for the queen', says the Waverley annalist. Her biggest success was with Clare, who defected after undergoing what the Dunstable annalist describes as 'a kind of apostasy'. According to the Battle chronicle, the Earl of Gloucester was won over 'by promises or favour of the queen'.[56]

By December, the standoff was over. The baronial side agreed to a compromise that provided for Richard of Cornwall to break any tie in the subsequent negotiations on the Provisions of Oxford and everything else. This all but guaranteed victory for the king. For Simon, it was another betrayal, for even his steadfast supporters Walter Cantilupe and Peter de Montfort went along with the agreement sealed at Kingston-on-Thames on 21 November 1261. Finding himself completely isolated politically, Simon made a speech about preferring to die landless than to abandon the truth and so took Eleanor and the children and abandoned England.[57]

In December, the king and queen left the Tower and took up their normal residence at Westminster, where the miserable face of winter painted on the mantle of her fireplace awaited Eleanor. There had been a personal loss for her through all of this. On 9 November, Sanchia of Provence died after a long illness, aged around 33. The sisters had remained close since she arrived in England eighteen years earlier, but the political situation did not allow Henry and Eleanor to attend her funeral at Hailes Abbey in Gloucestershire. They had masses said for her soul at the Tower and ordered a service conducted in her memory later at Westminster. Richard of Cornwall, who seems to have been an indifferent husband, was also absent, having chosen to attend business matters in London.[58]

The plan to restore the Crown to full power and authority had been wildly successful. The nobles were cowed, the number one troublemaker was in self-imposed exile, and the royal couple had pulled it off without any violence or bloodshed. Almost missed in the tension and excitement was Eleanor of Provence's other triumph that year, one that was equally controversial and left some members of the clergy so contemptuous of her that they began to denigrate her with innuendo.

It involved the hospital of St Katharine by the Tower of London, which had earlier turned to the queen with complaints that their patrons, the canons of Holy Trinity Aldgate, had acted disgracefully in imposing one of their own as the master of the hospital. Sometime just before the death of her daughter Katherine on 3 May 1257, Eleanor made a bid to take control of the hospital. In a letter to Fulk Basset, the Bishop of London and brother of Philip, she based her claim on the fact that the hospital had been founded by Queen Matilda, the wife of King Stephen, even though Matilda had entrusted it to Holy Trinity. Fulk took disciplinary action against the priory but seems to have ignored Eleanor's claim.

In 1260, the deceased Fulk was succeeded as bishop by Henry Wengham, long a close friend and adviser of the queen. After securing the support of two other bishops and members of her council, Eleanor struck the following year. She had these men summon the new Prior of Holy Trinity to get him to sign over the hospital to her. Although reluctant, he gave way and from that point on St Katharine's fell under the patronage of the queens of England.

The prior later claimed he cracked under pressure. The bishops and councillors repeatedly threatened him with the king's displeasure unless he cooperated. They gave no specific proof of what action Henry might take except to say that the king's will had the force of law and the queen was his 'night bird' (*nycticorax*), meaning she would exploit the mood in the royal bedchamber until she got her way. While the prior was clearly making excuses for his submissiveness, the view of Eleanor of Provence as a seductress now began to take hold among monastic chroniclers. Indeed, it was at this time that Battle Abbey insinuated she had used favours of this sort to get Richard de Clare to defect to the king.[59]

The scandalous talk, which must have reached her ears, was not going to slow her down. There was still unfinished business requiring her attention. Henry and Eleanor had not heard the last of Simon and Eleanor de Montfort, that they could be sure of, and the other bad influences on Edward also had to be dealt with before their son returned from the Continent and fell in with those ruffians again.

Experience might have informed the queen to proceed cautiously. The last time she attempted to purge Edward's household and cut loose his dangerous friends led to the revolution of 1258. She seems to have had little inkling that something similar might ensue from interfering in her son's life again. But she was who she was and nothing, not even a premonition of the consequences about to befall the realm on account of her actions, was likely to deter her.

9

Rapacious Turbulence 1262–1264

*More failed arbitrations, another trip to France,
a new breed of malcontents*

This was the second voluntary exile for Eleanor de Montfort. She went abroad first with Simon in 1239 after Henry denounced them at the queen's churching and did not return for four years. Her husband's standing and wider contacts in the country of his birth and upbringing gave the Montforts a greater freedom of opposition to Henry's regime not available to other English baronial families. They were, moreover, welcomed by Louis, who evidently gave them one of his castles in Normandy as their residence.

For Eleanor, home in France also put her in a better position to pursue her suit against her Lusignan half-brothers. The first arbitration had ended in no judgement or one not to her liking, so she renewed her efforts in 1262 and presented her case before the central court in Paris. She and Simon also wrote to Alphonse of Poitiers, the overlord of Angoulême, to enlist his support. All that came out of it was more arbitration.[1]

The arbitration they wanted the most took a step closer in January when Simon and Eleanor, then staying in Normandy, accepted Margaret's offer to adjudicate their dispute with Henry in Paris. There was no guarantee Henry was going to accept because it was not the best time for him to travel abroad. The reforms over the past four years had left a deep impression in the shires. So great was the concern that he might try to undo all the good work that in May he again publicly expressed his full observance of Magna Carta. He also ordered the arrest of anyone denouncing his resumption of personal rule. He had in mind the preachers who worked against him in the countryside at that time, no doubt with the full support of bishops like Walter Cantilupe of Worcester and Richard Gravesend of Lincoln. Both clerics were Simon's close friends and allies.[2]

Henry decided to accept so that he could use the arbitration to expose Montfort as a disloyal and dangerous subject in the eyes of the French court. The friendship Simon and Eleanor enjoyed with the King and Queen of France must have been galling to the King and Queen of England, but it did not alter the relationship between the royal couples. Henry and Eleanor's trip to Paris would be as much about seeing and being with Louis and Margaret as it was about dealing with that other pair. Certainly the exchange of gifts and letters hint at some subtle flirtation between Henry and Margaret. How far that might have worked in Henry's favour is debatable, because Simon had already shown that when it came to courtroom drama, he had no equal.[3]

The arbitration got underway in August 1262. Henry's proctors had prepared an elaborate case showing his generosity to Simon and all the insolence and ingratitude he received in return. Simon responded that the king got only what he deserved. He even suggested that it was Henry's idea that he and Eleanor get married. 'It pleased him graciously to give me his sister in marriage', he recalled in his deposition. He bitterly added that there were people at court who tried to discredit Eleanor when she claimed that her fee was a gift and not compensation for her dower. He also made sure to inform Margaret that it was her mother, Beatrice of Provence, who ultimately shamed Henry into treating his sister with the same kindness he showered on others.[4]

The proceedings were interrupted in early September when the English party was felled by an epidemic. Henry, Edmund and Mansel were all affected and some sixty individuals succumbed to the disease. It may have been thought that the king was on his deathbed and so it was time to act on his promise twenty years earlier to increase his wife's dower allotment. Her allocation in England was now extended to cover his lands in Ireland and Gascony as well, raising her settlement from the £1,000 at the beginning of her marriage to £4,000, a very impressive sum. The charter was enrolled on 10 October 1262, after Henry had fully recovered and was therefore cognizant of the details.[5]

All this extra money was to come out of Edward's inheritance, but he added his seal to the document. It could not have been out of gratitude to his mother for her recent labours to rescue him from bankruptcy. The climb down from opposition to his father had left Edward so demoralised that he resigned full control of his household and finances to his parents.

It began in the summer of 1261, when Eleanor cut him adrift from his Marcher friends and Henry went further by ordering an audit of their accounts. Leybourne and his brother-in-law Roger Clifford were among those targeted and disgraced. Edward failed to stand by them, either because he believed the charge that they had embezzled funds from him or it was all the malicious talk of his mother, as one chronicler asserts. Either way, they were left seething and embittered.[6]

This new group of malcontents received an unexpected addition to their ranks just as Henry and Eleanor sailed to France. On 14 July 1262, Richard de Clare died. Only 40-years old, he seems to have been ill for some time, probably having never fully recovered from what nearly killed him four years earlier in Winchester. His half-brother Henry of Almain accompanied Clare's 19-year-old son Gilbert to the king to be confirmed as the new Earl of Gloucester, but Richard had used reform to expand his estates at the expense of the Crown and there was also the dower allotment for Gilbert's mother Maud that needed to be considered. Henry wanted a survey done first, which is exactly what Gilbert did not want. Told to be patient, he went back to England angry and disappointed. Henry of Almain also felt snubbed, not just by the king, but by his cousin Edward as well. He too returned in a sour and festering mood.[7]

All this happened before Henry fell ill. By the time he recovered, Simon had abandoned the arbitration and was back in England. Henry suspected he was out to stir up trouble at the October Parliament, which he apparently did despite the treasurer receiving orders to authorise the payment of Eleanor's dower. Mansel urged Henry to go home to deal with the new unrest, but the king decided to make a pilgrimage to Reims.

Not until December was the English royal party ready to sail. Henry wrote to Louis to arrange a final meeting, adding his hope that Margaret would be there because 'we much desire to see her and bid mutual farewells'. She came to the meeting at Compiègne with a special parting gift for Henry, a ruby ring worth about £10,000 in today's money.[8]

Henry and Eleanor arrived on 20 December to a kingdom beset by problems. It was so cold that winter that the Thames froze over for three weeks and looked as if safe passage from side to side might be possible. On 7 February 1263, much of Westminster Palace outside of the Great Hall and exchequer caught fire. The most serious problem was in the marches, where fighting had broken out again after the Welsh tenants of Roger Mortimer, who was himself half-Welsh, rose in revolt earlier in November. Llywelyn was able to make great advances in part because the Marchers alienated by the Crown refused to help other local lords like Peter de Montfort and Peter d'Aigueblanche, the Bishop of Hereford, put up an adequate defence. Henry fell ill again and was unable to go there himself. He had to berate his son by letter into coming home and defending his lands.[9]

There was some good news from Scotland. On 21 January 1263, Margaret gave birth to a boy and heir named Alexander after his father. He was not Henry and Eleanor's first grandson. Earlier in July 1262, just as the king and queen arrived in France, Beatrice gave birth to her first child, a boy called Arthur after the tragic brother of Eleanor of Brittany. At this time Beatrice's mother-in-law wrote to Henry and Eleanor with news that their daughter was also ill, but improving. Arthur, she added, 'is a very good child, and very pretty, thank God'.[10]

The unfinished business of the Montforts beckoned and in January Henry made one last attempt at appeasement. He freely reissued the Provisions of Westminster as an act of good faith towards reform and dispatched two envoys to make Simon and Eleanor an offer of restitution. Interestingly, he told the envoys that they should consult Queen Margaret first. For her part, Margaret asked them not to speak to Louis about the matter unless she was present.

These conditions were met and Louis later had a private talk with Simon, who told him that he was sure Henry wanted only the best for him and Eleanor. There were others around the king, he believed, who were of a different mind. He asked Louis to bother no more and the envoys returned home with no deal. They did, however, bring Henry a letter from Margaret describing how she had sunk into her own sorrow on news of his illness, but with his recovery came hers as well.[11]

Whatever ailed the king, it seems to have been serious enough for the Tewkesbury annalist to pronounce him dead on 23 March 1263. He was remembered as a strenuous ruler and supporter of widows and orphans among other things. Other annals noted that Richard of Cornwall had returned from Germany and assumed that it was to succeed his brother.

This was strange since Edward was not only alive but he also arrived at this time. He had with him a body of foreign knights he intended to use in launching a counterattack against the Welsh. He did not bother with his former Marcher friends, who were best placed for the offensive. For Leybourne, Clifford and the others, this was the last straw, and Gilbert de Clare felt the same. When Henry ordered the magnates to Westminster to do homage to Edward, Gilbert, nicknamed 'Red' on account of his ginger hair, refused to oblige.[12]

While Edward struggled in his drive against the Welsh, these malcontents formulated a plan to avenge themselves on the royal family. They were joined by Henry of Almain and John de Warenne, who had also been curtly dismissed by the queen and Edward. None of these men had the prestige or skill to pull something like this off, but Simon de Montfort did. As a political exile of sorts, he would ennoble what was otherwise an ignoble cause. They sent feelers out and he responded. On 25 April 1263, the Montforts returned home, and England was about to be changed forever.[13]

Upheaval, Edward's heist, the infamous bridge incident, Montfort triumphant

It had been almost five years to the day since Simon and a group of magnates marched on Westminster and demanded reform. He had been one among peers, now he was the undisputed leader. The underlying goal then had been to get rid of the Lusignans, now it was to get rid of the Savoyards. The latter had had the Marchers purged, now it was their turn. The malcontents made an exception for the queen and her immediate family, but the others were fair game, including her uncle Boniface, the Archbishop of Canterbury.

The queen's English allies like Mansel, Walerand and Langley were also targeted. Simon and his cohorts had no fear that the rebellion they were about to raise would lead to the chopping block. Political executions were unheard of in that age, although that would change because of these events. The Provisions of Oxford demanded they proscribe their enemies and that was all they intended to do. Oxford, fittingly, was their staging point.[14]

But the driving force was not just the Marchers and their vendetta against the queen. Robert de Ferrers, the Earl of Derby, had his own vendetta against Edward, and John de Warenne, the Earl of Surrey, had one against Peter of Savoy. The churchmen in their group had vendettas against the pope and foreign priests, and the knights against their Jewish creditors. And of course, there was the biggest vendetta of them all, Simon's against the king.

Joining them were disgruntled agitators looking to settle scores with neighbours, relatives or local officials. Some did not have vendettas, like day labourers, drifters and louts from town and village. They were in it for the pillage and violence. There may have been some idealism in the younger novices among the barons, knights and clerks who really did believe in the Provisions of Oxford as something akin to Magna Carta, but the chronicler Thomas Wykes saw them as unwitting fools in Simon's hands and so dismissed them as gullible punks.[15]

In early June, the shock troops went into action against two high-profile Savoyards, Peter d'Aigueblanche in Hereford and Matthias Bezill in Gloucester. Both men were imprisoned, their lands plundered. By the middle of the month, a line of destruction began moving westward, gaining in strength and momentum thanks to what had become open season on any foreigner. Henry scrambled to confront the violence and tried to get Simon to talk about it. On 16 June, he sent him and Eleanor a safe-conduct to visit him and the queen and to bring their children and households, but unarmed, naturally. He saw the entire Montfort family as the command centre of this blitzkrieg and was probably hoping against hope he could persuade them to remember their ties of family. Certainly he saw his sister and her organisational skills as part of the operation, whether in requisitioning men and supplies or dispatching the messages that turned all the local uprisings into a full-scale upheaval.[16]

On 19 June, the king and queen moved to the Tower. Five days later Simon sent a letter, not to them but to the people of London demanding to know where they stood in this conflict. Fearing the anti-foreigner hysteria already sweeping through the city, the ruling class under Mayor Thomas Fitz-Thomas informed the king that they too wished to abide by the Provisions of Oxford. That left the royal party in the Tower desperate. Supplies and money were running low, none of the wealthy merchant families would extend them credit, and they were surrounded by an increasingly hostile crowd.[17]

An evacuation was ordered. Boniface had already fled to France, now Mansel followed with several 'ladies from overseas' placed in his care by the queen. Mansel was hated as any foreigner and his flight galvanised the Montfortians. Henry of Almain, probably at Simon's orders, took off after him, but the queen learned of his pursuit and had Almain arrested and imprisoned by a Savoyard knight upon his landing on the Continent.

Almain's father Richard of Cornwall had also left the Tower, telling Henry he would try to seek peace with Simon. In fact, he may have gone to warn him that Edward was talking about meeting the rebellious tide head on with his foreign knights. Never conspicuously loyal to his brother, Richard was placed at the conference in Oxford by the Dunstable annalist and the pope later denounced him for his role in the turmoil.[18]

Edmund had gone with Mansel and the ladies as far as Dover so he could secure it for the arrival of mercenaries. But bringing them in took time and money, none of which Henry had. The huddle in the Tower therefore decided on a new plan of action. On 29 June, Edward, Walerand and their knightly contingent rode to the New Temple on the outskirts of London's walls. Under the pretence of wanting to check up on the queen's jewels, they gained access to the vaults, broke open the chests, and hauled away £1,000 in deposits. They continued on to Windsor but were too late to intercept the advancing insurgents. Simon had turned his course southward to the Channel ports to cut off the king from receiving outside help.[19]

The situation in London had been jittery enough on account of the presence of Edward's foreign knights. Their departure was welcome, but when the populace learned that they and the heir to the throne had pulled off the heist at the New Temple, the city erupted in rioting and looting. The properties of royalists were specifically ransacked, but roving bands helped themselves to whatever lay in their path.

Simon by now was in reach of Dover and paused only long enough to allow his men to have a go at the estates of Boniface and his brother Peter, the latter having returned to his native Savoy the year before. Acting through the bishops, he sent terms to Henry calling on him to inviolably observe the Provisions of Oxford and expel all foreigners except those deemed fit to stay. On 4 July, the king told his proctors to sue for peace.[20]

Although he had little choice otherwise, Henry probably hoped that forgoing any prolonged standoff would help quiet the situation. If anything, it worsened with the approach of Montfort's army. Save for attendants and the garrison, Henry and Eleanor were all alone in the Tower, unnerved no doubt by the crowds roaming the streets below looking for foreigners to harass and despoil, all the while the officials looked the other way. According to *Flores*, 'whoever was unable to speak the English language, was considered a vile and contemptible person by the common people'.[21]

It seems improbable that Eleanor of Provence would have picked up no English after living over two decades in the country, especially in the company of servants and administrators all the time, but it would not have helped her in any case. The hatred of foreigners now focused on her because she was the most visible among them, the source of all the freeloading courtiers and priests speaking gibberish. As the consort who had the ear of the king, moreover, the queen was seen as equally responsible for the policies that had aroused Simon and his men to action. The Melrose chronicler did not mince any words about it. 'Eleanor, the Queen of England, was believed to be the root, the fomenter, and the sower of all the discord which existed between Henry, the King of England, and the barons of his realm.'[22]

On 12 July, Simon reached Canterbury and was informed that London stood with him. News of the complete isolation of the king and queen likely drew cheers and taunts from the crowds below. At some point Henry and Eleanor must have decided it was no longer safe for her in the city and the next day a barge with rowers and attendants left the wharf to ferry her upstream to Windsor.

Seeing what was up, the people on London Bridge and those in a sprint to join them picked up whatever objects were at hand. As the craft approached, they began cursing the queen with shouts of 'whore' and 'temptress' and pelting her and the other occupants with mud, stones and rotten eggs. They let loose a torrent of abuse and projectiles without a thought for the disaster it might cause or the consequences sure to follow from it. Twenty-seven years earlier, they had welcomed Eleanor, then a young girl from Provence, with a dazzling display of splendour and kindness. Now she was subjected to this appalling spectacle, but those Londoners who witnessed both events probably found the grimmer and grimier of the two to have been much more entertaining.

Mayor Fitz-Thomas had helped unleash the mob with his populism, now he had to find a way to save the queen from it if he hoped to keep his head, much less his job. He organised a rescue party, but the king, worried the mob might overwhelm them if they tried to dock at the wharf, ordered him to take her to St Paul's.[23] They eventually got her there and she later rejoined her husband at the Tower, presumably under armed escort.

The Montfortian army entered London in triumph on 15 July. Simon walked into the Tower the next day and asked Henry if he accepted the terms, which included freeing Henry of Almain and surrendering Dover. The king simply replied, 'Yes'. It is presumed that neither Eleanor was present at what must have been an angry and awkward interview.[24]

The Montforts were likely as shocked and dismayed as anyone over the indignity inflicted on the queen at the bridge. Simon's whole strategy of seizing control of the government had depended on no confrontation with the royal family. He counted on them retreating to the Tower and staying there out of harm's way until he came knocking at the gate. The shameful incident would cost him dearly in the eyes of Louis and Margaret and other admirers who were not necessarily committed to his cause. It also took the feud between the Montforts and royal family to an entirely new level of personal hostility and put an end to whatever equivalency Edward had about supporting his parents. From then on he was an implacable foe of his uncle and former ally, and London too for that matter.

No one needed to tell Simon that. His first order of business was prising Edward and his knights out of Windsor Castle. In that atmosphere, Henry was worried it could end badly like his siege of Bedford nearly four decades earlier. Having moved back to Westminster with Eleanor, he rode out to Windsor with Simon and his forces to make sure it did not end in a bloodbath. The castle was surrendered without a fight, something Edward had not planned for judging by the way he sulked off instead of taking official leave of his knights. It was up to the queen to step in and she did so gracefully, handing out gifts of rings to the knights before they were escorted to the coast and told never to return.[25]

Under Montfort's regime, letting Louis decide, reclaiming the kingdom

Eleanor of Provence seemed to have quickly recovered from the trauma of the bridge. She may have even beheld the annular solar eclipse on 5 August 1263 as a sign of better times ahead. As expected, Montfort had taken control of the ministries and royal castles, but perhaps in a move at reconciliation, he and his handpicked council awarded the marriage of 26-year-old Isabella de Forz to Edmund, now 18. Isabella had inherited two earldoms, Aumale from her husband William, and Devon from her brother Baldwin de Redvers, Eleanor's former ward, who died in the epidemic that almost killed Henry the year before.[26] Edmund would become an earl twice over by right of his wife and in this way receive the rich endowment he had been lacking, which perhaps had informed the decision to try and buy for him the kingdom of Sicily.

Through all the troubles of the past few years, Henry and Eleanor never abandoned the Sicilian project, and when Pope Alexander IV died in May 1261, they appealed to his successor, Urban IV, to re-issue their absolution from the Provisions of Oxford and to revive Edmund's claim to the island throne. Urban's decision was a long time coming in part because Simon had planted an agent in Rome to work against Henry's interests. The agent tricked Urban into confirming the king and queen's oath to the Provisions instead of absolving them of it. Henry's proctors eventually sorted it out, but that confusion alone must have convinced Urban that the Plantagenet couple and their son did not have it together to make Sicily work, if they ever did. On 28 July 1263, the pope wrote to say he was cancelling Edmund's claim, not adding that he had rightly concluded that only Charles of Anjou stood any chance of making it work.[27]

One act of the new government the queen could only have found distasteful was the appointment of Roger Leybourne as the steward of the royal household. The thug who helped mastermind her fall would be insinuated into her private life. In fact, he probably was not the council's choice for the position, rather the Marchers demanded it as reward for their support. They had never been reformers. They got mixed up with the Montfortians to teach the royal family a lesson. With that accomplished, they wanted to be friends again with the future king and Leybourne would use his proximity to Edward to make it happen. If that meant ditching the Provisions of Oxford, so be it.[28]

Simon might reasonably hope that the humiliation felt by Eleanor and her son went too deep for any grovelling the Marchers were prepared to do, but Henry was a different story. He had come further than any English king before him by virtue of his instinct for survival and forgiveness. He had persuaded Eleanor to drop her loathing for the Lusignans in order to win Edward back into the fold and that had been successful.

But where the Lusignans had been grasping competitors, the miscreant Marchers had abused her family and friends and had them imprisoned or chased out of the country. The thought of working with these swine was more than a matter of swallowing her pride and disgust. Try to think of the bigger picture, my lady, Henry might have urged her. Edward was easily won over and negotiations to reconcile him to the Marchers began in the middle of August.[29] Eleanor ultimately knew it was the only way to go, but better she did not have to look at Leybourne in the process.

The answer was to go abroad and stay there for the time being. Louis had a man in England at the time and it was possibly through him that Henry and Eleanor arranged to have Louis summon Henry to France. The higher French nobility would be gathered in Boulogne to discuss a new crusade and Henry as the Duke of Aquitaine was one of them. But Louis also let it be known that, as Henry's overlord, he wanted an explanation about all the disturbances going on over there. Simon was keen not to offend Louis and tried stalling him, but the council agreed that the royal family could go on their oath to return by a certain deadline. Simon would lead a baronial delegation to provide their side of the story.[30]

On 23 September, Henry, Eleanor, Edward and Edmund crossed over. Louis, Margaret, her mother Beatrice, and exiles like Mansel and Boniface were there to receive them. It can only be imagined how Eleanor recalled her terror at the bridge to her sister and mother. Both were scandalised. Twenty years previously Beatrice had made a personal appeal on behalf of Simon and Eleanor de Montfort and this is how they repaid her?

Margaret put her fury into action by pestering her brother-in-law Alphonse of Poitiers to requisition ships so they could prepare an invasion force if necessary. She also demanded and got Louis to arraign the Montfortians on charges of rebellion against their lord. Simon scoffed at the notion of any authority outside of England judging what went on inside it. In the proceedings that followed, Louis not only agreed with him, but according to the Tewkesbury annalist, he approved both the Provisions and rule of the native-born.[31]

The queens may not have been able to get Louis to condemn Simon, but Boulogne had been no defeat. As probably planned in advance, Eleanor did not follow her husband and son home. She had taken an oath to return, but dispensations from the pope were easy to obtain and hers came in December. By remaining on the Continent, she could build support against the Montfortians while removed from the dirty business of pardoning and absorbing the Marchers into a plan to drive Simon from power. Edmund also stayed behind to offer her the solace of family and to be surety for any extreme idea Simon may get about eliminating members of the royal family to seize the throne for his son Henry de Montfort, who was fifth in line.[32]

Events moved swiftly after Henry and Edward returned for Parliament on 13 October. The king made sure it was a stormy affair by refusing to countenance anyone but himself naming his ministers and household. The calls for justice by the people who had been despoiled during the disturbances left the Montfortians isolated. As if on cue, Edward stole away two days later and seized Windsor Castle. Henry followed him there the next morning with senior members of the nobility.

By the end of the month, the Marchers had received full pardons and joined them. Henry bribed his brother Richard of Cornwall into deserting Simon and Edward did the same to his cousin Henry of Almain and other followers of Montfort. Young Henry's conscience nevertheless compelled him to tell Simon how painful the decision had been for him. Simon just laughed and told him to get lost.[33]

While Henry set about reclaiming the offices of government and boxing the Montfortians into an ever smaller corner, Eleanor, Margaret and Louis appealed to the pope to dispatch a legate to England to help restore peace and tranquillity to the kingdom. Urban obliged on 22 November by appointing Frenchman Guy Foulquois, the Bishop of Sabina, to the post. One of the letters announcing his appointment was sent to Simon, who the pope understood was the 'chief among the disturbers of the realm'.

Given the violence meted out to Bishop Peter of Hereford, who fled to France the moment he was released from prison, and the general havoc wreaked on Church properties, Simon and his men could expect the severest of ecclesiastical penalties from the legate. Running out of options, they agreed that Louis could arbitrate the dispute between them and the king. Both sides would again go to France, only this time sworn to abide by whatever judgement Louis awarded.[34]

They had just been down that road and Simon had somehow persuaded Louis of the justice of his cause. Margaret and Eleanor were determined not to let that happen again when they all gathered in Amiens in January 1264. Henry was actually counting on Eleanor coming home before then and marched to Dover on 3 December to ensure her passage and that of the exiles. He had four earls and a large force of men with him but the Montfortian garrison was not impressed and refused to hand over the castle. Henry could not storm the place because there was a truce in effect, so he was forced to tell Eleanor to wait a little longer.[35]

Simon was at Kenilworth, presumably with his Eleanor although there is no indication of her whereabouts at this time. Their four oldest sons, aged from 19 to 25, had been very much a part of Simon's seizure of power and were rewarded as a result. The younger Simon received the custody of Mansel's lands and Amaury a prebend at St Paul's. This family enrichment naturally drew comment, even from those opposed to the king.

As the desertions mounted, Simon declared it made no difference, he was sworn to his cause and his sons (and wife) were standing firmly by him. But he realised the danger he was in. When Henry convened Parliament at Reading, he refused to attend for fear of being arrested. The king's attempt to take Dover sounded like war to him and he gathered what men and arms he could and went back to London.[36]

Henry ordered the mayor to throw them out and proceeded there himself to make sure it happened. At Croydon, he was informed that the Montfortians were encamped at Southwark and that a plot had been hatched to chain the gates to the bridge. Safety behind the walls of London would be barred to them. With the king coming up from the south and Edward from Windsor, Simon found he was trapped. Told to surrender, he said 'never' and prepared to make a last stand. He and his men made a lucky escape, however, when some citizens on the bridge managed to get the gates open at the last minute.[37]

Still anxious to keep Simon from appearing before Louis at the arbitration, Henry already had a Plan B in the works. It involved three of the nine manors Henry had been forced to cede to his sister four years earlier to gain her cooperation in the peace treaty negotiations. They were located in Herefordshire, not far from the landed estate of Roger Mortimer, a leading Marcher who had kept mostly aloof during the reform period and who did not associate with Leybourne's group.

The king told Mortimer he could have the three manors if he could take them, but it had to be now. Henry hoped Simon's pride would lead him to the marches to defend his properties rather than go abroad for the arbitration. Mortimer attacked, but Montfort, realising like everyone else that a favourable ruling from Louis depended on him being at Amiens, did not take the bait. As it was, he suffered a riding accident on his way to catch a boat over and was taken back to Kenilworth with a broken leg.[38]

Mise of Amiens, civil war, Battle of Lewes, Montfort's second regime

The queen and other exiles met Henry and Edward in Amiens in early January. Neither man was looking good after encountering a fierce storm in the Channel, but they probably began to feel better when they noticed Simon missing among the Montfortian delegation. Henry de Montfort was there, a very well-educated young man, but the presentation of their case was entrusted to Thomas Cantilupe, the nephew of Bishop Walter of Worcester. He had studied in France and knew Louis personally, so it was hoped that that might count for something as the arbitration got underway.[39]

Walter Merton, the chancellor, put forward the king's case to Louis. The Provisions of Oxford infringed traditional royal rights and were contrary to the nature of kingship in general, he said. In demanding the outlawry of anyone who opposed them, the barons had set the realm on a course for destruction. The Provisions ought to be quashed and the barons forced to pay damages.

For his part, Cantilupe described Henry's rule as oppressive and irresponsible. Had he been fairer with wardships, less beholden to foreigners, and vigilant about justice for all, there would be no Provisions. Cantilupe cunningly argued that the Provisions were basically the executive enforcement that Magna Carta had always lacked. He indicated to Louis that messing with the Provisions was messing with Magna Carta and that would be like opening up a whole new can of worms.[40]

Since his judgement in favour of Simon in September, Louis had been under pressure from Margaret, Eleanor and the pope to reverse himself and he chose to do so in the award he issued on 23 January 1264. He quashed the Provisions of Oxford in their entirety, as well as any statutes arising from them that called for the banishment of aliens. Although he did not have to justify his decision, Louis claimed he was doing nothing more than what the pope had already done before him. To the Montfortians, he added the nice-try-guys proviso that his ruling, known as the Mise of Amiens, was totally exclusive of Magna Carta and other ordinances that pre-dated the reform period. They had nothing to do with this case.[41]

Back home, the news was received with disbelief. The Dunstable annalist accused Louis of caving in to pressure from the two sister queens, while the Tewkesbury annalist put the blame solely on Eleanor of Provence. She deceived him with 'the serpent-like speech and fraud of woman', bewailed the anonymous monk. This allusion to Eve and the Garden of Eden was meant to cast whatever influence Eleanor may have had in a sinister light. She did not throw herself at the feet of the King of France and plead with him on behalf of her husband, which would have been understandable and forgivable, rather she beguiled him with honeyed phrases and fork-tongued persuasion. Evidently the temptress who had been stoned by the mob at the bridge had lost none of her seductive power.[42]

Although the Montfortians were sworn to abide by the arbitration, they used the link between the Provisions of Oxford and Magna Carta as an escape clause for their oaths and simply ignored the Mise of Amiens. The moment Simon received word of it he prepared for struggle. He made an alliance with Llywelyn and dispatched his two oldest sons and a squad of men to deal with Mortimer.

Fighting immediately broke out up and down the line of the River Severn. Edward went straight there from France but was outnumbered and had to appeal to Walter Cantilupe for a truce to avoid being captured by his cousin Henry de Montfort. Simon was furious with his son when he learned that he had let Edward escape.[43]

Henry spent three weeks in France after the ruling. He needed to raise money for the war ahead and for this he empowered Eleanor and her affinity of exiles to settle the balance of the treaty money owed by Louis and to pawn the crown jewels. He also put his foot down on Savoyard attempts to prosecute the Marchers for the destruction they had caused them. He demanded unity to suppress the Montfortians. In the middle of February, he said goodbye to Eleanor and Edmund and left, doubtless hoping he would send for them soon.[44]

As Simon had summoned the malcontents to Oxford the year before to launch their rebellion, the king gathered the feudal host there in preparation for taking the war to them. On 6 April, his army stormed well-defended Northampton in one day and bagged the entire Montfortian garrison, including the younger Simon, Peter de Montfort, and some eighty knights and barons. Henry's stunning victory threw London in a panic. Various mobs had already ransacked the properties of high-profile royalists like Richard of Cornwall. Now on 9 April, they fell upon the Jewish community and massacred more than 500 people. In attempt to regain the initiative, Simon attacked Rochester with Gilbert de Clare, but they were forced to withdraw to London when the royalist army arrived.[45]

By the first week in May, the situation looked bleak for them. They were trapped in London while the king secured the submission of the Channel ports and their fleets in anticipation of laying siege to the city. On 6 May, Simon took his men, now reinforced with units under his son

Henry and a battalion of London irregulars, and marched south towards the coast to gamble on one pitched battle with the king.

As the two armies encamped in and around Lewes for the epic showdown, Eleanor of Provence tried to recruit men and ships for an expeditionary force. Gaston de Bearn and his men were among those to respond and gathered around St Omer in mid-April.[46] She also appealed to Alphonse of Poitiers for assistance.

> To the renowned man, A[lphonse], son of the illustrious King of France [Louis VIII], the Count of Poitiers and Toulouse, E[leanor], by the grace of God, Queen of England, Lady of Ireland and Duchess of Aquitaine, greetings and affection of sincere love.
>
> We do not doubt that the iniquity and treason of certain barons of England who strive to disinherit our lord the King of England and his children by open war has reached your hearing and knowledge. We firmly believe that your goodness and magnanimity could not help but be compassionate and scandalised if you knew that such things were attempted against any king or prince, let alone our lord king to whom blood and special ties of love bind him to you and you similarly to him.

She asked him to impound English ships found in his ports for the duration of the war, citing that 'all things belong to the prince when there is urgent need' as if acting as an attorney specialising in Roman law. Alphonse was indeed scandalised, but more by her request. He informed her that it was his opinion and that of 'many good men' that getting involved in the war in England at this point would only result in great injury and danger.[47]

His rebuff was written on 12 May, the same day that Walter Cantilupe and other bishops undertook one last effort to establish peace between Henry and the Montfortians. It failed and the next day Simon and his men withdrew their homage to the king, who in turn defied them. On 14 May, both sides arrayed their forces outside Lewes, Henry having more men but Simon higher ground.

Edward's initial charge completely drove the Montfortian left wing off the field. That may have decided it then and there, but having understood that many of the fleeing foot soldiers were Londoners, Edward chose to have his revenge for the way they had treated his mother at the bridge. He led the Marchers and a sizable contingent of knights on a killing spree that took them well off the battlefield. Simon noticed the error and threw everything he had against the royalist centre corps. They were under the command of Richard of Cornwall, who had not been in combat for nearly forty years. Richard and his men broke and ran for it, with the King of Germany taking shelter in a windmill he found along the way.[48]

The left corps was then routed, but Henry, fighting at the front, managed a more dignified retreat to the priory at Lewes and set up a defensive perimeter there. Edward erred again when he chose to fight his way into the priory instead of regrouping at a nearby garrison and returning with a relief force. That left father and son in a hopeless position and the next day they agreed to terms of surrender.

They called for the council to go back to running the country, with the king now more or less a figurehead. Edward, Richard and Richard's children Henry of Almain and Edmund of Cornwall were to be held as hostages for the king's compliance. Henry received two concessions under the treaty, known as the Mise of Lewes. There would be more arbitration on the Provisions of Oxford, with a view towards a final settlement everyone presumably could live with, and the release of the Marchers and other prisoners.[49]

Three that got away and fled to France were Warenne, Valence and Hugh Bigod. They informed the queen of the disaster, who was naturally 'anguished and distressed' at the news. Wykes reports that they stayed with her for a while 'mourning happier times', but she must have quickly tired of their sorrow and self-pity.[50] None of them had ever been favourites of hers and their flight from the battlefield could only have lowered their estimation in her eyes. On top of that, there was work to be done.

She needed men and money to organise an invasion force, but before that, she needed to find out where Edward was. Surely there were royalist pockets that could be induced to try and spring him. Once free, he could rally the Marchers and other barons disaffected with Simon and overthrow his regime. That would save the expense and carnage of an invasion which, however successful, could end up costing her whatever popularity she had left in England.

Rescue attempt, the queen's invasion force,
diplomacy with the legate

Prior to the spring offensive, Edward took furlough to visit his wife and their 2-year-old daughter Katherine at Windsor. When he left to rejoin his father's army at Oxford, Eleanor of Castile was pregnant. Another occupant of the castle, Joan de Valence, was also expecting. Both women were probably overjoyed to watch the line of prisoners captured at Northampton, including the younger Simon de Montfort, marched into internment at the fortress.

Now, five weeks later, came the order to release them following the defeat at Lewes. Negotiations for the surrender of the castle went on for a month until the constable handed over command to Eleanor of Castile and left with the garrison. The next day, 17 June 1264, the younger Eleanor was told to take her daughter and household and go to live at Westminster Palace. Joan received more cursory treatment. She was told to find 'some convenient religious or other place near those parts, until God delivers her of the offspring wherewith she is great'.[51]

At this point Edward was forty-six kilometres away at Wallingford Castle, held there with the other hostages. Supervising their custody was Eleanor de Montfort, whom Simon chose for this role because she was Richard's sister and the aunt of the younger men. Eleanor's rank and ties of kinship to them eased the awkwardness of the situation. Her organisational skills meant she could make sure her incarcerated guests, especially her brother, had the lifestyle they were accustomed to before the war. Richard was, after all, a king and Wallingford his castle.[52]

That was about to change thanks to Eleanor of Provence. Having learned of Edward's whereabouts, she contacted the garrison at Bristol, where several loyalist knights had fled along with their wives after the battle. She informed their commander, the ever faithful Robert Walerand, that Wallingford was lightly defended and that if they moved quickly, they could free the prisoners there. Eleanor de Montfort was too good a manager to go lax on security, but Eleanor of Provence sought to encourage the garrison to undertake what was a difficult mission, riding some 100 kilometres in haste in order to surprise the guards at Wallingford.

Sometime in late June or early July, they left 300 hundred strong. Arriving before dawn, they were deprived of the element of surprise thanks to the abbot of nearby Reading alerting the defenders to the projected assault. They managed to fight their way into the outer ward, but could not advance under a hailstorm of stones pounding them from the ramparts of the inner ward. Finally Edward was produced to appeal to them to back off, else he would be put in a mangonel and shot to them with the next volley. Walerand and his men broke off the attack and returned to Bristol.[53]

The raid coincided with the Parliament that imposed a constitutional monarchy on the land. The council was again reinstated to run the country, only numbering nine members instead of fifteen, and it was subordinate to a triumvirate consisting of Simon, Gilbert de Clare and Stephen Berksted, the Bishop of Chichester. Henry was still the lord king and it was his seal that went on the writs, letters and charters issued by the chancery, but the Montfortians were in complete charge.

In early July, just after the adjournment, Simon and Gilbert headed west to deal with the Marchers, who were creating havoc in the Severn Valley. The pair and their armed force went by Wallingford in order to transfer Edward and the other captives to the more secure environs of Kenilworth. The chronicler Robert of Gloucester, writing in metered Middle English, says Countess Eleanor went with them, which makes sense since Kenilworth was her castle.

> þe kinges soster þe contasse sir simondes wif was þer mid hom & wat he miȝte dude hom of solas. (And the king's sister, the countess, sir Simon's wife, was there with them, and what she could she did for their comfort.)[54]

Eleanor retained control of Wallingford and can be found there and at her other residence of Odiham for much of her husband's supremacy. Her household still remained large, around 200 people, and she still had her youngest children Richard (11) and Eleanor (6) with her. Her ward Gilbert de Umfraville, whom she raised as one of her own, had gone north to take seisin of his estates near Scotland, while her older sons were a part of their father's administration and profiting mightily from it.

Henry de Montfort was named the warden of Dover and other Channel ports, the sheriff of Kent and constable of Corfe. The younger Simon was back in possession of Mansel's lands and was given custody Nottingham and Pevensey Castles. Since both were in loyalist hands, it was basically a challenge to him to take them if he could. Guy was given control over his uncle Richard of Cornwall's lands in Devon, while the churchman of the family, Amaury, received the rectory of St Wendron, a very wealthy benefice close to the southern tip of Cornwall.[55]

All this was not simple enrichment for the Montfort clan, rather Simon, whose last regime collapsed through betrayal, was determined to promote only people he could trust. Others naturally were not so sure, especially when no effort was spared to exude propriety in what was going on. A case in point was the younger Simon's suit against Marcher lord William de Braose for the destruction he had caused to his (Mansel's) manor of Sedgewick in Sussex. When Braose failed to appear, a packed jury of three staunch Montfortians, Simon's brother Henry one of them, ruled against him on 30 June 1264. Braose was ordered to pay the fantastic sum of £6,667 in damages, and until he did so, his son would be a hostage. The boy entered Eleanor de Montfort's household sometime afterward, an indication that she was willing to condone and participate in what others might have seen as a family racket.[56]

Nobody was more determined to break up that racket than Eleanor of Provence. The failure to liberate Edward was a huge disappointment and forced her to fall back on the invasion plans. By July men were starting to assemble in Flanders under the organisation of former Alpine warrior Peter of Savoy, who would probably take overall command.

The queen was mostly involved with procurement and raising money. She pawned the crown jewels, heavily borrowed and spent the balance of the treaty money. She acquired £5,000 from Louis for selling back to him the rights in the three French bishoprics ceded to Henry under the treaty. She made sure to insert a buy-back clause with a stiff fifty-percent penalty because her husband was very picky about his rights and she knew she would hear it from him the moment he found out about the deal.[57]

By mid-summer the threat of the invasion had become real enough for Simon to summon the feudal host on 7 July 1264, supplemented by conscription in every village. 'We know for a fact that a great horde of aliens is getting ready to invade the land', he declared. He went on to say everyone should forget about the harvest because these aliens would spare neither sex nor age in their thirst for blood.

The turnout between Dover and Canterbury was spectacular. Not since the Norman Conquest had the English nation rallied in such numbers to defend the realm. The irony was they were there to defend their homeland. Defending the Provisions of Oxford and Simon's grip on power came in a distant second.[58]

No mention was made of the queen for the obvious reason that the proclamation was made in the king's name. Her invasion force was said to have been equally impressive. According to *Flores*, she had assembled 'such a number of dukes and earls and such a fleet that it would scarcely appear credible to anyone'. Those who saw it were sure it would have no trouble sweeping away Montfort's peasant army.

She had been opposed in her efforts by Guy Foulquois, the legate appointed back in November. He was expecting to go to England to negotiate a peaceful settlement and did not think the sabre rattling helped the situation. Eleanor did not stand down, but agreed to defer to him before giving the order to launch.[59]

Foulquois moved to Boulogne in August, but Simon refused to admit him. He told the legate to disband the army and then they would talk. In the meantime, he sent him and Louis his terms for peace, known as the Peace of Canterbury. It called for the government that was currently in place, the triumvirate and council of nine, to remain until arbitration on the Provisions of Oxford, one of the concessions to Henry after the Battle of Lewes, had been implemented. In fact, Simon was being disingenuous. He had intentionally included Louis in the arbitration knowing he would refuse to become involved because it would reverse his judgement at Amiens. This way the Montfortians could continue to rule indefinitely.[60]

However anxious the queen was about this setback, the legate persisted in his diplomacy and Simon at least pretended to show good faith by moving Edward and Henry of Almain to Dover as if ready to release them. Almain was even allowed to go to France to take part in the discussions. Eleanor hoped to at least win Edward's freedom and at one point the legate offered to swap Edmund for him.

But all the proposals going back and forth suggest Simon was merely buying time. He could not free Edward because he was a security risk and he could not allow the legate into the country because he would excommunicate him and the bishops, his chief supporters. By stalling him long enough, the queen would no longer be able afford her army and it would disband on its own.[61]

By October, the legate had had enough, but then word came that the pope had died and Foulquois was needed back in Rome to help elect a new one. He left Eleanor of Provence high and dry, because her money had run out and her army drifted away. It was a bitter defeat. So much hope and exertion and she was right back to square one. If anything,

Simon was more powerful than ever, having proved he could protect England against invasion and interdict. Wykes is probably right to say the queen withdrew to France 'in confusion and distress', but *Flores* pays tribute to her as *virago potentissima*, a mighty warrior heroine.

> But this I may weave into my story to the praise and great glory of the noble Eleanor, Queen of England, who like a mighty warrior heroine vigorously and valiantly laboured for her lord and Edward.[62]

Two writs enrolled in the chancery on 18 November 1264, however, show how Eleanor de Montfort succeeded where Eleanor of Provence did not. One writ went to the queen, admonishing her not to alienate anything belonging to the Crown. This was a clear reference to her sale of Henry's rights in the three French bishoprics. The other writ empowered Hugh Despenser, Peter de Montfort and the Bishops of Worcester and London, all close friends of the Montforts, to look into Eleanor's dower and the losses she incurred on account of it and to compensate her accordingly. After more than thirty years, it looked like she would finally get justice.[63]

Christmas that year was spent at Kenilworth. It was a huge celebration, with more than 140 household knights among the revellers. Presumably royal captives Edward, Richard, Henry of Almain and Edmund of Cornwall were asked by the Montforts to join them. They were, after all, family.

The king was also family, but he spent the holidays alone in Woodstock. He was not one to mope around in adversity, however, and busied himself by having 100 pear trees planted in nearby Everswell. It would make a nice gift for his wife, because she did love her gardens.

Henry had no doubt Eleanor was coming back. In 1236, the year of their wedding, he had had a Wheel of Fortune painted in Winchester Hall, where he would soon belt the Earl of Leicester. He wanted the Wheel to remind all and sundry, especially ambitious folk like Simon and Eleanor de Montfort, that no matter how lucky or supreme you are, fate always has a way of catching up.[64]

10

Triumph, Grief and Sorrow
1265–1291

*The queen in Gascony, Simon's great Parliament,
Eleanor de Montfort's accounts*

Eleanor of Provence likely spent Christmas at the court of her sister in Paris. Perhaps they sadly reminisced how a decade earlier the royal couples got together for the first time, a glorious political and personal achievement that must have felt like ages ago now. The elephant Louis had given to Henry then was long dead, unable to cope with life in cold, foggy London, and for all they knew Margaret's slightly flirtatious gift to him of a bejewelled peacock had been appropriated by Simon, as he had appropriated the rest of Henry's kingdom.

Gascony was a different story. The queen ignored Simon's order to cease and desist from acting on behalf of the Crown and went to the province after the holidays to rule as the Duchess of Aquitaine. With the Lusignans in nearby Poitou, now her firm allies in this twisted tale, it put her in a position to organise another expeditionary force, smaller but ready to launch the moment the Montfortian regime showed any sign of weakness.[1]

The queen probably took her son Edmund, who turned 20 on 16 January, with her, but she lost her affinity of close advisers. Peter of Savoy returned to his homeland to rule as the count there and John Mansel died in the middle of that month. She must have taken the loss of Mansel hard. Able, discreet and utterly loyal, he had been, in her own words, a 'special and beloved' friend to her and Henry for more than twenty years.

Simon, on the other hand, had considered Mansel an enemy to be crushed and had doubtless taken satisfaction in giving his confiscated

166

lands to his namesake son. Mansel's death now allowed him to take his coveted church office of treasurer of York and give it to his son Amaury de Montfort. Henry had promised to give Roger Mortimer's son, another Edmund, such a benefice and deeply resented what he saw as Simon using appointments that were in the king's gift for his own family's benefit.[2]

It was not only the king offended by all the wealth and offices going to the Montfort children. Gilbert de Clare had profited from the distribution of spoils, including the lands, castles and wardships of William de Valence, John de Warenne and Peter of Savoy, but felt excluded from a government dominated by Montfortians and churchmen who treated him like an outsider. A rabid xenophobe, he sneered at Simon's foreign origins and charged him with using foreigners to garrison castles.

The Montfort sons were contemptuous of Gilbert and his high opinion of himself and so challenged him and his brother Thomas to a tournament in Dunstable for 17 February. Worried it would turn into an all-out brawl, Simon ordered a halt to it and threatened his sons with the dungeon if they did not obey. The ban coincided with his arrest of Robert de Ferrers, the Earl of Derby, who had been carrying on his feud with Edward by laying waste to his lands while he was locked away in Kenilworth. Gilbert thought he might be next and left for Gloucester to plot with the Marchers.[3]

They were just then in the middle of Parliament convened on 20 January 1265 principally to negotiate the terms for Edward's release. It was this assembly that won Simon his later fame as the founder of the House of Commons because, with dwindling support from the nobility, he summoned representatives of the towns and boroughs, for the first time on record, to treat on the business of government with the barons, knights and clergymen. Whether that innovation deserves greater recognition than Eleanor of Provence's Parliament with the first elected members is easily debatable, but in neither case were they out to make history. They just wanted backing for their proposals.[4]

Here one of the conditions for Edward's release was a land swap between him and Simon. He would exchange his lands in Cheshire, which Ferrers had lately ravaged, for some of Simon's manors scattered elsewhere. The deal was much more favourable to Simon, but he justified it on the grounds that Edward would only seek to overthrow the

Montfortian regime with his Marcher neighbours if he were allowed to go back there.

On Wednesday, 11 March 1265, the peace settlement was finalised in a ceremony in Westminster Hall. Henry and Edward swore to abide by the constitutional monarchy now in place and there were nine bishops on hand to pronounce sentences of excommunication against them and anyone who acted otherwise. Edward was then officially released to his father's household. It was all very cosmetic, because the heir to the throne was still restricted to the movements of the court.[5]

Eleanor de Montfort was not a witness to this abject humiliation of her brother and nephew. We know this because her household accounts for this period have survived and show that she was at Odiham on the day of the ceremony. These accounts were kept as a record of all the expenditures she made between 19 February and 29 August for both her family and household.

They also show regular expenditures made on behalf of the royal captives. Clearly Eleanor wanted to ease the plight she had helped to impose on her brothers and their children and made sure they continued to have fine food, wine and garments. For example, she sent spices and treats like pepper, ginger, almonds and raisins to Richard and Edmund of Cornwall at Kenilworth, along with sumptuous whale meat and sturgeon and quality cloth and linen to make robes and hoods for them.[6] This was not only because they were her close kin, but Simon wanted to project a regal air of continuity in a kingdom still struggling to come to terms with all the change and disorder of the last two years. Henry and Richard had to look and eat like kings despite having no more freedom to make decisions and roam about than an indentured peasant.[7]

Naturally Edward was not forgotten. Eleanor paid for the services of his barber, Master Roger, and courier costs indicate that she and her young daughter Eleanor wrote letters to him. Other recipients of letters from the countess include Margaret de Lacy and her daughter Maud, who was the dowager Countess of Gloucester and mother of Gilbert de Clare, and friends and political associates like Peter de Montfort, the Bishops of Lincoln and Worcester, and Thomas Cantilupe, who was serving as chancellor. Her networking role for the regime can also be seen in her entertainment of more than fifty visitors, among them the Countess of Oxford, whose husband Robert de Vere was a Montfortian newcomer, and Robert Bruce, grandfather of the future Scottish king, who had been captured at Lewes and was waiting for his son to collect his ransom.[8]

The typical outlays in the accounts are concerned with her family at home and wages for her staff and specialists, like 12 pence paid to her daughter's nurse during Easter and 32 pence to the barber brought in from Reading to bleed one of her damsels. The countess purchased 240 parchment sheets in London in order to have a breviary (devotional book) made for her daughter in Oxford, altogether costing 24 shillings (about £850 today). Two decades previously her friend Adam Marsh admonished her to dress frugally and modestly. It does not seem to have made any impression. Eleanor still enjoyed the finer things and for Easter bought a hood of black muslin for herself and fur of miniver for her daughter, together costing 31 shillings. She nevertheless did not neglect her duty to the poor and maintained on average 15 paupers in her household. She fed more for special observances, reaching a high of 800 on one day in April.[9]

With Parliament finished, Simon set out to visit his family in Odiham. Edward and Henry of Almain also went along, under an armed escort led by Henry de Montfort, and arrived on 17 March. That increased the number of horses in her stable from 44 to 172, meaning more expense for hay and oats. Two days later Simon arrived with 162 horses in his entourage, bringing the number of animals to feed up to 334. Among the items consumed by the guests and occupants on the first day alone were 1,700 herring, 36 pounds of almonds and 240 gallons of beer. The total cost of provisions for this small army on that one day, 19 March 1265, was 105 shillings, 5 pence (today £3,900). Simon apparently grumbled about the type of fish on the menu—it being Lent, there was no meat served—and had servants go to the ponds around nearby Farnham to bring back a better variety. They were fishing there for the entire two weeks of his stay.[10]

They all left on 1 April. The next day Isabella de Forz, the Countess of Aumale and Devon, arrived and spent Easter with Eleanor. Some 1,200 eggs, purchased for 48 pence, were dyed and passed out for the holiday. Isabella had Montfortian sympathies, but the invitation for her to visit may have been connected to Simon's decision to revoke Edmund Plantagenet's right to her remarriage and give it to his and Eleanor's second son instead. This would make Junior a very wealthy and powerful baron. Doubtless Simon discussed it with Eleanor, maybe asked her to hint at the prospect of the marriage to the countess, soften her up if necessary.

Isabella had no sooner left Odiham when Eleanor dashed off a letter to her son, presumably with intelligence about Isabella's willingness to become the wife of another Simon de Montfort. Junior was then at Pevensey, still trying to get the loyalist garrison there to surrender. The news probably was not good, because Isabella wanted nothing to do with the younger man. It did not stop him from pressing his suit and she later complained that she had to flee to Wales for safety.[11]

The quarrel with Gilbert de Clare dominated the political matters Simon discussed with Eleanor. He had decided to call a make-up tournament at Northampton in an attempt to appease him. If he refused to come, then he would go to Gloucester to deal with him and the Marchers in person. For security and to overawe the much younger man, he would take the entire court with him. That meant the king, Edward, the chancellor, justiciar, several councillors, all their retinues, and their sons Henry and Guy de Montfort. There were nevertheless dangers and he might have to call on his firm ally Llywelyn and local militias for support. For a man of his legendary confidence, which she as his wife of 27 years had to know all about, it would seem Simon had everything under control.[12]

Endgame, Battle of Evesham, Eleanor de Montfort leaves England forever

Working backwards from the events about to happen suggests that Eleanor of Provence helped to coordinate them from her base in Gascony. First, there was Ireland. In February 1265, William de Valence began moving men, horses and arms north from Poitou to his estates there. Ireland was still solidly loyalist thanks to the efforts of Geoffrey de Joinville, the brother of the future biographer of Louis IX. From his homeland in Champagne, Joinville had entered Henry's service through his brother-in-law Peter of Savoy and was rewarded with a marriage in 1252 that gave him control of Meath, north of Dublin. He then joined Edward's household and served with him in Gascony, but refused to follow him into rebellion in 1260. This endeared him to the queen and made him a lifelong friend.[13]

Joinville's wife was Anglo-Irish heiress Maud de Lacy. Through her he acquired various possessions in the marches, including Ludlow Castle. About twenty kilometres southwest of Ludlow is Wigmore which is where Roger Mortimer and his wife, another Maud, made their home. Maud Mortimer had been a friend of the queen for at least a decade and it was Roger who led a second Marcher uprising against Simon in November 1264. It was suppressed and Roger and the other Marchers were ordered to go into exile in Ireland for a year, but they had postponed it endlessly.[14]

On 27 April, Simon and the entire court arrived in Gloucester. They had come not only to negotiate with Gilbert, who did not show up for the tournament in Northampton, but to force the Marchers to abjure the realm as agreed. While the talks were going on, a mounted troop of men under William de Valence and John de Warenne landed at Pembroke on the southwest tip of Wales, which was in Gilbert's keeping. The Earl of Gloucester had not been negotiating in good faith and was seeking to overthrow the regime he had helped to install. To prevent this new threat from linking up to the Marchers, Simon moved the court to Hereford, but in doing so he put Edward within the grasp of his enemies.[15]

On 28 May 1265, Edward slipped his guard while out riding and escaped. It had been executed on the inside by Gilbert's brother Thomas, who for unfathomable reasons had still been trusted at court, and on the outside by the Mortimers. Roger and a party of horsemen, lurking in a nearby woods, met up with Edward and took him to meet Gilbert at Ludlow which is an indication of Joinville's involvement in the scheme to free him. There Edward agreed to Gilbert's demands, mainly that the restored royals get rid of all the foreigners. Eleanor of Provence would not have welcomed that news, but like everybody else she knew her son, the same as her husband, to be the type to promise anything on the spot and worry about the details later.[16]

Simon immediately realised he had been had and may have suspected that Henry of Almain had something to do with it. After leaving Odiham in April, Almain was dispatched to France in an attempt to restart talks with Louis. No progress had been made when Simon learned that Valence and Warenne had landed with their force sometime before 10 May. A week later he got a request from Almain to extend his stay and Simon reluctantly agreed. It seems that at some point Almain did in fact meet the queen, but it had to do with her idea of a marriage between him and

Constance de Bearn, the heiress of Gaston. The match would establish an English dynasty near the Pyrenees much as Simon and Eleanor de Montfort had planned one of their own in Bigorre.[17]

For all Simon knew, young Henry's request to stay longer in France was part of a wide-ranging conspiracy involving the queen. He sent orders to Kenilworth to put Almain's father and brother, Richard and Edmund of Cornwall, in chains in case there was a move to free them as well and he sent a message to his wife Eleanor to seek greater security than what Odiham offered. Simon Junior and his men arrived to escort her and her household to Porchester Castle near the coast, where he was the constable.

They left in haste on 1 June, travelling at night with her shepherd, Dobbe, to guide them. They moved again ten days later, reaching Dover on 15 June. The countess's retinue by then was so large that not all of them could find accommodation in the castle and had to sleep in the town. Naturally all expenses were documented, including a boat hired for 7 shillings, 7 pence to bring parts of her baggage there.[18]

The move to Dover reflected Simon's deteriorating position in the marches. After Edward's escape, he remained at Hereford, confident that with Llywelyn's help he could again emerge victorious. Edward and his supporters saw it as the perfect opportunity to trap him behind the Severn and they had pulled it off within days of Eleanor arriving in Dover. Junior now left his mother in order to raise troops and head west to his father's aid.

Simon finally left Hereford for Monmouth on 24 June, hoping to cross the Severn by boat to Bristol, and from there to join forces with his son. They arrived only to find that Gilbert had burnt the flotilla waiting for them and that he and Edward had a much larger army nearby at Newport ready to destroy them. Still holding on to the king, Simon beat a quick retreat back to Hereford.[19]

It turns out that Junior and his relief force, recruited mostly in London, got nowhere near Bristol. They stopped en route at Winchester, which the Londoners viewed as ancient rivals, and sacked the city and its Jewish community. Hearing of his father's failure to cross the river, Junior then headed north for Kenilworth, where other Montfortian troops were mustering.

Meanwhile his mother was having more success keeping the southeast coast secure and loyal. On 12 July, Eleanor entertained a large gathering of local officials and aristocrats at Dover, people like the wife of Lord Ralph Darcy. Her dinner party and household consumed half a roasted ox, two sheep, 41 litres of red wine, 19 of white, 170 litres of beer and 270 loaves of bread. On that day her husband and his men marched aimlessly around South Wales, unable to find any bread or beer and having to subsist entirely off meat and milk.[20]

By now the queen would have heard about this change in fortunes. She was still in Gascony, still exerting her authority from there, and her efforts got a boost that month from the new pope. He was none other than Guy Foulquois, the former legate, now Clement IV. He owed her, it might be said, on account of all the money she had spent on an invasion force that came to nothing because he insisted on negotiating.

Hearing of his election, Eleanor wrote to ask him to appoint a legate for England, but Clement still felt aggrieved over the way the English had treated him with contempt and said he needed a month to get over it. She was pleased by the cardinal he eventually appointed, Ottobuono de Fieschi, whom she had met when he visited with Thomas of Savoy six years earlier. On 19 July, Clement wrote to Ottobuono in France not to work for peace until 'that pestilent man (Simon de Montfort) and all his progeny have been plucked out of England'.[21] This was meant to inform the Montfortian bishops that their days were numbered.

The situation in Wales changed again on 31 July when Junior and his men arrived at Kenilworth. Edward now found himself between two substantial enemy forces. He needed to move fast because all his immediate strength was in the marches, whereas Simon could still draw on support from the Midlands, London, and the ports. Edward chose to strike at Kenilworth because he learned through one of his spies that many of Junior's men had not taken shelter within the castle, preferring the more comfortable accommodations in town.

Riding through the night from Worcester, he and the Marchers pounced on them in their sleep. They captured a large body of men and equipment, but Junior and a sizable force got away. Edward hurried back to Worcester, but his absence had allowed Simon to cross the Severn. He got his men on the move again, because he had to catch up with him before Junior regrouped. It was his fortune that Simon's men were too tired and hungry to go on after they reached Evesham. On the morning of 4 August 1265, Edward, Mortimer and Gilbert and their troops appeared on the high ground north of the town.[22]

They had the advantage of numbers, position and a mutual agreement to butcher their opponents, a frightful precedent for future English political history. In the fight that followed that morning, with a dark cloud hovering over the field, the Montfortians were mowed down in a horrific bloodletting. Long-time friends of the family Hugh Despenser and Peter de Montfort were killed. The king, looking like any other knight in armour, escaped with a wound to the shoulder, but his namesake godson Henry de Montfort was cut down. Eleanor nearly lost her fourth son Guy as well. He was severely wounded but survived.

Her husband went into the battle a marked man. Edward and Gilbert had assigned a death squad to take him out, although it was said that Mortimer did the actual killing with a blow to Simon's neck from behind. After that, he and his men fell on the body, hacking it into pieces, perhaps getting a good laugh when they found that he was wearing a hair shirt. (Yeah, right, Sir Simon!) Mortimer claimed the prized parts, Montfort's head and testicles, so that he might hand them to his wife Maud in person.[23]

There is no indication in Eleanor's accounts of when she learned of the slaughter. On 11 August, one week after the battle, she sent the Prior of Dover on a mission to her brother. The purpose for it remains a mystery. On that same day she withdrew to her chamber and no longer appeared in the Great Hall for meals. Thomas Wykes, who never missed a chance to snarl at Simon and their sons, says she put on a widow's habit, stopped eating fish and meat, and was inconsolable in general. She made two offerings for masses to be said for her husband's soul, 12 shillings, 9 pence on 19 August, and 7 shillings on 3 September. She returned to dine with her household on 21 August.[24]

A messenger arrived from Edward during her mourning. Judging by the later relationship between aunt and nephew, the message was probably in the nature of condolences, something like, 'I didn't want it to end this way. He was my godfather, after all'. Edward knew he was in a delicate position. The desecration of Simon's corpse was not just a public relations disaster, but it saddled him with a blood feud with the Montfort clan, and they were everywhere, in France, in the Holy Land. He now had to get his aunt to surrender Dover without making it worse.

It was the same with Junior, who was still a threat at Kenilworth. On 6 September, the younger Simon let his uncle Richard of Cornwall go free with an expressed promise to do what he could for his sister Eleanor and her family. Richard, who was nearly chopped up by the garrison in retaliation for Simon, was happy to oblige.[25]

By then Eleanor knew her time at Dover was running out. Her men were having to resort to 'booty' to keep everyone fed. She saw no future for her younger children or herself in England and began making plans for all of them to cross over. Young Richard, she decided, would go to Bigorre. Eleanor intended to cede the family rights to that county to the King of Navarre, hoping in return that Richard, still only 12, might grow up at court there or in Bigorre, perhaps reclaim the county when he got older. It is touching to read in the accounts her purchases of clothes for his journey, knowing well she might never see her youngest son again once he left for there.[26]

Passage was paid for Richard and Amaury and they had left by 28 September. It was on that day that Henry wrote to the bailiffs of Dover not to allow his sister or anyone else to leave without his permission. We can see why on 10 October, when the king wrote again, this time to Louis. Richard and Amaury had apparently taken £7,333 in cash with them, an enormous sum of money. Henry advised Louis to seize what he saw as their ill-gotten gains and use it to compensate French merchants for damages they had suffered from English privateers. Louis does not seem to have acted. Henry had already done the best he could do himself for a response. On 7 August, after regaining control of his seal, he dismissed Amaury as the treasurer of York, whence some of that money may have come, and gave the office to Edmund Mortimer, son of the man who had so vilely defiled Simon's corpse.[27]

By the middle of October, Edward appeared ready to lay siege to Dover. The reason was clear enough. His mother and brother had been in France for more than two years and were anxious to come home. It would be embarrassing if the queen were unable to step ashore at Dover like all dignitaries because her sister-in-law was still holding the fort there.

In fact, Eleanor de Montfort was holding out only for the sake of negotiating pardons for the people closest to her. At the top was Richard de Havering, her estates steward who had first entered her service more than thirty years ago. Edward interceded with the new chancellor to win pardons for him, his son John (who later became one of Edward's most trusted officials) and several others. Given assurances Henry would grant them, the time had come. On 28 October 1265, Eleanor and her daughter embarked for exile in France. Now 50 years old, King John's youngest child would never see England again.[28]

Return of the queen, the Disinherited, the Montforts in exile, death of Henry III

In addition to writing letters to Louis about his sister, Henry also wrote to Margaret to ask when he might expect the arrival of his wife. Margaret responded in a playful tone that evidently characterised their relationship. She wished Eleanor might stay with them longer, especially since Margaret believed (erroneously) that she was pregnant again, but she was also worried that Henry would tire of waiting around and marry someone else. Having heard that Gilbert's mother Maud, the very rich Countess of Gloucester, was prowling around, she vowed not to rest until her sister was safely back in Henry's company.[29]

Eleanor of Provence landed at Dover the day after Eleanor de Montfort left. Edward was there to greet his mother, his brother Edmund and the new legate Ottobuono. He escorted them to Canterbury, where they were received by Henry, Richard of Cornwall, and numerous well-wishers. She nevertheless came home to a land still deeply troubled. Within days of the slaughter at Evesham, the victors, led by Gilbert de Clare, rushed to seize the lands of the vanquished. Henry equivocated whether to make these seizures official policy, but the failure of the younger Simon to deliver Kenilworth seems to have settled it.

In September, at Parliament in Winchester, the Montfortians were disinherited of their ancestral lands. Not everyone was happy with it, Richard of Cornwall, Roger Bigod and Philip Basset among them, but the greedier ones like Mortimer would argue that they had done nothing to restore the king to power. In any event, all three eventually partook of it.[30]

The biggest beneficiary was Edmund. On 25 October 1265, three days before his arrival, Henry granted him Simon's old earldom of Leicester. He would finally have the endowment that had always eluded the desire of his parents. The queen also gained eight major lordships valued at £300 annually and, perhaps sweetest of all, London Bridge. The shopkeepers and merchants on the bridge who had allowed the rabble to abuse her when she tried to sail under it for Windsor, maybe even took part in it themselves, were now her tenants. They and the rest of London were also slapped with a fine of £13,333 for their transgressions and support for Simon in the civil war. Just over half that money would go to redeem the three bishoprics in France that Eleanor had sold to Louis to raise money for her invasion force.[31]

The Montfortians chose to fight on rather than abide by the confiscation of their lands and the younger Simon left Kenilworth to join a different guerrilla pocket. Edward forced their surrender and in December led his cousin to Northampton, where Henry, Eleanor and the court were spending Christmas, to work out a settlement. Already on 16 November, Henry granted his sister protection in the hope she might return and become reconciled with him. This would induce the surrender of the garrison at Kenilworth, who claimed they were holding the castle for Eleanor de Montfort specifically. She did not come, but her son accepted the terms offered to him.[32]

Junior was to leave the realm with a pension of £400 annually from Leicester provided he caused the king no more trouble. He returned with the royal family to London but suspected that Edward was plotting to have him locked up in the Tower. He slipped away to Winchelsea and escaped to France on 10 February 1266. By this time his brother Guy had recovered from his wounds and was transferred to prison in Dover. He too escaped and joined his family.[33]

In June, the queen was at Windsor while her husband, sons, legate and others moved into position around Kenilworth to invest the castle. There she was in charge of high-ranking prisoners who had been captured in the ongoing struggle of the Disinherited. They included Robert de Ferrers, the Earl of Derby, who had not been disinherited after being released from the Tower, but had such a loathing for Edward that he reignited their feud. It was a bout of gout that kept him from fleeing with his men when they were routed by forces under Henry of Almain at Chesterfield on 15 May.[34]

Also under the queen's charge at Windsor was her daughter-in-law Eleanor of Castile. It will be remembered how young Eleanor had to leave Windsor a year earlier after Lewes, pregnant and with her husband held prisoner. She gave birth to a daughter Joan, who died several weeks after Evesham, before Edward could see her. Eleanor conceived again shortly after she and her husband were reunited, and on 13 July 1266 she gave birth to a son named John. They had King John in mind, an odd choice given the unpopularity of Edward's grandfather among contemporaries. London welcomed the birth by taking the day off and celebrating in the street, seemingly oblivious to the date of the birth being the three-year anniversary of their assault on the queen at the bridge.[35]

On 15 September, as the siege of Kenilworth continued, the pope asked Louis not to allow 'the relict of Simon de Montfort' (Eleanor) and her son Simon to recover Leicester because it had been 'justly' lost. Louis, however, wanted a settlement, and ten days later Henry made an offer to the Montforts. He agreed to abide by whatever award the King of France thought was fair for them, just that he consider all the 'damages, trespasses and injuries' they had caused him.

Finally, Henry agreed to a settlement for everyone and on 31 October 1266 published what became known as the Dictum of Kenilworth. All Montfortians were allowed to redeem their lands by paying a fine based on the yearly value of their property times the level of their involvement in the rebellion. In this way, even high-ranking rebels like the Earl of Oxford were able to regain their lands and titles. The Montforts themselves were excluded because they were Louis's problem now.[36]

In May 1267, Louis sent a group of envoys to hammer out a deal. At some point in negotiations, Eleanor de Montfort had asked Eleanor of Provence to intervene for her. The two Eleanors could no longer be friends, but they shared enough mutual trust and sympathy to get over all the indignities and heartache they had suffered, which they themselves had helped to bring on, in order to reach an accord between their families. The queen arranged for the countess to receive £500 annually from her dower tenants. If she thought that was too little, Henry promised her proctors a day in court and to enforce whatever verdict was reached in the matter.[37]

By this time Eleanor de Montfort and her daughter were living in the Dominican nunnery of Montargis, founded by her husband's late sister Amicia. While attending to prayer and silence, she still received friends and families and managed her affairs and theirs. She renewed her suit against her Lusignan kin and was awarded lands in Angoulême worth £400 a year. She encouraged her son Amaury, who had become a chaplain in Rome, to seek rehabilitation for his father from the pope. On 11 May 1267, Clement asked Ottobuono to verify Amaury's claim that Simon had received absolution before Evesham, in which case he deserved a Christian burial.[38]

Henry could not have endeared himself to his sister by taking steps to suppress a miracle cult growing for Simon at Evesham, never mind not ensuring he received a decent burial, which is to say burial of what could be found of him. Eleanor felt strongly enough to bring suit against her brother at the papal court, and when Henry expressed amazement that the pope should even listen to her, he was curtly told that was none of his business.

The suit faded away and Amaury eventually gave up the religious life to pursue medicine in Italy. His brothers Guy and Simon were already there. They had found service under Charles of Anjou in his conquest of Sicily, with Guy, a veteran of Lewes and Evesham, distinguishing himself so well that Charles made him his vicar-general for Tuscany. He married into the local nobility and had two daughters.[39]

Nothing more was heard from Richard de Montfort after he left for Bigorre. Gaston de Bearn was still eager to claim the province for his own family and the English royals were eager for him to remain loyal to the Crown. The best way to secure both these interests was a marriage between Henry of Almain and Constance de Bearn, just as Eleanor of Provence had envisioned during her rule in Gascony. The wedding took place on 21 May 1269 at Windsor.[40]

Six weeks before that, on 9 April, Edmund got married at age 24. The bride originally intended for him had been the older Isabella de Forz, but she decided she was not going to marry anyone. Since her 15-year-old daughter Aveline was her heiress to the Aumale and Devon earldoms, Eleanor gladly worked in that direction. She put up the £2,000 for her marriage rights, half to Aveline's mother Isabella and half to her grandmother Amicia, the sister of Richard de Clare, who was also a friend of the queen.[41]

The children of Edmund and Aveline were going to be fabulously wealthy. They would have four earldoms between them, Aumale, Devon, Leicester and lately Lancaster, which Henry had granted to Edmund two years earlier. On 1 May 1269, that number grew to five through a judicial swindle. Robert de Ferrers had been finally freed from prison and told he could redeem his lands like anybody else, only his fine was an outrageous £50,000. Since neither he (nor anybody) was able to pay it, his earldom of Derby was forfeited to the current custodian, Edmund.

Edward and Henry of Almain were the perpetrators of the fraud, but Henry and Eleanor of Provence had at the least condoned it. Whether they might have thought to defend themselves by saying Ferrers brought it all on himself, which is true, Edmund now had the endowment his parents hoped he would. Not quite a kingdom, but rich enough.[42]

Edmund's wedding was held at Westminster Abbey. Henry had laboured hard on reconstructing it for the last quarter of a century, through poverty and rebellion, but enough of it was finished to stage ceremonies there, including the translation of Edward the Confessor to his new shrine on 13 October 1269. Everyone who saw it was floored. Henry had lost none of his flair for splendour and showmanship, going all the way back to his second coronation nearly fifty years before.

The event was nevertheless overshadowed by a fractious Parliament and Henry's struggle to obtain funding so that Edward, Edmund and a host of other young knights might join Louis on a second crusade. The money came through, but the crusade was another disaster. Louis, his son and most of their entourage had died of plague in the African heat, including the King of Navarre, to whose court Richard de Montfort had been sent, and Hugh Lusignan, the Count of Angoulême. The latter's death put Eleanor de Montfort back to square one with obtaining her inheritance in the county.[43]

The crusade was over by the time Edward arrived. He continued on to the Holy Land anyway, taking his wife with him, but dispatching Henry of Almain to Gascony to manage his affairs there. Edward suggested Almain might pursue reconciliation with their cousins Guy and Simon de Montfort while he was passing through Italy. It was foolish to say the least, because on 13 March 1271, Guy jumped Almain while he was at mass in Viterbo and hacked him to death. Having avenged their father, he and Simon went into hiding. Guy was protected by his Italian relatives, but Simon died later that year at a castle near Siena.[44]

Richard of Cornwall reeled from the murder of his son. It is unknown what Eleanor's response was or if she tried to reach out to her brother. She probably would have understood her sons' crime had it been Roger Mortimer or someone else who had had a hand in dismembering her husband's body. But Henry of Almain was her nephew and had been liked and trusted by Simon. That was probably because of all the people who turned their back on him, Almain alone had had the courage to tell him it in person.[45]

In early August, Richard received another blow when Edward and Eleanor of Castile's son John died, aged 5, while under his care at Wallingford. He found the king and queen overcome by grief when he brought the child's body to be buried at Westminster. Only a couple of weeks after the funeral came word that Edward and his wife had landed safely in the Holy Land. Not until they were on their way back more than a year later did they learn of the death of their son.[46]

The reasons are obscure why Eleanor of Provence had not been entrusted with the guardianship of John or her two new grandchildren, touchingly named Henry (3) and Eleanor (2). There could have been political concerns. Gilbert de Clare was still harping about getting rid of all foreigners and Edward was worried that naming his mother the guardian of the future king might give Gilbert an excuse to stir up trouble while he was gone. Eleanor of Castile may have had her own worries. Her mother-in-law had been famously protective of her children and the younger Eleanor did not want her own children, whom she might not see for the next few years, to become too attached to their grandmother while she was away.[47]

Had the people of London been asked why the queen was not given the guardianship of her grandchildren, they would have pointed to the bridge. Eleanor had been given control of it following the submission of the city, but in the five years since then she had collected all the rents but put nothing back into maintaining the structure or carrying out repairs on it. A delegation of citizens convinced her to hand the bridge over to two wardens for its upkeep, but she quickly repudiated the agreement. On 10 September 1270, Henry renewed her custody of the bridge for another six years.[48]

In April 1272, Richard of Cornwall died, aged 63. The queen's relationship with him had never been easy, but she had known him the longest of anyone in England apart from her husband. His death followed a string of losses in her own family. Eleanor's mother died in 1265, her sister Beatrice in 1267, uncles Peter of Savoy in 1268 and Boniface two years after that. Richard was succeeded as Earl of Cornwall by Edmund, his son with Sanchia, who was knighted by Henry on 13 October.

By then the king was ailing. Since he nearly died from his previous illness the year before, it was thought prudent to take more steps to secure his wife's future. Eleanor was given Windsor Castle, which had been her home since her young motherhood, and granted several wardships to ensure she had £1,000 every year to provision her household.[49]

After seeming to recover, Henry took a turn for the worse. The situation in London was tense just then over the mayoral election, with crowds demanding the incumbent step aside in favour of a Montfortian-style radical. A truce was called just in time, because the king was dying. It was not recorded, but the queen was almost certainly at his bedside. They had been married for 36 years, had been through some trying times, but their bond to each other remained firm to the end. Only a few years before, he mentioned to Louis in a letter how much joy he got from being in his wife's company. Henry died on 16 November 1272 and was buried four days later in Westminster Abbey, his last great show in a reign of 56 years.[50]

The lionesses in winter

Edward learned that he was king when he stopped in Sicily on the return voyage. Instead of rushing home, he used his time abroad to meet heads of state and manage affairs in Gascony. Apparently he also met Eleanor de Montfort near Paris in August of 1273. Likely it was through Margaret, who had renewed her friendship with Eleanor, that Edward undertook to see her. He did not hold his aunt responsible for the murder of Henry of Almain by her sons Guy and Simon, but he would not be persuaded that Amaury, who was in Padua at the time, had nothing to do with it. Edward agreed to confirm Eleanor in her dower rights, provided she behaved 'faithfully to us'. As a sign of good faith, he lent her £200 to be paid back with revenue from her dower lands, which was done the next year.[51]

Two months later the new King of France, Philip III, urged Edward to act further for the sake of his father Louis. It went back to 1259 and the agreement that £10,000 of the treaty money would be withheld as security for satisfying Eleanor's dower. She was now claiming that money from Louis's executors, but it had been withdrawn by Henry from the Temple in Paris after Evesham. Philip feared that his father's soul was in danger on account of it. With his usual speed, Edward ordered the Marshal heirs to pay up their debts to the countess. The following year, according to the Dunstable annalist, he completely restored her dower lands to her.[52]

On 2 August 1274, Edward and Eleanor of Castile returned to England with Alfonso, one of their two children born abroad, and with Beatrice and John of Brittany. Eleanor of Provence was then living at Windsor with three of her twelve grandchildren. These were Henry and

Eleanor, who had passed to her care after Richard of Cornwall's death, and Beatrice's 8-year-old son John, nicknamed Brito. Their grandmother took them to Canterbury to meet their parents, whom they had not seen in four years. The children then went back to living with her while preparations were made for the dual crowning of the new king and queen on 19 August.[53]

For Eleanor of Provence, it had to be an especially emotional and gratifying experience. With Margaret and Alexander in attendance, it was the first time in nearly fourteen years, not since October 1260, that she had all her children together. There had not been, moreover, a coronation in the land since her own in 1236, when she was a 12-year-old girl from a faraway land (which she never saw again) and Westminster Abbey looked a lot different than it did now.[54]

Tragedy then befell her family in quick succession. Six-year-old crown prince Henry took ill at his grandmother's residence in Guildford and died there in the middle of October. Less than a month later Edmund's wife Aveline died in childbirth along with the twins she was carrying. In Scotland, Margaret took to her bed that winter. She grew weaker and died on 26 February 1275. Beatrice's health also began to fail after giving birth to a daughter at Windsor. She died on 24 March. Eleanor's bereavement over losing both her daughters in the space of a month can only be imagined. Their deaths, said *Flores*, 'left a deep sorrow after the great joy of the coronation, for they were ladies in the flower of youth, of high character and distinguished beauty'.[55]

In April, Eleanor de Montfort was dying. It had been exactly thirty years since she visited Waverley Abbey on a wonderful, spiritually uplifting Sunday outing with her husband and two oldest boys. Now all three were dead. Her fourth son Guy was still entrenched in Italy, eluding punishment for his killing of Almain, and there was no word about Richard. That left only Amaury and her daughter with her at the end. One of Eleanor's last acts was to witness her daughter's marriage by proxy to Llywelyn, something that had been arranged between Simon and his erstwhile Welsh ally before Evesham. Young Eleanor was about 17, Llywelyn in his 50s.[56]

The Countess of Leicester died on 13 April 1275, aged 60. Queen Margaret paid her a final visit at Montargis and promised to intercede with Edward to make sure her will was carried out and to ask the king to admit Amaury to his grace. Edward, however, nabbed him and his sister as they tried to make their way to Wales later that year. Not for three years, until Llywelyn submitted to his authority, did Edward release young Eleanor so the couple could complete their marriage ceremony. He paid for their wedding in Worcester and gave Eleanor away, probably out of contrition for Evesham and fondness for his cousin. She died in 1282 giving birth to a daughter, the only grandchild born to her parents in Britain. After Llywelyn was killed that same year in a skirmish, Edward took their baby, called Gwenllian, to be raised in a nunnery in Lincolnshire. She died there in 1337.[57]

Amaury was imprisoned at Corfe mostly. He was released after six years, just months before his sister's death. Guy by then had been fully rehabilitated and was back to serving under Charles of Anjou. He was captured in a sea battle in 1287 and died in prison four years later, his ransom seemingly blocked by Edward. Amaury ended his days in Italy, tutoring Guy's daughters and, it was said, giving up the priesthood for knighthood.[58]

While Amaury was in prison, young Eleanor prevailed upon Edward to execute her mother's will, even threatening him with litigation. After her death, Amaury resumed the pressure. Eleanor de Montfort's debts included £63 she owed to the convent of St Antoine near Paris. Her heart was entombed within the church there, chosen, as with Montargis, because of its connection to her husband. Simon's sister Petronilla had been placed in St Antoine as a girl and went on to become the abbess there. In June 1286, Edward paid the debt while in Paris and then had the exchequer recover the money from the Marshal heirs. And so, after 55 years of anxiety, despair, pleas and threats, culminating in the blockage of the greatest peace treaty of the age, the case of Eleanor de Montfort's Marshal dower was at last closed.[59]

By contrast her sister-in-law Eleanor of Provence enjoyed immense wealth in her retirement. Her dower properties together with those bequeathed to her by Peter of Savoy earned her upwards of £6,000 a year. She still travelled about her dower lands, spending the most time at Guildford, Marlborough and Ludgershall, whereas she avoided Gillingham because of the 'greasy smoky vapours' that corrupted the air there in the evening. She could still be an exacting lord. In Havering, she summoned a group of men to tell her what they knew about trespasses in her woods. When they refused to answer, she had them locked up until she got the answers she wanted.[60]

In January 1275, just before the death of her daughters, Eleanor received a series of grants from her son. They included making her will, making up shortfalls in her dower income, and expelling the Jews from any town she held in dower. The last item is a reflection of the pace gathering throughout England and Europe to expel their Jewish communities, often at the initiative of Dominican and Franciscan friars, and it seems that Eleanor was susceptible to their teachings and pressure.

There is no obvious connection between this grant and the repressive measures enacted against the Jews that same year by Edward. He needed a tax and Parliament wanted to abolish Jewish credit. We cannot know Eleanor's private feelings about the issue, probably they were no different than the average pious Christian of the age. She took one Jewish family under her protection but could not save them or others when their community was expelled from England fifteen years later. She remained a patron of the home for converted Jews founded by her husband in 1232, which lasted until the early seventeenth century.[61]

Eleanor wrote to Edward on various matters, typically addressing him as 'our very dear son' (*nostre très cher fis*). She did not presume to dictate policy, but nor would she let him forget everything she had done to make sure he became king someday. She and her sister Margaret were still incensed over how Charles of Anjou had swiped Provence from them and were prepared to thwart him wherever they could. Eleanor expected Edward to toe the line here and he admitted that he was bound to her 'more than any living creature'. Margaret's attitude was the same. When Edward begged off sending her aid, she asked him to remember 'the events and adventures that happened in the other war caused by Count Simon'.[62]

As Eleanor turned 60, she began making plans to retire to the Wiltshire nunnery of Amesbury. It was a daughter house of the illustrious Fontevrault Abbey in France, which she and Henry had visited in 1254. This association and its organisation recommended it, but so too did its location. Not far away was Tarrant Abbey, which had come under her patronage just after her arrival in England and where her sister-in-law Joan, who might be said to have been her first English friend, was buried. Practically next door were Clarendon Palace, one of her favourite royal retreats, and Salisbury Cathedral, the dedication of which she attended with Henry in 1258.[63]

Also to be considered was the legend that Guinevere retired to a nunnery in Amesbury. Although this first appears in a later medieval tradition, it could have been circulating in Eleanor's time. She remained devoted to Arthurian romance and seems to have passed her enthusiasm on to her son the king. In 1278, Edward and Eleanor of Castile paid a visit to Glastonbury to see the graves of Arthur and Guinevere much as Henry and Eleanor had done forty-two years earlier.

No less important was the presence of Stonehenge, which was part of the nunnery complex. We know Henry had a mystical side, employing astrologers at court, collecting magic stones, and adorning the high altar of Westminster Abbey with a wondrous floor that evoked the cosmos and end of time. Surely Eleanor would have shared in this fascination of his during the course of their marriage and saw herself spending her final days wandering around the mysterious, ancient ruins.[64]

Forever attached to family, the queen dowager wanted two granddaughters to accompany her in taking the veil there, her namesake Eleanor of Brittany and Edward's daughter Mary, whose mother agreed to it only reluctantly. Eleanor of Provence herself did not actually enter the nunnery until 7 July 1286, two years after both girls and only then after arrangements had been made to ensure she and her granddaughters were well provided for there. To this end, she retained much of her dower property, which caused the Osney chronicler to dismiss her conversion as a sham. Among the properties she did relinquish were Cambridge, Guildford and, no doubt to the relief of the locals, Havering.[65]

These were anxious times for her family. Alfonso, the heir to the throne, died in 1284 while his parents were on campaign in Wales. The boy born to them a few months before that, named Edward, would be their last child. All three of Margaret's children had died by this time. Before he could beget another heir, Alexander suddenly perished in an accident, leaving the Scottish succession to fall on Eleanor's great-granddaughter Margaret, known as the Maid of Norway. In April 1290, it was decided to unite England and Scotland by marrying the 7-year-old girl to young Edward. The arrangements were made at Amesbury, in the presence of Eleanor of Provence, but she did not live to see the crisis that engulfed both kingdoms after the Maid died on her journey over.[66]

Meanwhile Edmund, now referred to as the Earl of Lancaster, had remarried and had three sons. At this time, Eleanor bought back Peter of Savoy's palace in London and gave it to him. In this way, the famed

Savoy Palace came to be owned by the future Dukes of Lancaster, of whom Edmund was the ur-ancestor. Eleanor loved all her children deeply, but there would always be that extra amount of affection for her youngest son, probably because he never got to be the King of Sicily and they had shared their exile in France together.[67]

On 11 May 1290, the body of Henry III was moved to his new tomb next to the shrine at Westminster Abbey. He looked intact, his beard lush and full, descriptions meant to win him the same canonisation about to be conferred on Louis. But they needed miracles and Eleanor was willing to believe the claims of a knight made several years earlier that his eyesight had been restored during a visit to her late husband. When Edward called the man a fake, she ordered her son to get out.

He did but grumbled that he knew his father well and was sure Henry would just as soon blind that scoundrel of a knight than give him his sight back. Edward meant no disrespect to his parents, he was just being realistic. Henry's famed humility and charity easily qualified him for sainthood, but he had no crusade to his credit, whereas Louis had two. They were unspeakable calamities, but two nevertheless.[68]

Henry and Eleanor's plans to be buried together in the abbey were then upset when Eleanor of Castile died in November 1290. In addition to erecting memorial crosses to his wife, Edward decided she would be buried in the abbey and had magnificent effigies prepared for her and his father. Since there could be only one Queen Eleanor lying in state in the abbey, his mother would have to be content with burial elsewhere. He probably told her this when he saw her for the last time, a few months before she died on 24 June 1291, aged around 68.[69]

There was still uncertainty about where Eleanor's final resting would be. The nuns of Fontevrault Abbey wrote to Edward, who was in Scotland at the time, to have her body brought there. She would join Henry II, Eleanor of Aquitaine, Richard the Lionheart and Isabella of Angoulême in the nearest thing the English royal family had to a mausoleum. Her husband had planned to change that with his elaborate reconstruction of Westminster Abbey, but even he had willed his heart to Fontevrault. Devoted to him to the last, Eleanor had kept it all the years of her widowhood.

Not sure what to do, the nuns of Amesbury had her embalmed pending Edward's decision. In December, the abbess of Fontevrault travelled to England but left with only Henry's heart. Eleanor of Provence had already been buried three months earlier on 8 September 1291 in front of her two sons and a host of prelates and magnates. She was laid to rest at Amesbury with all due ceremony, while her gold-encased heart went to the London church of the Franciscans, where her beloved daughter Beatrice was buried. Her destiny, for better or worse, was England.[70]

Epilogue

After her death, Eleanor of Provence was memorialised by a single cross. We know of it only because in 1294 Edward granted her grandson Brito, who had grown up under her care at Windsor, an oak from the surrounding forest to repair the cross that had been erected to her. There is nothing left of it, nor of her tomb at Amesbury, which was destroyed by the marauding Tudors. A beautiful Cedar of Lebanon tree stands today on the site of the high altar, where she was probably buried. An avid gardener, she would be pleased at how exquisite the surrounding landscape looks. Everything is peaceful and tranquil, a jewel hidden away from the noise and tumult of nearby Stonehenge.

But had Eleanor been interred in Westminster Abbey as originally intended, she might be better remembered today. Certainly she would be better appreciated for her accomplishments. She had not only revived the long dormant queenship of medieval England, but made it an equal partner in the monarchy. That in turn qualified her to assume the regency when the time came, despite expecting a child. Neither she nor her contemporaries could know it, but her role as acting head of state became a milestone in the political transformation of the country.

What seems impressive to us at a distance was not always viewed the same in her own day. Eleanor's wilfulness and temperament often elicited profound disdain from her contemporaries. They were apt to blame her for the problems that beset the later years of her husband's reign. To acerbic commentators, it was only logical. Henry was a former boy king who eschewed war and knightly pursuits, who saw his rule mainly as the manifestation of peace, charity and splendour. He was, in a word, a simple guy, nobody too exciting but somebody they could live with. Then along comes this woman from France and the next thing they know the country is plunged into turmoil. Had to be her and all those relatives she imported.

It is, of course, the simplest of falsehoods. Henry was all of the above, but he was sharp, gifted and determined to restore Plantagenet pride and prestige on the Continent. Marrying Eleanor was part of that plan and he more or less expected to incorporate her very able family in that arrangement. It worked insofar as it led to peace and friendship with France, one of the great achievements of the age, which was due in no small part to Eleanor and her sister Margaret fostering the feeling of family and togetherness between their two kingdoms.

Family had always been the strong suit of Eleanor's queenship. After giving the country four heirs by her early 20s, she insisted on being a mother first and foremost. She was a naturally doting and affectionate parent and together with Henry gave England its first truly cohesive royal family. He was vital to this, not just because he was forever faithful, but he deeply loved and respected his wife and would never subject her to the same indignity that the vast majority of English queens had had to endure. This allowed her to devote her energy and interests to her children, friends, household and realm at large.

It was that faith and loyalty in their marriage that led Henry to name Eleanor his regent when he left the country. This was one of the more remarkable instances in the history of the English monarchy. Having just given birth to her fifth and last child, she was expected to obtain funds for her husband's overseas expedition. In doing so, she became not only the first woman to summon and lord over Parliament, but the first person ever to summon Parliament with a democratic mandate. Nobody had planned for it, it was just the way it turned out, but as with any discovery or innovation, whoever is first gets the honours and this one is all hers.

The chroniclers who recorded these events saw nothing objectionable about women in positions of authority. Henry had female castellans and sheriffs during his minority and his earlier miscues may have been avoided had his mother been given an active role in his upbringing. Instead he was dominated by old men who led him to one problem after another until he got rid of them and instituted his personal rule. Eleanor entered his life shortly afterwards and for the next quarter of a century England enjoyed its first long stretch of peace and prosperity in the thirteenth century.

Eleanor played her own part in bringing it to an end, however. She was tough on her tenants, too adamant about her queen's gold, and not very mindful of her shady business practices. All three of these issues were subsequently addressed in the reform period, but the period itself was launched as the result of a misfire with her fingerprints all over it. Worried that Edward was going in the wrong direction, she joined a conspiracy to oust her rivals from court. She succeeded, but at a cost not just to the independence of her queenship, but her husband's kingship as well.

There was nothing at the outset of reform to suggest they had anything to fear. The council would rule, but under the king's lordship. It soon became apparent that some people, Simon de Montfort in particular, had other ideas. As far as he was concerned, Henry had failed him and his wife. They had clamoured about their claims year after year to no avail. The only way the Montforts were to get any justice in this world was if the king and queen went about feeding the poor and receiving guests and looking regal before their subjects, but otherwise leaving all decisions of state in the council's hands. The peace treaty with France had the potential to be manipulated to make that happen, and this is where our other Eleanor re-emerges.

The last we heard of Eleanor de Montfort, she had died at Montargis in France. The nunnery there survived much longer than Amesbury, but ultimately met the same fate during the French Revolution. Whatever trace there was of Eleanor disappeared in the ruins, but they did yield a bit of parchment curious by any standards of scholarship. It was the record of her household accounts.

It remains a mystery why she took these accounts with her into exile. They probably served as a diary of sorts of her last days in England, when all her immediate family was intact. The accounts have proved an invaluable resource in our understanding of medieval life and they show her to have been a competent and energetic estates manager, but that could have been almost any lord in that age, even Eleanor of Provence. It is the circumstances that brought the parchment and Eleanor de Montfort to the nunnery in the first place that bring her to life.

We see her first as 'treasure' of the realm, a princess to be viewed and married off to a stranger in a strange land for the benefit of the kingdom. She escaped the tragic destiny of her older sisters, even found happiness in the political marriage that was arranged for her, but it was cut short by her husband's untimely death. This set off a chain of events that would one day destroy the close and tender bond between her and her brother Henry. It started with Richard Marshal swindling her out of her dower and ended with the vow of celibacy she undertook to reconcile his quarrelsome family.

Whatever agency she played in these events, she was clearly unhappy. But inasmuch as Eleanor of Provence's queenship was made possible only by Henry, so too could Eleanor the chaste widow turn to him for help. He allowed her to marry Simon de Montfort despite the outrage it was sure to cause. Giving her another chance for family and children, with a foreign parvenu and adventurer, should have made her and Simon eternally grateful, but the scandal of the queen's churching, with its overtones of innuendo, corrupted their relationship forever.

Bad luck certainly did not help, like all the Marshal sons dying without heirs and Gascony spiralling out of control at the worst possible time. However it all came to pass, Eleanor de Montfort decided she had had enough. When it came time to ratify the peace treaty with France, something which Eleanor of Provence put all her hopes in, Eleanor de Montfort refused to cooperate. Her very emphatic statement to Henry, Louis and all the proctors waiting for her to play the role of the obliging princess was simple: You want peace, talk to me first.

And we can be sure this is Eleanor's voice and not her husband's. The existence of letters to her from her friend Adam Marsh reveal a woman who was going to wear what she wanted and say what she wanted regardless of the predominant place given to men in her world. This has moved some modern observers to see in her an attitude bordering on shrillness, but this neglects the gracious and amiable woman who is also present in these letters, who cannot hide the fears and concerns she has for her family.

Eleanor's gamble to hold the peace treaty hostage to her rights did not succeed and satisfaction eluded her to the end. What role she played in her husband's subsequent defiance we do not know, just that it was Henry's turn to decide he had had enough. Reform in the hands of someone like Simon de Montfort meant the end of monarchy as they knew it. The king's overthrow of the Provisions of Oxford proved to be a wildly unpopular move, but since he had shared in creating and promoting all the good legislation, the pundits assumed his hand had been forced, not by the behaviour of radicals like Simon, but by his wife the queen. The Montforts helped make it look that way by going into exile, as if adopting the guise of victims of oppression.

This is the point where Eleanor of Provence becomes the target for both chroniclers and insurgent barons. In the case of the former, it goes back to the great scandal of the age. In 1254, while Eleanor was regent and engaged as the impresario of Parliament, Henry accepted the throne of Sicily for their son Edmund. That was not the scandal, and had all the cards fallen into the right places, the glory for her family and England would have been beyond measure. The scandal was the papacy that made the offer. They had already imposed insufferable taxes and provisions on the English clergy. Sicily now made them obscene. The history of the age being written by monks, they found the whole business abhorrent and could not see how their king could sign on to such a deal. But of course, his wife.

The insurgent barons did not have to pay these taxes, but they were angry at the queen just the same because she cut them off from Edward. Her reasons were those any mother might have. Edward had caused her endless worry with his disobedience for much of the reform period and she figured his unruly friends were behind it. His submission to her led them to seek revenge. Under Simon's leadership, they teamed up with the xenophobic clergy and made Eleanor of Provence the symbol of all the ills afflicting the land. When word had it that she was vulnerable, the crowds gathered on London Bridge and pummelled her with stones and abuse.

Terrifying as it must have been, it did not stop her. She went right to work on bringing Simon down and kept at it until it was his turn to be brought low, on the fields of Evesham. While she could not have wished that disgraceful end on him and his family, important was the safety of her husband and son and restoration of the kingdom to its rightful place and balance. She returned from exile with no bitterness of heart, save for that wretched bridge, and finished her days in the England that was her home.

For Eleanor de Montfort, going back would be harder because of her unenviable position of being the sister of the king and wife of the man who tried to overthrow him. No matter who won, she lost, and we can glean a sense of unease and regret in her efforts to make her brother's captive monarchy as palatable as possible. In choosing exile when it was over, she was probably thinking of her children first and foremost, because she certainly did not withdraw to the nunnery in France with her spirit crushed. She went right back to contesting her rights, even reaching out to Eleanor of Provence to help settle her affairs in England.

Her brother would not have denied her had she turned to him, but it was beside the point. She trusted her sister-in-law.

And so the story of the two Eleanors comes to a poignant end, with one, defeated but resilient, turning to the other, victorious but magnanimous, two extraordinary lives at the centre of some of the most exciting events of the Middle Ages. While it is not always easy to separate women of achievement in that era from the men around them, their case stands out. Eleanor de Montfort showed us what strong and vigorous lordship looked like, Eleanor of Provence strong and vigorous queenship. It is a remarkable legacy that speaks to the ages.

Appendix 1

The Queen's Summons to Parliament
(Matthew Paris Additamenta no. 141, pp. 286–7)

During her regency, Eleanor of Provence summoned two Parliaments as acting head of state, making her the first woman to do so. For the second assembly in the spring of 1254, she dispatched orders to the sheriffs to elect local knights and send them to Westminster to treat on her plan to bring aid to the king for the defence of Gascony. This marks the first time any Parliament met with a democratic mandate. A copy of the writ was entered in the Close Rolls (*CR 1253–54*, pp. 114–5) with Eleanor's name and that of Richard of Cornwall on it. Chronicler Matthew Paris was impressed with what appeared to be a constitutional innovation and included another copy of the writ in his *Additamenta*, this one bearing only the name of the queen as witness.

H[enricus] Dei gratia, etc., vicecomiti Hertfordiae salutem
   Cum comites et barones et caeteri magnates regni Angliae nostri nobis firmiter promiserint quod erunt Londoniis a die Paschae proximo futuro in tres septimanas cum equis et armis bene armati, ad tendendum sine ulla dilatione versus Portesmue ad transfretandum ad nos in Wasconia contra regem Castellorum, qui terram nostram Wasconiam in manu forti in aestate proximo futura hostiliter est ingressurus, et tibi mandaverimus quod omnes illos de balliva tua qui tenent viginti libratas terrae de nobis in capite vel de illis qui sunt infra aetatem et in custodia nostra ad idem destringeres; tibi districte praecipimus quod praeter omnes praedictos venire facias coram consilio nostro apud Westmonasterium in quindena Paschae proximo futuri quatuor legales et discretos milites de comitibus praedictis, quos iidem comites ad hoc elegerint vice omnium et singulorum eorundem comitum, videlicet duos de uno comitatu et duos de alio, ad providendum una cum militibus aliorum comitatuum quos ad eundem diem vocari fecimus quale auxilium nobis in tanta necessitate

194

impendere voluerint; et tu ipse militibus et aliis de comitibus praedictis necessitatem nostram et tam urgens negotium nostrum diligenter exponas, et eos ad competens auxilium nobis ad praesens impendendum efficaciter inducas, ita quod praedicti quatuor milites praefato consilio nostro ad praedictum terminum praecise respondere possint super praedicto auxilio pro singulis comitum praedictorum.

Teste Alienora regina nostra apud Windsiure, xiv. die Februarii, anno regni nostri xxxviii°

Henry by the grace of God, etc., to the Sheriff of Hertfordshire, greetings.

Since the earls and barons and the other nobles of our kingdom have firmly promised that they will be in London on Easter day next for three weeks, with horses and arms, ready and well furnished for going without delay to Portsmouth, to cross with us (the queen) to Gascony against the King of Castile, who is about to enter our land of Gascony during the ensuing summer with a strong force and in hostile manner, and we have also ordered all those in your jurisdiction who hold twenty librates of land of us in chief or of others who are under age and in our ward to muster, by distraint if necessary; we charge you that in addition to all the aforesaid that you shall have two lawful and discrete knights specially elected by the counties, for each and all in their counties, appear before our council at Westminster within a fortnight at Easter to consider, together with the knights of the other counties whom we have had summoned for the same day, what aid they will be willing to grant us in our great need. And you yourself shall diligently explain our necessity and very urgent affairs to the knights and the others coming from the counties, and effectually persuade them to grant us a sufficient aid; so that on the date fixed the knights, in the name of their counties, shall be able to provide a definitive answer in the matter of this aid.

By the witness of Queen Eleanor at Windsor, the 14th day of February in the thirty-eighth year of our reign.

Appendix 2

Eleanor of Provence to Henry III
(Royal Letter no. 447, 1244/1245)

Henry III had secured the election of his wife's uncle Boniface of Savoy to become the Archbishop of Canterbury, figuring he would tolerate the king's influence over other church elections. In 1244, Henry convinced the chapter of Chichester to elect one of his officials, Robert Passelewe, as their new bishop, but Boniface had only just arrived in England and so asked a panel of bishops to convene a confirmation hearing for Passelewe. They rejected him, and Boniface not only accepted their finding, but also their own choice of bishop. Henry was livid, and Eleanor of Provence undertook to write this letter to her husband to let him know she was on his side.

Excellentissimo ac reverendisimo domino suo Henrico, Dei gratia regi Angliae illustri, domino Hiberniae, duci Normanniae Aquitaniae, et comiti Andegaviae, sua humillima consors et devotissima Alianora, eadem gratia regina Angliae, salutem et debitam cum omni reverntia subjectionem.

Dominationi vestrae notum facimus nos per Dei gratiam et liberos nostros sanos esse et incolumes, quod de vobis scire toto cordis et animi affectu desideramus; regiae majestati vestrae significantes quod electus Cantuariensis praeterita die nuntios suos cum literis suis nobis destinavit, et per ipsos nobis significavit, quod quorundam relatu didicerat nos pro facto suo de episcopatu Cycestrensi contra ipsum fuisse commotas, et petiit quod super hoc non molestaremur, nec contra ipsum moveremur. Cui per nuntios et literas nostras significavimus, quod non fuit mirum si contra ipsum moveremur, cum vos super hoc offendisset, nec posset aliquo modo nostram habere benevolentiam, dummodo vestram sustineret indignationem. Quibus etiam auditis et intellectis, in propria persona ad nos accessit, nobis significans quod super praedictis et omnibus aliis vestram pro posse suo adimpleret voluntatem. Cui persuasimus quod vestram adimpleret voluntatem si nostram vellet sedare indignationem; quia dum discordia inter vos et ipsum duraret, nostram iram nec indignationem eidem nullo modo remitteremus. Excellentissimae igitur dominationi vestrae omni qua possumus affectione supplicamus, quatenus statum vestrum, quem Deus prosperum faciat et felicem, et vestrae voluntatis beneplacitum nobis crebo, si placet, significare dignemini. Valeat excellentia vestra semper in Domino.

To her most excellent and reverend lord, Henry, by the grace of God illustrious King of England, Lord of Ireland, Duke of Normandy, Aquitaine, and Count of Anjou, his most humble consort and most devoted Eleanor, by that same grace Queen of England, greetings and owed subjection with all reverence.

We make known to your lordship that by the grace of God we and our children are healthy and well, which we want you to know with all the affection of heart and spirit; and we impart to your majesty that the elect of Canterbury sent us his messengers with letters on a day past and let us know by them that he had learned from certain people that we had been moved against him over the episcopacy of Chichester, and he asked that we be neither angry about it, nor turned against him. We let him know through messengers and our letters that it was no wonder if we were moved against him since he had offended you over this, nor could he gain our benevolence in any way as long as he suffered your indignation.

Having heard and understood these things, he came to us in person, telling us that he would satisfy your will over said matters and all others, as far as he could. We persuaded him that he must satisfy your will if he wished to quiet our indignation; since while discord lasted between you and him, our wrath or indignation against him would not in any way abate. We therefore beg your most excellent lordship with all the affection we can, that you deign to let us know your state, may God make it prosperous and happy, and the pleasure of your will over this, quickly, if it please you.

May your excellence always be well in the Lord.

Appendix 3

Eleanor de Montfort's Confraternity

(MS Clairambault 1021)

The elegant Latin script of these letters details the prayers and masses to be said for the souls of Simon and Eleanor de Montfort in the afterlife and for the feeding of the poor on their behalf. They were issued in 1257 by St Albans Abbey. The text begins with Simon and ends with her.

Hec eadem per omnia in omnibus presentium tenore concesserunt dicti abbas et conventus nobili comitisse, Domine videlicet Alienore uxori domini comitis prenotati, filiis quoque ac filiabus de utroque eorum progenitis, unanimiter concesserunt communia tricenalia in eorum exitibus ab hac vita.

All these same things in all respects in everything the said abbot and convent have conceded to the noble countess, namely to Eleanor the wife of the aforementioned lord count, and also to the sons and daughters begotten by either of them, they have unanimously granted common trentals when they depart from this life.

Appendix 4

Eleanor de Montfort's Litigation

(MS Clairambault 1188, f. 13–16)

Throughout much of her life, Eleanor was involved in a number of arbitrations and suits. Many of the records survived in the Montfort family archives and were copied as part of the collection that exists today at the Bibliothèque nationale de France. Below is Eleanor's seal used to attest the suit she launched in 1260 against her Lusignan relatives for a share of their mother's estate.

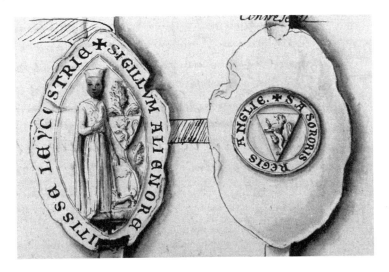

In July 1259, an arbitration panel was commissioned to rule on the issue of Eleanor's Marshal dower, by then 25-years old. The attesting seals, a few in bad shape, belong to 1) Boniface of Savoy, 2) Walter Cantilupe, 3) Richard de Clare, 4) Roger Bigod, 5) Peter of Savoy, 6) Humphrey de Bohun, 7) William de Forz, 8) John de Plessis, 9) Philip Basset, 10) John Mansel, 11) Roger Mortimer, 12) James Audley, 13) Richard de Grey, 14) Peter de Montfort.

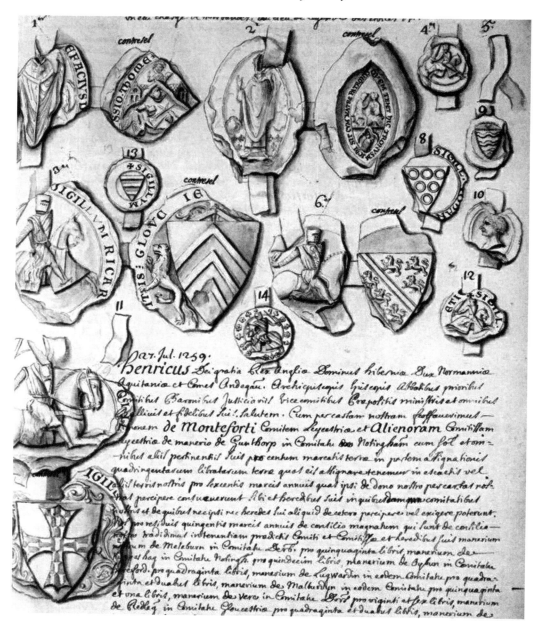

Appendix 5

Eleanor de Montfort's Household Roll
(BL Add. MS 8877)

After the downfall of her husband's regime, Eleanor left England with
her daughter to live at the nunnery of Montargis in France. The record of
her household accounts were discovered there five centuries later when
the nunnery was destroyed during the French Revolution. They show
the expenditures made by Eleanor's household on a daily basis between
late February and August 1265. The entries were made by one of two
clerks, Christopher or Eudes, and show the day in question, location of
the household, what was consumed from stores or purchased, and any
special guests. The bottom entry reproduced from the section of the roll
below indicates that the day was 23 February and her household was
at Odiham.

Dɪᴇ Lᴜɴᴀᴇ, pro Comitissa ; Panis, i. quart. et dimid., de instauro. Vinum, ij. sext. i. lagen. *Bracinium*. v. quart. Ordei., vij. quart et dimid. Avenae. *Coquina*. iiijᶜ. Alleces. Piscis, ex emptione, viij.s. *Mareschalcia*. Ad xxxiij. Equos foenum de instauro. Avena, ij. quart et i. bus.

Summa, viij.s.

Monday, for the Countess: Grain, 1½ quarters from stores. Wine, 2 sextaries, 1 gallon. *Brewing*. 5 quarters of barley, 7½ quarters of oats. *Kitchen*. 400 herrings. Fish, by purchase, 7s. 9d. *Stables*. For 33 horses, hay from stores. Oats, 2 quarters, 1 bushel.

Sum 8s

List of Illustrations

1. Family trees, author's work.
2. Effigy of King John in Worchester Cathedral, author's collection.
3. Effigy of Isabella of Angoulême at Fontevrault Abbey, author's collection.
4. Genealogical membrane of King John and his children and grandchildren, British Library, MS Royal 14 B VI Membrane 6.
5. Coronation of King Henry III, British Library, Cotton MS Vitellius A XIII
6. Effigies of William Marshal and William Marshal II, author's collection.
7. Seal of Simon de Montfort, British Library, Additional Charter 11296
8. Marriage of Henry III and Eleanor of Provence, British Library, MS Royal 14 C VII f. 124v.
9. Painted Chamber, water colour painted by William Capon, 1799
10. 'Queen Eleanor' herb garden at Winchester Hall, author's collection.
11. Winchester Hall, author's collection.
12. La Réole Castle in France, author's collection.
13. Henry and Eleanor in a boat returning from Gascony, British Library, MS Royal 14 C VII f. 134v.
14. Children of Henry III and Eleanor of Provence, British Library, MS Royal 14 B VI Membrane 7.
15. Windsor Castle, author's collection.
16. Kenilworth Castle, author's collection.
17. Odiham Castle, author's collection.
18. London Bridge, British Library Yates Thompson 47 f. 94v.
19. Tower of London and London Bridge, British Library, MS Royal 16 F II f. 73.
20. Henry visiting Louis and Saint-Denis, British Library, MS Royal 16 G VI f. 426.

21. Civil war in England, Royal 16 G VI f. 427v.
22. Wallingford Castle, author's collection.
23. Dover Castle, author's collection.
24. Westminster Abbey, author's collection.
25. Site of burial place of Eleanor of Provence in Amesbury, author's collection.
26. Stonehenge, author's collection.
27. Corbel of Eleanor of Provence (© Dean and Chapter of Westminster).

Notes

1 No Greater Treasure

1. *Tewkesbury*, p. 84; Green, 'Account of the Discovery of the Body of King John'.
2. Wilkinson, *Eleanor de Montfort*, pp. 4–6.
3. Vincent, *Peter des Roches*, pp. 153–4.
4. Clanchy, *Memory to Written Record*, pp. 189–90.
5. Wilkinson, *Eleanor de Montfort*, pp. 11–12.
6. Baker, *Henry III*, p. 36.
7. Stacey, *Politics*, p. 20. Isabelle and Henry's brother Richard had been the 'spares' for the deal.
8. Wilkinson, *Eleanor de Montfort*, pp. 19–20.
9. https://epistolae.ccnmtl.columbia.edu/letter/457.html. [Accessed 3 December 2018]
10. *Royal Letters I*, p. 92; Vincent, 'Isabella of Angoulême', pp. 207–08.
11. Carpenter, *Minority of Henry III*, p. 196; Wilkinson, *Eleanor de Montfort*, p. 8.
12. *Dunstable*, p. 58; Carpenter, *Minority of Henry III*, pp. 186, 196, 200; *Royal Letters I*, pp. 70, 150.
13. *Lanercost*, p. 29.
14. Wilkinson, *Eleanor de Montfort*, pp. 18–9; *Royal Letters I*, p. 160; *Flores*, p. 139. Hubert's first wife was Beatrice de Warenne, who died around 1214, and his second wife the aged Isabella, heiress of Gloucester and King John's first wife. She died a few days after her wedding to Hubert in 1217.
15. Wilkinson, *Eleanor de Montfort*, pp. 24–5.
16. Ibid., pp. 21–4.
17. Carpenter, *Minority of Henry III*, pp. 271–2; *Royal Letters I*, pp. 244–6.
18. Wilkinson, *Eleanor de Montfort*, p. 25.
19. *CPR, 1216–25*, pp. 426, 437; *Gervase*, p. 113.
20. Carpenter, *Minority of Henry III*, pp. 343–75, 376–88. Henry hanged all but three of the surviving garrison of 88 knights. Fawkes was banished from the realm and died reputedly of fish poisoning two years later.
21. Huffman, *Social Politics*, pp. 228–44.

22. *Wendover*, p. 176.
23. Powicke, *King Henry III*, pp. 178–9. Henry also entertained a proposal from Ottokar I, the King of Bohemia, that he marry his daughter Agnes as part of England joining a princely confederation of the empire. Ottokar was in fact using him to make Agnes more attractive in the eyes of the real catch he wanted, Emperor Frederick, but Agnes turned them all down and became a nun.
24. *CPR, 1225–32*, pp. 80–1.
25. *CChR 1226–57*, p. 13; Ellis, *Hubert de Burgh*, pp. 110–1, 197–8.
26. *Wendover*, pp. 487–9; Denholm-Young, *Richard of Cornwall*, pp. 9–14.
27. Morris, *Bigod Earls*, pp. 4–5, 43–4, 100. Supposedly no suitable noble had been found for Isabelle by 1223, so she was returned to Scotland. Her marriage to Roger Bigod was probably the work of Hubert de Burgh, who would thus become the brother-in-law to the King of Scotland and to the powerful northern baron that Bigod was to become. The couple was childless, and in 1245 Roger tried and failed to get the marriage annulled. They reconciled in 1253 and died together in 1270, her death preceding his by a few months.
28. Pollock, *Scotland, England and France*, pp. 112–3.
29. *CChR 1226–57*, p. 102; Wilkinson, *Eleanor de Montfort*, pp. 28–9. Eleanor's own mother Isabella was probably close to twenty before she had Henry, her first child.
30. *Dunstable*, p. 92; Carpenter, *Minority of Henry III*, pp. 164–5, 367. John gave some of Marshal's manors to Fawkes de Bréauté. At the end of the war, Marshal reaffirmed the grant to Fawkes in an act of foolishness, says the Dunstable annalist. Not until Fawkes fell from grace in the spectacular siege of Bedford did Marshal get the manors back.
31. Powicke, *King Henry III*, pp. 179–80.
32. *CPR, 1225–32*, p. 400; *CR, 1227–31*, p. 323.
33. *Royal Letters I*, pp. 364–5; *Wendover*, p. 531; Green, *Lives of Princesses*, p. 55; Wilkinson, *Eleanor de Montfort*, p. 30.
34. Wilkinson, *Eleanor de Montfort*, pp. 27–8.
35. *Royal Letters I*, pp. 370–1; *Wendover*, pp. 534–8; Wilkinson, *Eleanor de Montfort*, p. 35.
36. Denholm-Young, *Richard of Cornwall*, pp. 18–9.
37. *Tewkesbury*, p. 78; *Wendover* (*Paris*), p. 539; Wilkinson, *Eleanor de Montfort*, pp. 37, 151.
38. Vincent, *Peter des Roches*, pp. 272–3; *Wendover*, p. 542; Denholm-Young, *Richard of Cornwall*, pp. 20–1.
39. Labarge, *Montfort*, pp. 27–31.
40. *Wendover*, p. 543.
41. Vincent, *Peter des Roches*, pp. 277–8.
42. Maddicott, *Montfort*, pp. 50–3.

43. *Wendover*, p. 542.
44. Wilkinson, *Eleanor de Montfort*, pp. 41–2.
45. Ellis, *Hubert de Burgh*, pp. 127–43.
46. Wilkinson, *Eleanor de Montfort*, pp. 43–4. She had received 51 deer by the end of August 1233.
47. Carpenter, *Struggle for Mastery*, pp. 312–5.
48. *Wendover*, pp. 569–91; Vincent, *Peter des Roches*, pp. 386–91.
49. Wilkinson, *Eleanor de Montfort*, pp. 42–3; Vincent, *Peter des Roches*, pp. 469–70.
50. *CPR, 1232–47*, pp. 65–6; *Paris II*, p. 442; Wilkinson, *Eleanor de Montfort*, pp. 45–6.
51. *Wendover*, pp. 607–09.
52. Wilkinson, *Eleanor de Montfort*, pp. 54–5.
53. Ibid., pp. 50–1.
54. Pollock, *Scotland, England and France*; pp. 125–6.
55. Nelson, 'A Queen and Sister: Joan, the wife of Alexander II of Scotland'.
56. Wilkinson, *Eleanor de Montfort*, pp. 56–7.

2 An Elegant Sort of Beauty

1. Vincent, *Peter des Roches*, pp. 463–4.
2. *Paris I*, pp. 237–9.
3. *CPR, 1232–47*, p. 74; *Foedera I*, p. 216.
4. *Foedera I*, p. 218. Louis VI was the father Louis VII, who was the father of Alice of France, the mother of Marie de Dammartin, the mother of Joan; Louis VI was also the father of Peter de Courtenay, who was the father of Alice de Courtenay, the mother of Isabella of Angoulême, the mother of Henry.
5. *Wendover*, p. 610; Cockerill, *Eleanor of Castile*, pp. 35–6. The wedding of Isabella and Frederick took place in Worms on 15 July 1235.
6. *Puylaurens*, pp. 82–3.
7. Labarge, *Saint Louis*, pp. 54–5.
8. Cox, *Eagles of Savoy*, p. 44.
9. *Joinville*, pp. 311–12.
10. Cox, *Eagles of Savoy*, pp. 6–7, 14–5; *Royal Letters I*, pp. 77–8.
11. Cox, *Eagles of Savoy*, p. 46. There has long been a tradition that Eleanor, although only 12-years old, set out to snare Henry by writing a verse poem called *Blandin of Cornwall* and sending it to Richard of Cornwall in the hope that the married Richard would pass it on to his brother. Modern scholarship has discounted it as a fine yarn. Howell, *Eleanor of Provence*, p. 7.
12. Howell, *Eleanor of Provence*, pp. 3–7.
13. Norgate, *Minority of Henry III*, pp. 157–8. Since the monarch had been traditionally crowned in Westminster Abbey by the Archbishop of Canterbury,

Pope Honorius ordered the second coronation to remove any doubts about the legality of the first ceremony in Gloucester in 1216.

14. *Foedera I*, p. 217.
15. *Wendover*, pp. 607–08.
16. Vincent, 'Inventory of Gifts to Henry III', pp. 133–5, 146. Relations between England and Savoy went way back, at least to 1173 and negotiations to contract a marriage between Henry's father John, then 7-years-old, and a daughter of the then count. As king, John was known to keep magic stones in his treasury, including one that was said to imbue the wearer with invincible power. In his charges against Hubert de Burgh in 1232, Henry claimed that his former minister had given this particular stone to Llywelyn, which would account for the recent success of the Welsh against the English.
17. *Foedera I*, p. 218; Cockerill, *Eleanor of Castile*, pp. 36–7.
18. *Foedera I*, p. 220. The Record edition of the *Foedera* cited here provides the date as 15 October 1236, the Haugue edition (p. 120) gives 11 October 1236.
19. *CChR 1226–57*, p. 218; Howell, *Eleanor of Provence*, p. 13.
20. *Flores*, p. 177; *CPR, 1232–47*, p. 103.
21. *Paris I*, pp. 7–8.
22. *CPR, 1232–47*, pp. 132–4.
23. Howell, *Eleanor of Provence*, p. 15.
24. Carpenter, *Minority of Henry III*, p. 305; Vincent, *Peter des Roches*, pp. 243–6; Vincent, 'Henry III and the Blessed Virgin Mary', pp. 129–40. Henry had a number of half-sisters, probably as many as six, sired by John before his marriage to Isabella of Angoulême and those born to Isabella after her remarriage to Hugh Lusignan.
25. *Dunstable*, p. 57–8; Norgate, *Minority of Henry III*, pp. 129–30, 157–8.
26. *Paris I*, pp. 9–10; *Coronation Records*, pp. 61–2; Howell, *Eleanor of Provence*, pp. 18–9.
27. *CR, 1234–37*, p. 229; Howell, *Eleanor of Provence*, p. 20.
28. *Coronation Records*, pp. 63–4.
29. Steane, *Archaeology of the Medieval English Monarchy*, p. 73; Hyams, 'Henry III in Bed', pp. 93–7.
30. *Paris I*, pp. 10–11.
31. Ibid., pp. 12–14.
32. *Dunstable*, pp. 145–6; Stacey, *Politics, Policy, and Finance*, pp. 96–116.
33. Howell, *Eleanor of Provence*, p. 7. It was perhaps on this first visit to the Severn that Eleanor developed a taste for the eel-looking lamprey pulled from the river, at least to the exclusion of other fish. In March 1237, the Sheriff of Gloucester was ordered to keep the supply of lampreys to Westminster coming, because all other fish seemed tasteless to the king and queen (*CR, 1234–37*, p. 420).
34. *CPR, 1232–47*, p. 158; *Paris I*, pp. 36–7; Nelson, 'A Queen and Sister'.

35. *Foedera I*, p. 221.
36. *CPR, 1232–47*, pp. 161, 166; *CR, 1234–37*, p. 387; Wilkinson, *Eleanor de Montfort*, pp. 55–6.
37. *CR, 1234–37*, p. 309; *CLR, 1226–40*, p. 243; Howell, *Eleanor of Provence*, p. 24.
38. Howell, *Eleanor of Provence*, pp. 23, 104–05; Tout, *Administrative History, Vol. V*, pp. 232–5; *Paris I*, p. 173.
39. *Paris I*, pp. 49–50; Stacey, *Politics, Policy, and Finance*, pp. 112–3.
40. Bémont, *Montfort*, pp. 53–4; Maddicott, *Montfort*, pp. 47–9. To get them to surrender their claims to Leicester, Montfort had to pay Ranulf of Chester £200 and his older brother Amaury £500. Moreover, he received only half of Leicester, as his great-aunt Margaret inherited the other half upon the death of her childless brother Robert de Beaumont.
41. *CChR 1226–57*, p. 230.
42. *Paris I*, pp. 54–5, 68; *Flores*, p. 183.
43. *CPR, 1232–47*, pp. 199, 203; *Foedera I*, p. 233; *Dunstable*, p. 146; *Paris I*, pp. 69–70.
44. *CPR, 1232–47*, pp. 184–5; *Melrose*, pp. 180–1; *Paris I*, p. 54.
45. Carpenter, *Minority of Henry III*, p. 260. Joan of Wales died on 2 February 1237. She may have been the daughter of Clemence Fougeres, making Clemence the grandmother of Helena. In 1200, John married Clemence to Ranulf of Chester, whose own marriage to Constance, the mother of Eleanor of Brittany, had been annulled. Ranulf was said to be 'small in stature' and 'impotent', hence no children with either of his wives. Both Clemence and Helena were dowager countesses of Chester at the time of the Christmas court of 1237–38.
46. *CPR, 1232–47*, p. 204; *Lanercost*, pp. 11–12.

3 Too Much Goodwill

1. *Paris II*, p. 442.
2. *Paris I*, pp. 71–9, 117; *Dunstable*, pp. 146–7; *Flores*, p. 183; *Tewkesbury*, p. 105. Paris says the archbishop left the week before Christmas.
3. *CPR, 1232–47*, pp. 125–6; see above, p. 27.
4. See above, p. 18.
5. *Paris I*, p. 117. For the description of Montfort, *Lanercost*, p. 39; Rishanger, *De Bellis*, p. 6.
6. *CR, 1234–37*, p. 292; Wilkinson, *Eleanor de Montfort*, pp. 62–3.
7. Binksi, *Painted Chamber*, pp. 13–15.
8. *Paris I*, p. 117.
9. *CPR, 1232–47*, pp. 199–200; *Tewkesbury*, p. 105; Powicke, *King Henry III*, pp. 760–8. There was plenty more controversy surrounding the marriage of Richard de Clare. In 1232, he was 10-years old and the ward of Hubert de

Burgh. When Hubert fell into disgrace, his wife Margaret of Scotland had the boy married to her only child with Hubert, a daughter named Megotta, who was of the same age. Hubert later recovered his land and respectability, but nearly lost them again when Henry learned of the secret marriage of the young couple. Megotta was on her deathbed on 26 October 1237 when the council decided that they should try to interest Isabella of Angoulême and Hugh Lusignan in a marital alliance between Clare and one of their daughters. If that did not happen by January 1238, then young Clare was to marry Maud de Lacy. Maud's father was instructed to fine with the king £3,333 for the marriage, of which £1,333 was automatically pardoned. The Lacy-Clare marriage took place on 26 January 1238.

10. *CPR, 1232–47*, pp. 208–09.
11. *Paris I*, pp. 120–3.
12. *CPR, 1232–47*, p. 22;. Stacey, *Politics, Policy, and Finance*, p. 123.
13. *CLR, 1226–40*, p. 329; Crouch, *Acts and Letters of the Marshal Family*, p. 30.
14. *Foedera I*, p. 235.
15. *Melrose*, p. 181; *Paris I*, pp. 123–4; *CPR, 1232–47*, p. 214; *CLR, 1226–40*, p. 316.
16. *CLR, 1226–40*, pp. 311, 410; *CPR, 1232–47*, p. 214; *Paris I*, pp. 124, 130; Wilkinson, *Eleanor de Montfort*, p. 65. Henry lent the Montforts another £1,565, all of it later pardoned, and according to Paris, Simon extorted £333 from one of his tenants in Leicester. Paris also says that Simon 'pined away with deep grief' on account of having become estranged from Richard of Cornwall, the nobles, and interestingly, the king. He adds that he 'set sail by stealth', as if a wanted man.
17. *CLR, 1226–40*, pp. 315–6, 319, 320–1, 344.
18. *Paris I*, pp. 138–9. The damsel was Margaret Biset, who had previously served Isabella, Henry's sister. While at the Tower that year, Henry made a gift of £13 to another of Eleanor's damsels, Emma Biset, possibly Margaret's sister, after she lost her eyesight (*CPR, 1232–47*, p. 103; *CLR, 1226–40*, p. 315).
19. *Flores*, p. 187; *Royal Letters II*, pp. 15–6. *Flores* says an accomplice was caught the following year who tried to implicate several nobles in the plot. He later admitted perjury and was dragged and hanged in London. Not until 1242 was the outlaw gang, led by William de Marisco, rounded up and executed. See Powicke, *King Henry III*, pp. 740–59; *Paris I*, pp. 408–09; *Paris II*, p. 58.
20. *CPL I*, p. 172; *Paris I*, pp. 124, 130. The treatise was by Master Peter Lombard.
21. *Paris I*, p. 155; Stacey, *Politics, Policy, and Finance*, p. 124.
22. *CLR, 1226–40*, pp. 337, 356.
23. *CLR, 1226–40*, p. 389; *Paris I*, pp. 155, 160; Kanter, 'Peripatetic and Sedentary Kingship', pp. 19–26.
24. *CLR, 1226–40*, pp. 406, 418; *Paris I*, pp. 172–3.

25. *Flores*, p. 189; *Paris I*, pp. 134–5, 165, 172–3. Eleanor de Montfort was still referred to as 'the Countess of Pembroke' in Chancery rolls as late as 1256 (*CPR, 1247–58*, p. 457), typically as the Countess of Leicester and Pembroke.
26. *Paris I*, pp. 132–3, 135–7.
27. *CLR, 1226–40*, pp. 400–03.
28. *Paris I*, p. 194.
29. *Paris I*, p. 236; Stacey, *Politics, Policy, and Finance*, p. 128; Maddicott, *Montfort*, pp. 24–5.
30. *Dunstable*, p. 151; Bémont, *Montfort*, pp. 60–1.
31. *Paris I*, pp. 166–7, 241; Cox, *Eagles of Savoy*, pp. 70–6.
32. *CLR, 1226–40*, pp. 409, 444; *CR, 1237–42*, p. 236; *Tewkesbury*, p. 113; *Paris I*, pp. 255, 287.
33. *CR, 1237–42*, pp. 234–5; *Paris I*, p. 259; Baker, *Montfort*, p. 227.
34. *CLR, 1240–45*, p. 100; *Dunstable*, p. 152. Paris says Simon received £1,000 for selling his noble woods to the Hospitallers.
35. *Paris I*, pp. 195–6, 266–8, 287–9.
36. Ibid., pp. 264–5, 268–270; Cox, *Eagles of Savoy*, p. 135.
37. *CR, 1237–42*, p. 217; *Tewkesbury*, p. 116; *Paris I*, p. 290; Howell, *Eleanor of Provence*, p. 30; Labarge, *Saint Louis*, p. 57.
38. *Lanercost*, p. 39; *Paris I*, pp. 309–11.
39. *Paris I*, pp. 318–20; Cox, *Eagles of Savoy*, pp. 40–3, 82–6; Stacey, *Politics, Policy, and Finance*, pp. 140–1. For all his warlike reputation, Peter had never been knighted. Henry gave him the honour, along with fifteen other youths, on 5 January 1241. Peter was induced to stay with custody of Richmond, which had formerly belonged to his brother William (*CChR 1226–57*, p. 252), was given the wardship of John de Warenne, the future Earl of Surrey (*Foedera I*, p. 243), and made the warden of the Channel ports (*CPR 1232–47*, p. 266).
40. *CPR 1232–47*, p. 241; *Paris I*, pp. 334–6; *Dunstable*, pp. 156–7; *Gervase*, pp. 190–2; Powicke, *King Henry III*, pp. 270–3; Cox, *Eagles of Savoy*, p. 110.
41. *CPR 1232–47*, p. 244; *Paris I*, pp. 458–9.
42. *Paris I*, pp. 322, 359–60, 379; *CPR 1232–47*, pp. 261, 266; *Tewkesbury*, pp. 119, 120.
43. *Paris I*, pp. 308, 315, 318, 337, 362–71, 385–6; Denholm-Young, *Richard of Cornwall*, pp. 42–3.

4 Flowers Among Women

1. *Osney*, p. 77; *CLR, 1240–45*, p. 324; Carpenter, 'Meetings of Kings Henry III and Louis IX', pp. 3–5, 17.
2. *CLR, 1240–45*, pp. 124, 204, 306.

3. *Paris I*, pp. 394–6; Stacey, *Politics, Policy, and Finance*, pp. 160–200; Howell, *Eleanor of Provence*, pp. 34–5; Clanchy, *England and Its Rulers*, pp. 239–40.
4. *CPR, 1232–47*, pp. 280, 294; *CChR 1226–57*, p. 268; *Paris I*, pp. 397–402.
5. *Paris I*, pp. 416–31; Powicke, *King Henry III*, p. 215.
6. *CLR, 1240–45*, pp. 153; Bémont, *Montfort*, pp. 64–6 ; Maddicott, *Montfort*, pp. 30–1; Turner, *Manners*, pp. xviii–xix.
7. *Paris I*, pp. 420–1.
8. *CPR, 1232–47*, p. 318, 320, 437; *CLR, 1240–45*, p. 198; *Letters of Adam Marsh II* (no. 153), pp. 372–3; *Paris I*, pp. 434–6; *Paris II*, pp. 115–6; Denholm-Young, *Richard of Cornwall*, pp. 48–9.
9. *CPR, 1232–47*, pp. 394, 401–02; *Paris I*, p. 447 ('The queen was great either with child or some other infirmity.')
10. *CPR, 1232–47*, p. 405; *Paris I*, pp. 455, 459–61.
11. *CPR, 1232–47*, p. 377; Bémont, *Montfort*, p. 68, (first edition, p. 335).
12. *CPR, 1232–47*, p. 433; *CChR 1226–57*, p. 278; *Paris II*, p. 52; Maddicott, *Montfort*, pp. 33, 54. Paris says that Richard of Cornwall was angry not to have been given the wardship himself.
13. *Paris II*, pp. 7–13, 22–6; Stacey, *Politics, Policy, and Finance*, pp. 221–2, 245–6.
14. *Paris I*, pp. 530–3.
15. *Letters of Robert Grosseteste* (no. 103), pp. 327–8.
16. *Paris II*, pp. 5, 40–1 49–50, 61.
17. *Royal Letters II* (no. 447), pp. 42–3; https://epistolae.ctl.columbia.edu/letter/588.html. [Accessed 3 December 2018]
18. *Paris II*, pp. 133–4.
19. *CLR, 1240–45*, p. 275.
20. Ibid., pp. 284, 292. Perhaps as a gift for his wife, Henry undertook the construction of walled gardens for Eleanor that year at Clarendon and Woodstock (*CLR, 1240–45*, pp. 291, 307).
21. *CR, 1237–42*, pp. 236, 476, 523.
22. *CPR, 1232–47*, p. 434; *Paris II*, pp. 23–6. Henry's charter of 20 August 1245 granting Chester to Edmund was never enrolled and is known only from the cartulary roll of Peter of Savoy. My thanks to Huw Ridgeway for letting me see his compilation of the roll.
23. Maddicott, *Montfort*, pp. 46–50, 67; Labarge, *Montfort*, p. 87. The values were calculated using http://www.nationalarchives.gov.uk/currency–converter. [Accessed 3 December 2018]
24. *Waverley*, p. 336.
25. *Letters of Adam Marsh I*, xiv–xvii, *II* (no. 60), pp. 158–9.
26. *Letters of Adam Marsh II* ((no. 157), pp. 379–83.
27. Ibid., (no. 160), pp. 386–7.
28. *Paris II*, pp. 441–3.

29. Maddicott, *Montfort*, pp. 84–7.
30. Ibid., pp. 54–5.
31. *CPR 1232–47*, pp. 415, 416, 449, 453; *CLR, 1245–51*, pp. 46, 85, 118, 142, 178–9.
32. *CPR 1232–47*, p. 485; Wilkinson, *Eleanor de Montfort*, p. 87.
33. *Letters of Adam Marsh II* (no. 151), pp. 370–3, (no. 161), pp. 388–9.
34. Vaughan, *Life of Matthew Paris*, p. 126.
35. Verini, 'Visions of Medieval Queenship: Gender and Genre in *La Estoire de Seint Aedward le Rei*', pp. 5–32.
36. *Paris I*, p. 404; *Paris II*, p. 182. In fact, Sanchia retreats almost entirely into the background after the first child she bore to Richard of Cornwall died only a month old.
37. Cox, *Eagles of Savoy*, pp. 146–9; *Paris II*, pp. 113–14, 129–30.
38. *CPL I*, p. 227; Howell, *Eleanor of Provence*, p. 40; Denholm-Young, *Richard of Cornwall*, p. 52.
39. See above, p. 56; *Paris II*, pp. 133–4.
40. *Waverley*, p. 337; *CLR, 1245–51*, p. 65; *Paris II*, p. 177.
41. *CLR, 1245–51*, pp. 71, 78, 288.

5 Seriously Aroused Displeasure

1. *CLR, 1240–45*, p. 293.
2. *Paris I*, p. 49.
3. *Paris II*, pp. 230–1.
4. *Paris III*, pp. 14–15; Ridgeway, 'King Henry III and the "Aliens"', pp. 84–5; Howell, *Eleanor of Provence*, pp. 56–7. In addition to Mansel and Kilkenny, other rising men at court included Paul Pevre, John of Lexington, Henry Wengham, and Lawrence of St Martin. They joined the already established guard of Bertram de Criol, Nicholas de Molis, Ralph Fitz-Nicholas and Robert Passelewe.
5. *Paris II*, pp. 240–2.
6. Ibid., pp. 274–6.
7. Maddicott, *Montfort*, pp. 130–1.
8. *Paris II*, pp. 231, 252.
9. *CR, 1247–51*, pp. 3–4, 22; *CPR 1247–58*, p. 5.
10. Baker, *Montfort*, pp. 228–9; see above, p. 63.
11. Bémont, *Montfort*, pp. 75–6.
12. *Paris II*, pp. 288–9, 312.
13. Labarge, *Montfort*, pp. 112–14; *CChR 1226–57*, p. 345.
14. *CPR, 1247–58*, p. 57; *Paris II*, p. 331.
15. *Royal Letters II*, pp. 361–2; Bémont, *Montfort*, p. 37.

16. *Paris II*, pp. 314, 329–30; *Waverley*, p. 342.
17. *Paris II*, pp. 372–82.
18. *CR, 1247–51*, pp. 283, 454, 464; *CLR, 1245–51*, pp. 358, 362; *Paris II*, pp. 412–13.
19. *Letters of Adam Marsh I* (no. 25), pp. 58–9, (no. 52) pp. 146–7.
20. *CPR 1247–58*, pp. 55, 67; *CR, 1247–51*, pp. 254, 321; *CLR, 1245–51*, p. 288.
21. *CPR 1247–58*, p. 68; *CR, 1247–51*, p. 302. *Letters of Adam Marsh I* (no. 52) pp. 146–7; *II* (no. 155) pp. 376–7.
22. *Letters of Adam Marsh II* (no. 138) pp. 336–7; (no. 141) pp. 348–9.
23. *Paris II*, pp. 397–8; Ridgeway, 'The Ecclesiastical Career of Aymer de Lusignan', pp. 151, 155.
24. Ibid., pp. 395–8, 420–2.
25. *Letters of Adam Marsh II* (no. 158) pp. 384–5; (no. 159) pp. 386–7.
26. *Paris II*, pp. 464–5.
27. Green, *Lives of Princesses*, pp. 178–9.
28. *Paris II*, pp. 468–71; *CLR, 1251–60*, pp. 8, 10.
29. *CPR 1247–58*, pp. 123, 129.
30. *Paris II*, pp. 476–7; Bémont, *Montfort*, pp. 97–9.
31. *Letters of Adam Marsh II* (no. 224) pp. 540–1.
32. *Letters of Adam Marsh I* (no. 47) pp. 128–9.
33. *CPR 1247–58*, pp. 124, 129, 132; *CR, 1251–53*, pp. 203–05; *Royal Letters II*, pp. 68–85; *Paris II*, pp. 476–7, 483, 485–7; Bémont, *Montfort*, pp. 97–103.
34. *Paris II*, pp. 487–93, 507–10; Bémont, *Montfort*, pp. 104–15; Maddicott, *Montfort*, p. 119.
35. *Letters of Adam Marsh I* (no. 30) pp. 88–91; *II* (no. 134) pp. 326–9.
36. Green, *Lives of Princesses*, pp. 104–05. There is speculation whether the birth of Richard de Montfort actually occurred the year earlier, in 1251. This is due to Marsh writing in *Letter 30* that Simon crossed over on 13 June 1252 'safe and cheerful, with Henry, his eldest son ... and in the loving company of his consort'. It is unlikely Eleanor would have gone to the Continent if she were that far pregnant at the time. There is an allocate on 11 October 1251 for purchasing victuals for the 'purification of the king's sister' (*CLR, 1245–51*, p. 380), which would coincide with Richard's birth then, but it seems to refer to Henry's half-sister Alice de Warenne. Prior to the allocate, Henry ordered a bed, mattress and gowns for Alice, presumably with a view to her going into confinement (*CR, 1247–51*, p. 479).
37. *CPR, 1232–47*, p. 283; *CPR, 1247–58*, p. 121.
38. *CR, 1251–53*, pp. 202, 208; *Paris II*, pp. 494–5.
39. *CPR, 1247–58*, pp. 140, 160, 168; *Paris II*, pp. 536–7.
40. *Paris III*, pp. 1–2.
41. Ibid., p. 113; *CR, 1251–53*, p. 273.

42. *Paris III*, pp. 3–6; *CR, 1251–53*, pp. 272, 273. Marsh writes that the king lashed out at him as well, calling him an enemy and traitor and forbidding Boniface from asking him to join his household (no. 186, pp. 446–9).
43. *Letters of Adam Marsh II* (no. 186) pp. 450–1; Howell, *Eleanor of Provence*, pp. 68–9; Ridgeway, 'The Ecclesiastical Career of Aymer de Lusignan', pp. 165–6.
44. Russell and Heironimus, *Shorter Latin Forms of Master Henry of Avarances*, pp. 141, 152–3.

6 Historic Undertakings

1. *CLR, 1251–60*, p. 110; Howell, *Eleanor of Provence*, pp. 79–80, 101.
2. See above, p. 69. Eleanor de Montfort's fifth child was the daughter she and Simon lost in Bordeaux. Both Eleanors may have had miscarriages in the intervening years, but the later claim that the king and queen had two sons born after Edmund, given the names Richard and John, and later two more sons named William and Henry in the following decade, has no foundation in any chronicles or government records at the time. Margaret Howell gives the issue full treatment in 'The Children of King Henry III and Eleanor of Provence', pp. 57–72.
3. Howell, *Eleanor of Provence*, pp. 95–6.
4. Mitchell, *Studies in Taxation*, p. 257; Strickland, *Lives of Queens*, p. 111. On 16 July 1253, Eleanor was allowed to make her own will up to 3,000 marks (£2,000) over and above her possessions (*CPR, 1247–58*, p. 213).
5. *CPR, 1247–58*, p. 209 (also p. 206).
6. Ibid., pp. 210, 214.
7. *Royal Letters II*, p. 99; *CR, 1251–53*, p. 485; *Paris III*, pp. 30–1.
8. *CPR, 1247–58*, p. 244; *Paris III*, pp. 16–17.
9. *CPR, 1247–58*, pp. 242, 250; *Paris III*, pp. 56–7.
10. *Letters of Adam Marsh II* (no. 186) pp. 448–9; Wilkinson, *Eleanor de Montfort*, pp. 90–1.
11. *CR, 1251–53*, pp. 503–04; *CPR, 1247–58*, pp. 222, 238, 391; *Mayors and Sheriffs*, p. 22.
12. *CR, 1253–54*, p. 7; *CPR, 1247–58*, p. 267; *CLR, 1251–60*, p. 154; *Paris III*, pp. 56, 60.
13. *Foedera I*, pp. 290–1.
14. *Paris III*, pp. 226–7; *CPL I*, p. 153; D'Avray, 'Dissolving Royal Marriages', pp. 82–98. Gregory's letters are dated 27 April 1236.
15. *Royal Letters II*, pp. 101–02; *Paris III*, pp. 61–3, 439–40; Maddicott, *Origins of the English Parliament*, pp. 211–18.
16. *CR, 1253–54*, pp. 114–16. 'A(lienor) regina nostra'.

17. *CPR, 1247–58*, pp. 279–80.
18. *Foedera I*, pp. 295–7; *CPR, 1247–58*, p. 310.
19. *CPR, 1247–58*, pp. 270–1; Howell, *Eleanor of Provence*, p. 113.
20. *CPR, 1247–58*, pp. 364, 367, 369, 528; *CLR, 1251–60*, pp. 154, 162, 167. Eleanor also needed to bring a tremendous quantity of supplies, including 100 gallons of vinegar, 1,000 pounds of lard, 30,000 eggs, and 15 tonnes of flour.
21. *CPR, 1247–58*, pp. 368, 374–7; *CR, 1253–54*, pp. 74–5, 176.
22. *Paris III*, pp. 80–1.
23. *CPR, 1247–58*, p. 311; Cockerill, *Eleanor of Castile,* pp. 82–5.
24. *Foedera I*, pp. 297, 301–04; *Paris II*, pp. 537–8; *Paris III*, pp. 89–91; Howell, *Eleanor of Provence*, p. 131.
25. Carpenter, 'Henry III and the Sicilian Affair', pp. 1–11; Maddicott, *Montfort*, p. 125.
26. *CR, 1251–53*, p. 433; *Paris III*, pp. 86, 96, 97.
27. *CPR 1247–58*, p. 383; *Burton*, pp. 327–8; *Paris III*, pp. 98, 104–10, 115; *Flores*, pp. 343–5; *Political Songs*, p. 67.
28. *CPR, 1247–58*, p. 293.
29. *CPR 1247–58*, p. 321; *Dunstable*, p. 192.
30. *CPR, 1247–58*, pp. 398–9; Labarge, *Montfort*, pp. 128–40.
31. *Manners*, p. 5; Labarge, *Montfort*, pp. 89–92.
32. *CR, 1251–53*, p. 286; *CLR, 1251–60*, p. 96; *CPR, 1247–58*, p. 225; *Mayors and Sheriffs*, pp. 23–4; *Paris III*, pp. 113–14; Barrow, 'Peter d'Aigueblanche's Support Network', pp. 32–3.
33. *Paris III*, pp. 125–6; Carpenter, 'The *vis et voluntas* of King Henry III', pp. 2–3.
34. *CPR, 1247–58*, pp. 423, 424, 425, 426, 441; *CR, 1254–56*, pp. 216, 218; *Melrose*, pp. 206–07; *Paris III*, pp. 128–30; *Dunstable*, p. 198.
35. *CLR, 1251–60*, pp. 240, 244.
36. *Foedera I*, pp. 316–22; *Burton*, pp. 336, 348–53; *Paris III*, p. 102.
37. *CPR, 1247–58*, p. 444; *Paris III*, pp. 137–8, 141–3. In October 1254, while still in Bordeaux, Henry granted the principality of Capua to Thomas of Savoy on behalf of his son as incentive for Thomas to make the business a success (*Foedera I*, p. 308).
38. *CLR, 1251–60*, p. 244; *CPR, 1247–58*, pp. 401, 448; Madox, *Histories and Antiquities of the Exchequer*, pp. 350–2.
39. *CPR, 1247–58*, pp. 451, 452; *Paris III*, pp. 138–41; *Burton*, pp. 340–8.

7 An Arduous and Difficult Matter

1. *CPR, 1247–58*, pp. 493–4; *CR, 1254–56*, pp. 426–7, 438. Wilkinson, *Women in Thirteenth-Century Lincolnshire*, pp. 47–56.

2. *CPR, 1247–58*, p. 534, 536; *CLR, 1251–60*, p. 347; Waugh, *Lordship of England*, pp. 57–8, 200.

3. *CPR, 1247–58*, p. 493; *Layettes III*, no. 4279; Labarge, *Montfort*, pp. 133–7.

4. *CChR, 1226–57*, p. 460; Maddicott, *Montfort*, pp. 142–3.

5. MS Clairambault 1021, f. 42; Wilkinson, *Eleanor de Montfort*, p. 85.

6. *Foedera I*, p. 341; *CR, 1254–56*, pp. 444–5; *Diplomatic Documents I, 1101–1272*, no. 282; Lloyd, 'King Henry III, the Crusade and the Mediterranean', pp. 114–15.

7. *CR, 1254–56*, pp. 389–90.

8. *Foedera I*, p. 342; Denholm-Young, *Richard of Cornwall*, pp. 87–8; Baker, *Henry III*, pp. 234–5.

9. *Paris III*, pp. 174–5; 214.

10. Morris, *Great and Terrible King*, pp. 22, 25.

11. *Paris II*, pp. 358–9, 531–2; Howell, *Eleanor of Provence*, pp. 125–6.

12. Coss, 'The Knightly Class in Thirteenth-Century England', pp. 166–74.

13. *CLR, 1251–60*, p. 360; *Paris III*, pp. 224, 225; Denholm-Young, *Richard of Cornwall*, p. 94; Howell, *Eleanor of Provence*, p. 76.

14. *CR, 1254–56*, pp. 123, 287–8; *CLR, 1251–60*, p. 270.

15. *Paris III*, pp. 232, 241; *CLR, 1251–60*, pp. 376, 385, 448; *CR, 1256–59*, p. 222; Badham, Oosterwijk, 'The Tomb Monument of Katherine, Daughter of Henry III and Eleanor of Provence', pp. 4–10.

16. Howell, *Eleanor of Provence*, pp. 45–6, 101–02, 151.

17. *Trivet*, pp. 280–1; Baker, *Henry III*, pp. 187–8.

18. *CR, 1256–59*, pp. 219–20; *Paris III*, pp. 131–2.

19. See above, pp. 73, 102, 133, 187.

20. Cockerill, *Eleanor of Castile*, pp. 102–03.

21. *Dunstable*, pp. 200–01; *Tewkesbury*, p. 158; *Paris III*, pp. 148, 156–7, 201, 204–05; 217–8; Prestwich, *Edward I*, pp. 14–6.

22. *CR, 1256–59*, pp. 107–08; *CPR, 1247–58*, p. 554; *Flores*, pp. 354–5; *Paris III*, pp. 200–01, 204–05, 238, 243, 245, 246; Smith, *Llywelyn ap Gruffudd*, pp. 97–9.

23. *Dunstable*, pp. 203–04; *CR, 1256–59*, p. 80; Smith, *Llywelyn ap Gruffudd*, pp. 102–05.

24. *CChR, 1226–57*, pp. 438–9; *CChR, 1257–1300*, pp. 3–5. Clare received £3,333 for the Gilbert-Alice match, which turned out to be a total failure. Isabel the marchioness died in 1270, aged around thirty.

25. *Paris III*, p. 250.

26. *CPR, 1247–58*, p. 616.

27. *Flores*, p. 422; *CR, 1256–59*, p. 147; Howell, *Eleanor of Provence*, pp. 146–7. Hamo would join Edward's crusade to the Holy Land in 1270 and die there two years later after marrying the widow of Hugh II of Cyprus, the son of the Queen Plaisance who had floated the idea of a marriage between her and Eleanor's son Edmund.

28. *Paris III*, pp. 167, 239; *CPR, 1247–58*, p. 589; Ridgeway, 'What Happened in 1261?', pp. 100–01.
29. Ridgeway 'Foreign Favourites and Henry III's Problems of Patronage, 1247–1258', pp. 591–607.
30. *Paris III*, pp. 270–1; Howell, *Eleanor of Provence*, pp. 147–8.
31. *CPR, 1247–58*, pp. 271, 308; *Paris III*, p. 268; Howell, *Eleanor of Provence*, p. 129.
32. *CPR, 1232–47*, pp. 508–09; Ridgeway's 'Foreign Favourites and Henry III's Problems of Patronage', p. 595; Maddicott, *Montfort*, p. 136.
33. Stacey, *Politics Policy, and Finance*, p. 219; Ridgeway's 'Foreign Favourites and Henry III's Problems of Patronage', pp. 596, 605.
34. *CPR, 1247–58*, p. 609; Maddicott, *Montfort*, p. 137.
35. *CPR, 1247–58*, p. 542; *CR, 1256–59*, p. 73.
36. *Paris III*, pp. 233–4.
37. *Paris III*, pp. 296–7; *CPR, 1258–66*, p. 2; Ridgeway, 'Ecclesiastical Career of Aymer de Lusignan', pp. 166–7.
38. *Foedera I*, p. 370; *CR, 1256–59*, pp. 294–6, 299; *Melrose*, p. 208.
39. *Paris III*, pp. 268, 279; Baker, *Montfort*, pp. 216–7.
40. *Tewkesbury*, pp. 163–4; *Paris III*, pp. 279–80. Tewkesbury also says the king asked for an unheard of one-third tax on movables and immovables. Henry's last tax from Parliament was in 1237, a thirtieth on movables only, and yielded £22,000 based on an assessment of £660,000 (Mitchell, *Studies in Taxation*, pp. 354–5). Asking for a third based on that figure meant £220,000, or the end of all his problems. The most likely source for this account in the annals, embellished or fictional, is Richard de Clare or someone in his entourage, for his family had close connections to Tewkesbury. Interestingly, on the date Henry agreed to reforms, he also stood surety for the money Clare owed for the Montferrat marriage (*CPR, 1247–58*, p. 662). For the view that the confrontation in Tewkesbury is accurate, see Carpenter, *Reign of Henry III*, pp. 187–9.
41. *CPR, 1247–58*, p. 626. Plessis first appears in the king's service in 1228. In late 1242, Henry granted him the marriage of Margaret de Beaumont, the Countess of Warwick. It is unclear whether the marriage went forward, but Plessis carried the title of Earl of Warwick until his death in 1263 (*CPR, 1225–32*, p. 227; *CR, 1242–47*, p. 9; *CPR, 1247–58*, p. 76). See also Waugh, *Lordship of England*, pp. 86–7.
42. *Paris III*, pp. 285–6; *Flores*, pp. 355–6.
43. *Burton*, pp. 446–53, trans. 501–05.
44. *CPR, 1247–58*, p. 637; *Burton*, pp. 447, 449.
45. *DBM*, pp. 91–3.
46. *Foedera I*, p. 374; *DBM*, pp. 93–5; *CPR, 1247–58*, pp. 639, 664; *Robert of Gloucester II*, p. 734; *Tewkesbury*, p. 165.

47. *CPR, 1247–58*, pp. 640, 641; *Paris III*, pp. 291–2.
48. *DBM*, pp. 78–9, 94–5. It was supposed to be paid on fines to the Crown, but apparently Eleanor considered reliefs to be fines as well and had been demanding payment any time an heir came into his inheritance.
49. *CPR, 1247–58*, pp. 631, 632.
50. *Burton*, p. 449.
51. *DBM*, pp. 92–3.
52. *Paris III*, pp. 265–6, 283–4, 291, 298–9; Baker, *Henry III*, pp. 258–60.
53. *Paris III*, pp. 294–5.
54. *CPR, 1247–58*, p. 627.
55. *Paris III*, pp. 306–07; Baker, *Henry III*, pp. 261–2. The other members of the delegation were Roger Bigod and two bishops, Walter Cantilupe of Worcester who was also a councillor, and Richard Gravesend of Lincoln. Both churchmen were firm allies of Montfort.
56. *Diplomatic Documents,* no. 209, pp. 204–05; *CPR, 1247–58*, p. 663; *CPR, 1258–66*, p. 51.
57. *Foedera I*, pp. 373, 379; *Paris Additamenta*, pp. 476–82; Bémont, *Montfort*, pp. 162–5.

8 Great Indignation and Fury

1. *CPR, 1247–58*, p. 666; *Tewkesbury*, pp. 165; *Paris III*, pp. 296, 297, 310–1, 318–9. The German delegation that informed Richard of his election said it had been unanimous, but the vote was 4-3 and the elector casting the deciding vote for Richard switched it to Alfonso of Castile two months later. Not until April 1259, nearly two years after Richard's coronation, did the pope finally send him his congratulations (*Foedera I*, p. 382; *Paris III*, pp. 207–09).
2. *Paris III*, p. 316.
3. MS Clairambault 1188, f. 81; Baker, *Montfort*, pp. 221–3.
4. *Foedera I*, p. 380; *CPR, 1247–58*, p. 663; *CPR, 1258–66*, p. 14; *Flores*, p. 359.
5. *CPR, 1258–66*, p. 18.
6. *Paris III*, pp. 324, 327; *Flores*, p. 362.
7. *CLR, 1251–60*, p. 460; *CPR, 1258–66*, pp. 25–7, 46, 52–3; *Flores*, p. 365.
8. *CChR, 1257–1300*, pp. 18, 20; *CPR, 1258–66*, pp. 34–5; *CR, 1256–59*, pp. 426, 433. The grant was made temporarily because it was not clear whether the manors were part of the royal demesne or not. In 1257, one year before the start of the reform period, all councillors, including Simon, swore an oath not to accept or allow alienations from the royal demesne. When later accused of violating that oath, Simon pointed out that the grant was actually a lease, then said the manors were granted to Eleanor in any case. Not all his fellow councillors were so sure (*Burton*, p. 396; *DBM*, pp. 196–9; Maddicott, *Montfort*, pp. 188–9).

9. MS Clairambault 1188, f. 15; Maddicott, *Montfort*, pp. 182–3; see above, pp. 25, 105. Humphrey de Bohun was named to the panel after Richard of Cornwall and Richard de Clare, another Marshal heir, declined to be involved.
10. *Diplomatic Documents*, no. 209, pp. 204–05; *CPR, 1258–66*, pp. 121, 379; Baker, *Montfort*, p. 118.
11. *Flores*, pp. 366–7; Maddicott, *Montfort*, pp. 183, 190.
12. *CPR, 1258–66*, p. 45.
13. MS Clairambault 1188, ff. 13–4; Carpenter, *Reign of Henry III*, pp. 241–51.
14. *DBM*, pp. 200–05; *CPR, 1258–66*, p. 59; *CR, 1259–61*, p. 12.
15. *CPR, 1258–66*, pp. 106–07; *DBM*, pp. 202–05; *Foedera I*, p. 392; MS Clairambault 1188, f. 14; *Flores*, p. 371; *Mayors and Sheriffs*, p. 46.
16. *DBM*, pp. 206–07; Labarge, *Montfort*, pp. 160–1.
17. *Diplomatic Documents I*, no. 313.
18. *Paris*, pp. 326–7.
19. Ibid., pp. 223, 303.
20. Howell, *Eleanor of Provence*, pp. 116, 275.
21. *CPR, 1258–66*, pp. 12, 21.
22. *DBM*, pp. 152–3.
23. *Burton*, p. 471
24. *CPR, 1258–66*, pp. 63–4; Howell, *Eleanor of Provence*, pp. 163–4. As Edward's acting steward, Leybourne caught some of Clare's men trying to raid Bristol Castle during the autumn of 1259. According to the *Annals of London*, he hanged the lot of them without trial (*London*, p. 54; Treharne, *Baronial Plan*, p. 193).
25. *Foedera I*, p. 386; *CPR, 1258–66*, p. 25.
26. *Flores*, p. 370.
27. *CPR, 1258–66*, pp. 16–7.
28. *Foedera I*, p. 391; *DBM*, pp. 204–05; *CPR, 1258–66*, p. 211; Ridgeway, 'Politics', p. 357.
29. Howell, *Eleanor of Provence*, pp. 165–6; Carpenter, 'The Meetings of Kings Henry III and Louis IX', p. 23.
30. *Flores*, pp. 373, 375.
31. *Foedera I*, p. 395.
32. *Flores*, pp. 367–9; *Royal Letters II* (nos. 526, 533), pp. 138–40, 150–2; *CPR, 1258–66*, pp. 35, 113.
33. *DBM*, pp. 165–9.
34. *Flores*, pp. 378–9; *Mayors and Sheriffs*, pp. 46–7; *DBM*, pp. 186–9, 206–09.
35. *CPR, 1258–66*, pp. 114, 116, 119, 121, 123; *DBM*, pp. 178–81, 208–11.
36. *Dunstable*, p. 215; *Flores*, pp. 379–80; *Wykes*, pp. 123–4; Treharne, *Baronial Plan of Reform*, p. 221–33.
37. *DBM*, pp. 204–05, 216–7; Maddicott, *Montfort*, pp. 199–200.

38. *Dunstable*, p. 217; *Flores*, pp. 380–1; *DBM*, pp. 194–211; Labarge, *Montfort*, pp. 187–8.

39. *Flores*, p. 384.

40. Ibid., pp. 384–5; *CPR, 1258–66*, p. 90; *Foedera I*, p. 410; Howell, *Eleanor of Provence*, pp. 173–4. Mansel, the illegitimate son of a country priest, was brought up at court and is first found at the exchequer in 1234 (*Foedera I*, p. 414). Henry named Mansel's namesake nephew as the keeper of the bishopric until the election was confirmed. As in the days of old, he did it on his own authority without approval from the council, an act which did not go unnoticed.

41. *Flores*, pp. 388–9; *CPR, 1258–66*, pp. 105, 128; *Foedera I*, p. 402.

42. *CPR, 1258–66*, pp. 94–5, 96; *Flores*, pp. 386–7, 390; *Mayors and Sheriffs*, pp. 48; Green, *Lives of Princesses*, p. 204; Ridgeway, 'King Henry III's Grievances', p. 230. Henry later complained that the appointment of steward was his prerogative and this action was another infringement by the council, but he was probably happy not to have Simon glowering at him the whole time.

43. *Flores*, p. 386; *CPR, 1258–66*, p. 97; Maddicott, *Montfort*, pp. 201–02. William de Forz was the Earl of Aumale. He accompanied Henry and Eleanor to France but died in Amiens on the way back.

44. Treharne, *Baronial Plan of Reform*, p. 244. Treharne gives the dates 10 August to 3 October 1260.

45. *Dunstable*, p. 216–7; *CPR, 1258–66*, pp. 126, 141. The Dunstable annalist says Edward and his retinue fared poorly in the tournaments. He was wounded many times and lost all his equipment. Concerning the appointment of Guy Lusignan, it will be remembered how Edward created a scandal in 1258 when he appointed Geoffrey Lusignan his seneschal and this helped lead to the expulsion of the brothers. See above, p. 119.

46. MS Clairambault 1188, f. 16; Labarge, *Montfort*, pp. 191–2; Denholm-Young, *Richard of Cornwall*, p. 97.

47. *Flores*, p. 389; *Wykes*, pp. 125–6; Ridgeway, 'Ecclesiastical Career', pp. 175–6.; *CR 1259–61*, p. 467. Writes *Flores* about the death of Aymer de Valence: 'And so as he was on his way with all speed into England, with full powers, by the will of God he ended his life in France, and received honourable burial, as he was well entitled to, at Paris, in the church of Saint Genevieve. And his death, though mournful to some persons, appeared nevertheless to many, and especially to those of the English, who were the framers of the Provisions of Oxford, a salutary event.' Ridgeway has shown that Aymer was a well-educated and very efficient administrator of the diocese.

48. *Flores*, pp. 390–1; *CPR, 1258–66*, p. 175; Green, *Lives of Princesses*, pp. 205–06.

49. *CR 1259–61*, pp. 340, 377, 457; *Flores*, pp. 391–2.

50. *CPR, 1258–66*, pp. 150, 151, 152; *DBM*, pp. 240–3; *Flores*, p. 394; Howell, *Eleanor of Provence*, pp. 181–2.

51. *Flores*, pp. 392–5; *CPR, 1258–66*, p. 170; *London*, p. 57; Ridgeway, 'Politics', pp. 385–7; Prestwich, *Edward I*, pp. 35–7; Cockerill, *Eleanor of Castile*, p. 132.
52. *CPR, 1258–66*, pp. 136, 145–6; *DBM*, pp. 240–7; *Gervase*, p. 211; *Flores*, pp. 397–8; 'King Henry III's Grievances', pp. 227–38.
53. *CPR, 1258–66*, pp. 162, 166, 165, 169.
54. *Diplomatic Documents I*, no. 325; Howell, *Eleanor of Provence*, pp. 88–90, 184–5.
55. *Foedera I*, pp. 407–09; *Gervase*, p. 213; *Mayors and Sheriffs*, p. 52; *Robert of Gloucester II*, pp. 736–7; *CPR, 1258–66*, p. 220.
56. *DBM*, pp. 246–9; *Waverley*, p. 355; *Battle* in Bémont, *Montfort* (first edition), p. 374; *Dunstable*, p. 217; Treharne, *Baronial Plan*, pp. 268–70.
57. *Foedera I*, pp. 411, 415; *CPR, 1258–66*, p. 195; *Royal Letters II*, pp. 194, 196; *Wykes*, p. 128; *Gervase*, p. 213; *Dunstable*, p. 217.
58. *Osney*, p. 128; Howell, *Eleanor of Provence*, p. 185.
59. Howell, *Eleanor of Provence*, pp. 283–5.

9 Rapacious Turbulence

1. MS Clairambault, ff. 16, 18, 19, 21, 23, 31; Labarge, *Montfort*, pp. 192–3; Maddicott, *Montfort*, p. 217.
2. *CR, 1261–64*, pp. 120–1; *Foedera I*, p. 419.
3. See above, pp. 85, 135.
4. Bémont, *Montfort*, p. 197, (first edn), pp. 333–43; Baker, *Montfort*, pp. 225–9.
5. *Mayors and Sheriffs*, p. 53; *Dunstable*, p. 219; *CPR, 1266–72*, pp. 734, 736–7; Howell, *Eleanor of Provence*, pp. 187, 190.
6. *Gervase*, pp. 214, 220–1; *CPR, 1266–72*, p. 727.
7. *Dunstable*, p. 220; *Gervase*, pp. 215–6. William de Valence also interceded for Gilbert de Clare.
8. *Foedera I*, p. 422; *CR, 1261–64*, p. 152; *Gervase*, pp. 217; Carpenter, 'The Meetings of Kings Henry III and Louis IX,' pp. 22, 24. Eleanor drew her £400 dower from the exchequer throughout the period of their exile (*CLR 1260–67*; pp. 36, 77, 89, 111).
9. *Mayors and Sheriffs*, pp. 54–5; *Flores*, p. 402; *Royal Letters II*, pp. 230–3; *CR, 1261–64*, pp. 272–3; Treharne, *Baronial Plan*, pp. 291–9.
10. *Melrose*, p. 214; *Royal Letters II*, p. 374.
11. *CPR, 1258–66*, pp. 240–1; *Royal Letters II*, pp. 242–3; *Mayors and Sheriffs*, p. 56; *Flores*, p. 403; Carpenter, 'The Meetings of Kings Henry III and Louis IX,' p. 25.
12. *CPR, 1258–66*, pp. 285–6; *Gervase*, pp. 219; *Burton*, p. 500; *Dunstable*, p. 220; *Flores*, p. 403; Carpenter, 'Reign of King Henry III,' pp. 253–9.
13. *Dunstable*, p. 221.

14. *Mayors and Sheriffs*, p. 56; *Dunstable*, pp. 221–2.
15. *Wykes*, pp. 133–4; Prestwich, *Edward I*, p. 43; Ridgeway, 'What Happened in 1261?', pp. 100–01.
16. *Flores*, pp. 404–06; *Mayors and Sheriffs*, p. 57; *Gervase*, pp. 221–2; *Wykes*, p. 135; *CPR, 1258–66*, pp. 263–6.
17. *Mayors and Sheriffs*, pp. 57–8; *Dunstable*, p. 222.
18. *Gervase*, p. 222; *Melrose*, p. 235; *Dunstable*, pp. 221, 223; *Flores*, p. 406; *CPL I*, p. 402; *Royal Letters II*, pp. 247–8.
19. *Dunstable*, p. 222; *Gervase*, p. 222; *CPR, 1258–66*, p. 279. Gervase puts the haul at £10,000 and the date 26 June.
20. *Flores*, p. 406; *CPR, 1258–66*, pp. 268, 269; Maddicott, *Montfort*, p. 229.
21. *Mayors and Sheriffs*, p. 59; *Flores*, p. 406.
22. *Melrose*, p. 215.
23. *Gervase*, p. 223; *Wykes*, p. 136; *Dunstable*, p. 223. The St Albans writer of the *Flores Historiarum* says that Eleanor was 'irritated by womanly feelings of annoyance' and 'strove with all her might' against the negotiated settlement (pp. 406–07). This has led historians to assume that she quarrelled with her husband and left the Tower in a huff. The vehemence of the crowd suggests she and Henry were worried for her safety in London and Boniface for one was wise to have fled. During the Peasants' Revolt of 1381, a mob dragged the Archbishop of Canterbury Simon Sudbury out of the Tower and chopped his head off in a gruesomely sloppy manner.
24. *Dunstable*, p. 224; *Mayors and Sheriffs*, pp. 57–8.
25. *Flores*, pp. 407–08; Howell, *Eleanor of Provence*, p. 198; see above, p. 19.
26. *CPR, 1258–66*, p. 275. *Flores* dates the eclipse to 6 August (p. 408).
27. *Foedera I*, p. 428; *Royal Letters II*, pp. 188–92; Treharne, *Baronial Plan of Reform*, p. 276.
28. *Gervase*, p. 224.
29. *Foedera I*, p. 430.
30. *CPR, 1258–66*, p. 275; *Royal Letters II*, pp. 249–50; *Mayors and Sheriffs*, p. 61; Treharne, *Baronial Plan of Reform*, pp. 319–20.
31. *Flores*, p. 409; *Gervase*, pp. 224–5; *Dunstable*, p. 225; *Tewkesbury*, p. 176; Howell, *Eleanor of Provence*, p. 200.
32. *Wykes*, pp. 136–7; *CPL I*, p. 397. Wykes (p. 123) suggests that Simon opposed the Treaty of Paris in the hope that the kingdom might pass to his son some day.
33. *CPR, 1258–66*, pp. 284, 291; 302–04; *Mayors and Sheriffs*, p. 62; *Gervase*, pp. 224; *Dunstable*, p. 225; *Flores*, p. 409; *Rishanger De Bellis*, p. 17. The London chronicler says Edward gained leave from Parliament by saying he wanted to visit his wife. Eleanor of Castile was then at Windsor with their daughter Katherine (Cockerill, *Eleanor of Castile*, p. 133).

34. *CPL I*, pp. 396–8; *Royal Letters II*, pp. 251–2; *Flores*, p. 409; *Dunstable*, p. 233.
35. *Gervase*, pp. 229–30; *Dunstable*, p. 225; *Wykes*, p. 137.
36. *CPR, 1258–66*, p. 273; *CPL I*, p. 417; *Tewkesbury*, p. 180; *Rishanger De Bellis*, p. 17; *Dunstable*, p. 225.
37. *Royal Letters II*, pp. 250–1; *Dunstable*, p. 226; *Gervase*, p. 231; *Flores*, pp. 409–10.
38. *DBM*, pp. 264–7; *Tewkesbury*, p. 179; *Dunstable*, pp. 226–7; *Flores*, pp. 410–1. Carpenter, 'A Noble in Politics: Roger Mortimer', pp. 199–201.
39. *Dunstable*, p. 227; *Gervase*, p. 232; Labarge, *Montfort*, p. 221.
40. *DBM*, pp. 252–79; Maddicott, *Montfort*, pp. 260–1; Stacey, 'Crusades, Crusaders', pp. 139–42.
41. *DBM*, pp. 280–91.
42. *Tewkesbury*, pp. 177, 179; *Dunstable*, p. 227; *Wykes*, p. 139; Howell, *Eleanor of Provence*, p. 205.
43. *Rishanger De Bellis*, pp. 17, 20; *Gervase*, p. 233; *Flores*, pp. 410–1; *Dunstable*, pp. 227–8; *Mayors and Sheriffs*, pp. 64–5.
44. *CPR, 1258–66*, pp. 293, 295, 317, 378, 379, 381, 382; *Gervase*, p. 233.
45. *Foedera I*, pp. 436, 437; *CPR, 1258–66*, p. 306; *Gervase*, pp. 232–3; *Wykes*, pp. 140–7; *Flores*, p. 411–4, 432; *Dunstable*, pp. 229–31; *Rishanger de Bellis*, p. 23–5; *Guisborough*, pp. 310–2; *Mayors and Sheriffs*, p. 66.
46. Howell, *Eleanor of Provence*, pp. 208–09.
47. https://epistolae.ctl.columbia.edu/letter/648.html. [Accessed 3 December 2018]
48. *Rishanger De Bellis*, pp. 27-31; *Mayors and Sheriffs*, p. 66; *Wykes*, pp. 148–51; *Political Songs*, p. 69; *Flores*, pp. 415–9; Blaauw, *Barons' War*, pp. 168–9; Carpenter, *Battles of Lewes and Evesham*, pp. 22–3, 26; *Guisborough*, pp. 313–8; *Melrose*, p. 219.
49. *Mayors and Sheriffs*, p. 67; Maddicott, 'The Mise of Lewes, 1264', pp. 588–603; Carpenter, *Reign of King Henry III*, pp. 281–91.
50. *Dunstable*, p. 233; *Wykes*, pp. 151–2.
51. *CPR, 1258–66*, pp. 324, 325; *Foedera I*, pp. 441, 443.
52. *Dunstable*, p. 233; *Wykes*, p. 153; *Flores*, p. 419. Richard was first taken to the Tower of London, Edward and Henry of Almain to Dover. The Dunstable annalist says they were moved to Wallingford for fear of a revolt breaking out at Dover.
53. *Robert of Gloucester II*, pp. 751–2; *Flores*, p. 423.
54. *DBM*, pp. 294–301; *CR, 1261–64*, p. 396; *Flores*, p. 423; *Mayors and Sheriffs*, pp. 69–70; *Robert of Gloucester II*, p. 752, Powicke, *King Henry III*, pp. 476–7.
55. *CPR, 1258–66*, pp. 319, 321, 335, 336, 355, 364, 371, 599, 613–4; Maddicott, *Montfort*, pp. 309–10, 324. Gilbert made an informal relief to Simon of £800 to take seisin of his lands, half of which he paid. Of the other half, half of that (£200) was pardoned after Evesham, half he was ordered to pay John

Balliol as his fine for siding with Simon. He got off lightly compared to other Montfortians, but he had never actually taken up arms against the king, just harassed his loyalist neighbour Balliol.

56. Maddicott, *Montfort*, pp. 325–6.
57. *CPR, 1258–66*, p. 474; Howell, *Eleanor of Provence*, pp. 212–5.
58. *Foedera I*, p. 444; *Mayors and Sheriffs*, pp. 71–3; *Flores*, p. 420; *Dunstable*, p. 233.
59. *Flores*, p. 420; Howell, *Eleanor of Provence*, pp. 218–9.
60. *CPR, 1258–66*, pp. 347, 365–6; *Gervase*, p. 239; *Wykes*, p. 155; *Dunstable*, p. 233–4; Maddicott, *Montfort*, pp. 292–5. Louis had not even bothered to respond to any of the initiatives. On 6 July, he received a letter, purportedly from Henry but more likely Simon, that his connivance in allowing Queen Eleanor to assemble troops was endangering the lives of Edward and Henry of Almain as hostages for the Mise of Lewes (*CR, 1261–64*, p. 389). Neither Louis nor Eleanor gave any indication they were worried that Simon would actually execute the heir to the throne.
61. *Foedera I*, p. 446; *CPR, 1258–66*, pp. 370–1; *Flores*, pp. 421–2; *Wykes*, p. 156; Powicke, *King Henry III*, 477–82; Maddicott, *Montfort*, pp. 296–9.
62. *Foedera I*, p. 447; *Flores*, p. 421; *Wykes*, p. 155.
63. *CPR, 1258–66*, pp. 388–9, 474; *Foedera I*, p. 448.
64. *Flores*, p. 424; Howell, *Eleanor of Provence*, pp. 74–5; *CLR, 1226–40*, p. 405.

10 Triumph, Grief and Sorrow

1. *Foedera I*, p. 450; *Flores*, p. 424; Howell, *Eleanor of Provence*, pp. 225–6; see above, pp. 98, 165.
2. *Melrose*, p. 235; *CPR, 1258–66*, pp. 404, 436.
3. *CPR, 1258–66*, pp. 322, 326, 333; *Foedera I*, p. 450; *Rishanger*, pp. 31–2; *Robert of Gloucester II*, pp. 752–3; *Dunstable*, p. 238; *Flores*, p. 436; *Wykes*, p. 160.
4. *CR, 1264–68*, pp. 84–7; *Mayors and Sheriffs*, p. 75; *Dunstable*, pp. 235–6.
5. *Foedera I*, pp. 451–4; *CPR, 1258–66*, p. 412; *Mayors and Sheriffs*, pp. 76–7; *Flores*, p. 424.
6. Wilkinson, *Eleanor de Montfort*, pp. 109–10; Labarge, *Montfort*, p. 90.
7. *Manners*, pp. 14, 23, 25–6, 31, 71; Wilkinson, *Eleanor de Montfort*, pp. 114–5.
8. *Manners*, pp. 8, 9, 11, 18, 24, 31, 37; Wilkinson, *Eleanor de Montfort*, pp. 112, 113, 114.
9. *Manners*, pp. 9, 18, 20, 24, 31; Wilkinson, *Eleanor de Montfort*, pp. 119, 122.
10. *Manners*, pp. 13, 16; Labarge, *Montfort*, p. 94.
11. *Manners*, pp. 15, 16; Wilkinson, *Eleanor de Montfort*, pp. 107–08; Powicke, *King Henry III*, pp. 707–08.

12. *CPR, 1258–66*, pp. 423, 425; *Wykes*, pp. 161–2; Powicke, *King Henry III*, pp. 492–4; Maddicott, *Montfort*, pp. 330–2.

13. Howell, *Eleanor of Provence*, pp. 51–2, 223–7.

14. Howell, *Eleanor of Provence*, p. 225; *Flores*, pp. 422–4; *Wykes*, p. 159; *Dunstable*, pp. 234–5; *Robert of Gloucester II*, p. 752.

15. *CPR, 1258–66*, pp. 423–4; *Wykes*, p. 162.

16. *CR, 1264–68*, pp. 119–20, 121–2, 124–5; *Wykes*, pp. 163–5; *Flores*, p. 437; *Robert of Gloucester II*, pp. 757–8; *Song of Lewes*, p. 42 (418–20, 431–5).

17. *CPR, 1258–66*, p. 425; *Royal Letters II*, p. 282; Howell, *Eleanor of Provence*, pp. 228–9.

18. *Manners*, pp. 41, 42–7; Wilkinson, *Eleanor de Montfort*, p. 116; Maddicott, *Montfort*, p. 335.

19. *Wykes*, pp. 166–8; *Rishanger*, p. 34.

20. *Mayors and Sheriffs*, p. 78; *Wykes*, pp. 169–70; *Manners*, p. 62; Labarge, *Montfort*, p. 95.

21. *CPL I*, p. 419; Howell, *Eleanor of Provence*, p. 229.

22. *Flores*, p. 437; *Mayors and Sheriffs*, p. 79; *Wykes*, p. 171; *Dunstable*, p. 239; *Melrose*, pp. 221–2.

23. *Flores*, p. 438; *Mayors and Sheriffs*, pp. 79–80; *Dunstable*, p. 239; *Wykes*, pp. 172–4; *Rishanger*, p. 34; *Robert of Gloucester II*, p. 765; *Osney*, pp. 170–1; *Oxendes*, pp. 228–9; Baker, *Montfort*, pp. 199–203.

24. *Manners*, pp. 66, 68, 81, 83; *Wykes*, p. 179; Wilkinson, *Eleanor de Montfort*, pp. 123–4.

25. *Wykes*, p. 175; *Manners*, p. 67; Powicke, *King Henry III*, pp. 505–06; *Rishanger* (p. 37) says Edward openly wept at the funeral of Henry de Montfort at Evesham. This may have been a sham, as a plea for reconciliation to avert a blood feud, because Wykes claims (p. 153) that young Henry, whom he disparages throughout his chronicle, treated Edward harshly while he was imprisoned at Dover. If true, it could have been Henry's payback to Edward for making him look like a fool when he reneged on their truce at Gloucester at the start of the war, see *Dunstable*, p. 228. Henry was, moreover, Edward's jailer during his supervised release.

26. *Manners*, pp. 74, 83–4; Labarge, *Montfort*, p. 139.

27. *Manners*, pp. 74; *Royal Letters II*, p. 292; *CR, 1264–68*, p. 136; *CPR, 1258–66*, pp. 436, 451; *Foedera*, p. 461.

28. *Wykes*, pp. 178; *Royal Letters II*, p. 291; *Oxendes*, p. 230.

29. Howell, *Eleanor of Provence*, pp. 231–2. In granting Maud her one-third dower after Richard de Clare's death, Henry assigned her the cream of Gloucester properties, something that did not endear her son Gilbert to the Crown. In April 1264, Eleanor de Montfort was in contact with Maud and her mother Margaret de Lacy as the crisis between Simon and Gilbert intensified.

Both Maud and Margaret were thought to have Montfortian sympathies, but the role of Thomas de Clare in Edward's escape suggests that their loyalty to the regime mirrored that of Gilbert's. See Wilkinson, 'Aristocratic Women in Politics, 1258–1267', pp. 162–4.

30. *Wykes*, pp. 179, 183; *Gervase*, p. 243; *Mayors and Sheriffs*, pp. 80–1; *Flores*, p. 439; *Robert of Gloucester II*, p. 768; Knowles, *Disinherited III*, pp. 10, 23, 36; Morris, *Bigod Earls*, pp. 94–5.

31. *CPR, 1258–66*, p. 470, 530, 658–62; *CPR, 1266–72*, p. 459; *Foedera*, p. 465 (dates the grant of Leicester to 26 October); *Mayors and Sheriffs*, p. 85; Howell, *Eleanor of Provence*, p. 241–3.

32. *CPR, 1258–66*, p. 506; *Rishanger*, p. 43; *Flores*, p. 443.

33. *Royal Letters II*, pp. 304–05; *Foedera I*, p. 465; *Dunstable*, p. 240; *Wykes*, pp. 181–2, 190; *Gervase*, p. 244; *Rishanger*, p. 42; *Mayors and Sheriffs*, p. 87. In May, Henry ordered the ports to be on the alert in case the brothers tried to re-enter the realm with their followers. Louis wrote at the same time to say he had prevented the crossing of such 'enemies', but he also implored Henry to make peace with his sister and nephews.

34. *Wykes*, pp. 188–9; *Mayors and Sheriffs*, p. 91.

35. *CPR, 1258–66*, p. 617; *Mayors and Sheriffs*, p. 92; Cockerill, *Eleanor of Castile*, p. 144, 149. Henry always honoured his father and Edward may have wanted to do him a good turn, especially since they would have had less troubles had Edward consistently honoured his own father.

36. *CPR, 1258–66*, pp. 641, 678; *CPL I*, p. 434; *DBM*, pp. 316–37; *Flores*, pp. 445–6.

37. *CPR, 1266–72*, pp. 140–1.

38. *CPL I*, p. 434; *Gervase*, p. 247; Wilkinson, *Eleanor de Montfort*, pp. 130–2.

39. *CPL I*, p. 422; *DBM*, pp. 322–3; *Flores*, p. 449; Labarge, *Montfort*, pp. 268–9; Powicke, *King Henry III*, pp. 607–08.

40. *CPR, 1266–72*, p. 323; *Wykes*, pp. 222–5; Denholm-Young, *Richard of Cornwall*, pp. 141, 144.

41. *CChR, 1257–1300*, pp. 121–2; *CPR, 1266–72*, p. 358; Howell, *Eleanor of Provence*, pp. 244–5.

42. *CChR, 1257–1300*, p. 78; *CR, 1268-1272*, pp. 122–6; Powicke, *King Henry III*, pp. 523–6.

43. *Wykes*, pp. 226; *Mayors and Sheriffs*, pp. 113, 121–2, 137–8; *Rishanger*, p. 65; Powicke, *King Henry III*, pp. 572–4; Tyerman, *God's War*, pp. 808–13; Prestwich, *Edward I*, pp. 73–4.

44. *Wykes*, pp. 239–40, 241–2; *Flores*, p. 452; Blaauw, *Barons' War*, pp. 336–53.

45. *Mayors and Sheriffs*, p. 140.

46. Ibid., p. 146.

47. *Wykes*, pp. 246; Howell, *Eleanor of Provence*, p. 250.

48. *Mayors and Sheriffs*, pp. 146–7; *CPR, 1266–72*, p. 459. Eleanor of Provence is said to be a finalist for the 'My fair lady' of the nursery rhyme 'London Bridge is Falling Down'.

49. *CPR, 1266–72*, pp. 682, 684; *Wykes*, p. 247; *Osney*, p. 253.

50. *CR, 1264–68*, p. 552; *Mayors and Sheriffs*, pp. 153–9; *Wykes*, p. 252.

51. Green, *Lives of Princesses*, p. 158; Labarge, *Montfort*, p. 270.

52. Green, *Lives of Princesses*, p. 159; *Dunstable*, p. 258.

53. Howell, *Eleanor of Provence*, p. 288; Cockerill, *Eleanor of Castile*, pp. 187–8.

54. *Wykes*, pp. 259–60; *Mayors and Sheriffs*, p. 178.

55. *Flores*, p. 468; *Wykes*, pp. 261–2; Green, *Lives of Princesses*, pp. 220, 264; Howell, *Eleanor of Provence*, pp. 289–91.

56. *Dunstable*, p. 265; Green, *Lives of Princesses*, pp. 159–60; Wilkinson, *Eleanor de Montfort*, pp. 135–6.

57. *Wykes*, pp. 267, 277, 291; *Dunstable*, p. 259; *Flores*, p. 469; *Rishanger*, p. 86–7; *Oxendes*, p. 239, 248; Maddicott, *Montfort*, p. 371.

58. *Rishanger*, pp. 79, 99; *Wykes*, p. 287; *Flores*, pp. 455–6; *Trivet*, p. 308; Bémont, *Montfort*, pp. 261–73.

59. *CPR, 1281-92*, p. 289; Labarge, *Montfort*, p. 271; Bémont, *Montfort*, pp. 259; Maddicott, *Montfort*, p. 102; Wilkinson, *Eleanor de Montfort*, pp. 1, 137.

60. Howell, *Eleanor of Provence*, pp. 292–4.

61. *CPR, 1272–81*, p. 76; *Oxendes*, p. 248; Howell, *Eleanor of Provence*, pp. 277–8, 299–300.

62. Howell, *Eleanor of Provence*, p. 295; https://epistolae.ctl.columbia.edu/letter/536.html. [Accessed 3 December 2018]

63. *Tewkesbury*, p. 166; Howell, *Eleanor of Provence*, pp. 303–05.

64. Scudder, *Le Morte Darthur*, p. 357; Morris, *Great and Terrible King*, p. 165; Baker, *Henry III*, pp. 338–9; see above, pp. 20, 35, 205.

65. *Flores*, p. 482; *Wykes*, p. 307; *Osney*, p. 329; Howell, *Eleanor of Provence*, pp. 300–02.

66. *Foedera I*, p. 731; *Flores*, p. 486; Morris, *Great and Terrible King*, pp. 192–4, 234–7.

67. *CPR, 1281–92*, p. 189; *French Chronicle of London*, p. 239.

68. *Trivet*, p. 302; Carpenter, *Reign of Henry III*, pp. 423–4.

69. *Flores*, p. 486; Howell, *Eleanor of Provence*, pp. 307–11.

70. *Osney*, pp. 329–30; *Dunstable*, p. 366; *Lanercost*, p. 141; *Foedera I*, p. 758; Strickland, *Lives of Queens*, pp. 159–60; Howell, *Eleanor of Provence*, pp. 304–07, 310–11.

Bibliography

Primary Sources

'Annals of Burton', *Annales Monastici*, Vol. I, ed. H. R. Luard (London, 1864)

'Annals of Dunstable', *Annales Monastici*, Vol. III, ed. H. R. Luard (London, 1866), trans. David Preest in a new edition released by The Boydell Press (2018) ed. Harriet Webster.

Annals of Nicholas Trivet, ed. T. Hog, Historical English Society, ix (London, 1845)

'Annals of Tewkesbury', *Annales Monastici*, Vol. I, ed. H. R. Luard (London, 1864)

'Annals of Waverley', *Annales Monastici*, Vol. II, ed. H. R. Luard (London, 1865)

'Annals of Winchester', *Annales Monastici*, Vol. II, ed. H. R. Luard (London, 1865)

Calendar of the Charter Rolls, 1903 (**CChR**)

Calendar of the Liberate Rolls, 1930 (**CLR**)

Calendar of Papal Letters, 1893 (**CPL**)

Calendar of the Patent Rolls, 1908 (**CPR**)

Close Rolls of the Reign of Henry III, 1932 (**CR**)

Chronicle of John of Oxendes, ed. H. Ellis (London, 1859)

Chronicle of Lanercost, ed. J. Stevenson (Maitland Club, 1839)

Chronicle of Melrose, trans. J. Stevenson (1856)

Chronicle of the Mayors and Sheriffs of London, 1188–1274, French Chronicle of London, ed. H. R. Riley (London, 1863)

'Chronicle of Osney', *Annales Monastici*, Vol. IV, ed. H. R. Luard (London, 1869)

'Chronicle of Thomas Wykes', *Annales Monastici*, Vol. IV, ed. H. R. Luard (London, 1869)

Chronicle of Walter of Guisborough, ed. H. Rothwell (Camden Society, 1957)

Chronicle of William de Rishanger, ed. J. O. Halliwell (1840)

Diplomatic Documents, 1101–1272, ed. P. Chaplais (1964)

Documents of the Baronial Movement of Reform and Rebellion (**DBM**), ed. R. F. Treharne, I. J. Sanders, Clarendon Press (Oxford, 1973)

Documents of the Christian Church, ed. H. Bettenson, C. Maunder, OUP (Oxford, 1963).

English Coronation Records, ed. L.G.W. Legg (London, 1901)

Flores Historiarum, trans. C. D. Yonge (London, 1853)

Foedera, Conventiones, Literae, ed. T. Rymer (London, 1816)

Green, V., *Account of the Discovery of the Body of King John* (London, 1797)

Historical Works of Gervase of Canterbury, Vol. II, ed. W. Stubbs (London, 1880)

Layettes Du Trésor Des Chartes, ed. M. Alexandre Teulet (Paris, 1863)

Letters of Adam Marsh, Volume I and II, ed. and trans. C. H. Lawrence, Clarendon Press (Oxford, 2006)

Letters of Robert Grosseteste, Bishop of Lincoln, ed. F.A.C. Mantello, F. M. Goering, University of Toronto Press (Toronto, 2010)

Manners and Household Expenses of England in the Thirteenth and Fifteenth Centuries, ed. T. H. Turner (Roxburghe Club, 1841).

Matthew Paris' English History from 1235 to 1273, Vol. I, II, III, trans. J. A. Giles (London, 1854)

Memoirs of the Lord of Joinville, trans. Ethel Wedgwood (London, 1906)

Metrical Chronicle of Robert of Gloucester, ed. W. A. Wright (London, 1887)

Political Songs of England, ed. T. Wright (London, 1839)

Roger of Wendover's Flowers of History, Vol. I, II, trans. J. A. Giles, (London, 1859).

Royal Letters, ed. W. W. Shirley (London, 1866).

Shorter Latin Forms of Master Henry of Avarances Relating to England, ed. J.C. Russell and J. P. Hieronimus, The Medieval Academy of America (Cambridge, 1935)

Song of Lewes, ed. C. L. Kingsford (Oxford, 1890)

Secondary Sources

Badham, S. and S. Oosterwijk, 'The Tomb Monument of Katherine, Daughter of Henry III and Eleanor of Provence, (1253–7)', *Antiquaries Journal*, 92 (2012)

Baker, D., *Henry III* (Stroud: The History Press, 2017)

—— *Simon de Montfort and the Rise of the English Nation* (Stroud: Amberley, 2018)

Barrow, J., 'Peter d'Aigueblanche's Support Network', in *Thirteenth Century England XIII*, (eds) J. Burton, F. Lachaud, P. Schofield, K. Stober and B. Weiler (Woodbridge: The Boydell Press, 2001).

Bémont, C., *Simon de Montfort* (Oxford: Clarendon Press, 1930)

Binski, P., *The Painted Chamber at Westminster*, Society of Antiquaries of London (London, 1986)

Blaauw, W. H., *The Barons' War* (London, 1871)

Carpenter, D., 'A Noble in Politics: Roger Mortimer', in *Nobles and Nobility*, (ed.) A. Duggan (Woodbridge: The Boydell Press, 2000)

—— 'Henry III and the Sicilian Affair', Henry Fine Rolls Project (November 2012)

—— *The Battles of Lewes and Evesham* (Keele, 1987)

—— 'The Meetings of Kings Henry III and Louis IX', in *Thirteenth Century England X*, (eds) M. Prestwich, R. Britnell and R. Frame (Suffolk, 2005)

—— *The Minority of Henry III* (London: Methuen Publishing, 1990)

—— *The Reign of Henry III* (London: The Hambledon Press, 1996)

—— *The Struggle for Mastery, Britain 1066–1284* (London: Penguin Books, 2004)

—— 'The *vis et voluntas* of King Henry III: The Downfall and Punishment of Robert De Ros', Henry Fine Rolls Project (November 2012)

Chaplais, P., 'The Making of the Treaty of Paris (1259) and the Royal Style', *The English Historical Review*, Vol. 67 (1952)

Clanchy, M., *England and its Rulers, 1066–1307* (Chichester: Wiley-Blackwell, 2014)

—— *From Memory to Written Record: England 1066–1307* (Oxford: Blackwell Publishers, 1979)

Cockayne, G., *Complete Peerage of England, Scotland, Ireland, Great Britain and the United Kingdom* (London: George Bell, 1895)

Cockerill, S., *Eleanor of Castile: The Shadow Queen* (Stroud: Amberley, 2014)

Coss, P. R., 'Sir Geoffrey de Langley and the Crisis of the Knightly Class in Thirteenth-Century England', *Past and Present*, lxviii (1975)

Costain, T. B., *The Magnificent Century* (Garden City: Doubleday & Company, 1951)

Cox, E., *The Eagles of Savoy* (Princeton: Princeton University Press, 1974)

Crouch, D., *The Acts and Letters of the Marshal Family* (Cambridge, 2015)

D'Avray, D., *Medieval Christianity in Practice* (Princeton: Princeton University Press, 2009)

Denholm-Young, N., *Richard of Cornwall* (New York: William Salloch, 1947)

Ellis, C., *Hubert de Burgh: A Study in Constancy* (London, 1952)

Gransden, A., *Historical Writing in England* (Abingdon: Routledge, 1996)

Green, M., *Lives of the Princesses of England*, Vol. II (London: Henry Colburn, 1850)

Harcourt, L. W. V., *His Grace the Steward and Trial of Peers* (London: Longmans, 1907)

Harding, A., *England in the Thirteenth Century* (Cambridge: Cambridge University Press, 1993)

Howell, M., *Eleanor of Provence* (Oxford: Blackwell Publishers, 2001)

—— 'The Children of King Henry III and Eleanor of Provence', in *Thirteenth Century England IV*, (eds) P. R. Coss and S. D. Lloyd (Woodbridge, 1992)

Huffman, J. P., *The Social Politics of Medieval Diplomacy: Anglo-German Relations (1066–1307)* (Ann Arbor, 2000)

Hutton, W. H., *Simon de Montfort and His Cause, 1251-1266* (London: David Nutt, 1907)

Hyams, P., 'Henry III in Bed', in *Anger's Past: The Social Uses of an Emotion in the Middle Ages*, (ed.) B. H. Rosenwein (Ithaca, 1998)

Kanter, J., 'Peripatetic and Sedentary Kingship: The Itineraries of John and Henry III', in *Thirteenth Century England XIII: Proceedings of the Paris Conference, 2009*, (eds) J. Burton, F. Lachaud, P. Schofield (Woodbridge: The Boydell Press, 2011)

King, E., *Medieval England, 1066–1485* (Oxford: Phaidon Press, 1988)

Knowles, C. H., 'The Disinherited, 1265–1280: A Political and Social Study of the Supporters of Simon De Montfort and the Resettlement after the Barons' War' (Doctoral thesis, University of Wales, 1959)

Kushner, T., *The Jewish Heritage in British History: Englishness and Jewishness* (Abingdon: Frank Cass & Company, 1992)

Labarge, M. W., *Saint Louis: The Life of Louis IX of France* (London, 1968)

—— *Simon de Montfort* (London: Eyre & Spottiswoode, 1962)

Laborderie, O. D., D. A. Carpenter, and J. R. Maddicott, 'The Last Hours of Simon de Montfort: A New Account', *English Historical Review 15* (2000)

Lloyd, S., *English Society and the Crusade, 1216–1307* (Oxford: Clarendon Press, 1988)

Maddicott, J. R., *Simon de Montfort* (Cambridge: Cambridge University Press, 1994)

—— 'The Mise of Lewes, 1264', *English Historical Review*, Vol. 98 (1983)

—— *The Origins of the English Parliament, 924–1327* (Oxford: Oxford University Press, 2010)

Madox, T., *Histories and Antiquities of the Exchequer* (London, 1769)

Marsh, F. B., *English Rule in Gascony, 1199–1259* (Ann Arbor: University of Michigan, 1912)

Mitchell, S. K., *Studies in Taxation under John and Henry III* (New Haven: Yale University Press, 1914)

Morris, M., *A Great and Terrible King* (London: Windmill Books, 2009)

—— *The Bigod Earls of Norfolk* (Woodbridge: The Boydell Press, 2005)

Mundill, R. R., *The King's Jews: Money, Massacre and Exodus in Medieval England* (London: Continuum, 2010)

Nelson, J., 'A Queen and Sister: Joan, the Wife of Alexander II of Scotland', *Henry III Fine Rolls Project*

Norgate, K., *The Minority of Henry III* (London, 1912)

Oram, R., *Alexander II: King of Scots 1214–1249* (Edinburgh, 2012)

Perry, F., *Saint Louis* (New York, 1900)

Pollock, M. A., *Scotland, England and France after the Loss of Normandy, 1204–1296* (Woodbridge, 2015).

Powicke, M., *King Henry III and the Lord Edward Vol. I, II* (Oxford: Clarendon Press, 1947)

—— *The Thirteenth Century* (Oxford: Oxford University Press, 1962)

Prestwich, M., *Edward I* (Berkeley: University of California Press, 1988)

Prothero, G. W., *The Life of Simon de Montfort* (London: Longmans, Green and Co., 1877)

Ramsay, J., *The Dawn of the Constitution* (Oxford: Oxford University Press, 1908)

Ray, M., 'Three Alien Royal Stewards', in *Thirteenth Century England X: Proceedings of the Durham Conference 2003*, (eds) M. Prestwich, R. H. Britnell, R. Frame (Woodbridge: The Boydell Press, 2005)

Ridgeway, H., 'Henry III (1207–1272)', *Oxford Dictionary of National Biography* (2004)

—— 'Henry III and the "Aliens", 1236–1272', in *Thirteenth Century England II*, (eds) P. R. Coss and S. Lloyd (Woodbridge: The Boydell Press, 1988)

—— 'King Henry III's Grievances against the Council in 1261', *Historical Research*, Vol. 61 (1988)

—— 'The Lord Edward and the Provisions of Oxford (1258)', in *Thirteenth Century England I*, (eds) P. R. Coss and S. D. Lloyd (Woodbridge: The Boydell Press, 1986)

—— 'What Happened in 1261?', in *Baronial Reform and Revolution in England, 1258–1267*, (ed.) A. Jobson (Woodbridge: The Boydell Press, 2016)

Runciman, S., *The Sicilian Vespers* (Cambridge: Cambridge University Press, 1992)

Sabapathy, J., *Officers and Accountability in Medieval England 1170–1300* (Oxford: Oxford University Press, 2014)

Sadler, J., *The Second Barons' War: Simon de Montfort and the Battles of Lewes and Evesham* (Barnsley: Pen & Sword, 2008)

Scudder, V., *Le Morte Darthur of Sir Thomas Malory*, (London, 1921)

Smith, J. B., *Llywelyn Ap Gruffudd: Prince of Wales* (Cardiff: University of Wales Press, 1998)

Stacey, R., 'Crusades, Crusaders and the Baronial *Gravamina* of 1263–1264', in *Thirteenth Century England III: Proceedings of the Newcastle upon Tyne Conference, 1989* (3), (eds) P. R. Coss, S. D. Lloyd (Woodbridge: The Boydell Press, 1991)

—— *Politics, Policy, and Finance under Henry III, 1216–1245* (Oxford, Oxford University Press, 1987)

Steane, J., *The Archaeology of the Medieval English Monarchy* (New York, 1999)

Strickland, A., *Lives of the Queens of England from the Norman Conquest*, Vol. II (1840)

Stubbs W., *The Constitutional History of England*, Vol. II (Oxford: Clarendon Press, 1880)

Tout, T. F., *Chapters in the Administrative History of Medieval England: The Wardrobe, the Chamber and the Small Seals*, Vol. 1 (Manchester, 1920)

Treharne, R., *The Baronial Plan of Reform* (Manchester: Manchester University Press, 1932)

Tyerman, C., *God's War: A New History of the Crusades* (Harvard, 2008)

Vaughan, R., *Matthew Paris* (Cambridge: Cambridge University Press, 1958)

Verini, A., 'Visions of Medieval Queenship: Gender and Genre in *La Estoire de Seint Aedward le Rei*', *Medieval Feminist Forum*, 50.2 (2015)

Vincent, N., 'Inventory of Gifts to Henry III, 1234–5', in *The Growth of Royal Government under Henry III*, (eds) D. Crook and L. J. Wilkinson (Woodbridge, 2015).

—— 'Isabella of Angoulême: John's Jezebel', in *King John: New Interpretations*, (ed). S. D. Church (Woodbridge, 1999)

—— 'King Henry III and the Blessed Virgin Mary', in *The Church and Mary: Studies in Church History*, (ed.) R. N. Swanson (Woodbridge 2005)

—— *Peter des Roches: An Alien in English Politics, 1205–1238* (Cambridge: Cambridge University Press, 1996)

Warren, W. L., *King John* (Berkeley: University of California Press, 1978)

Waugh, S. L., *The Lordship of England: Royal Wardships and Marriages in English Society and Politics, 1217–1327* (Princeton: Princeton University Press, 1988)

Westerhof, D., *Death and the Noble Body in Medieval England* (Woodbridge: The Boydell Press, 2008)

Wild, B., 'A Captive King: Henry III between the Battles of Lewes and Evesham', in *Thirteenth Century England XIII: Proceedings of the Paris Conference 2009*, (eds) J. Burton, F. Lachaud, P. Schofield, K. Stöber, B. (Woodbridge: The Boydell Press, 2011)

Wilkinson, L. J., *Eleanor de Montfort: A Rebel Countess in Medieval England* (London: Continuum Books, 2012)

—— *Women in Thirteenth-Century Lincolnshire* (Woodbridge: The Boydell Press, 2007)

Index